QUESTIONS GOD ASKS,
QUESTIONS SATAN ASKS

"Before we can find the right answers, we need to be clear about the questions. Doug Rumford is a skilled teacher in the art of questioning and a wise interpreter of God's Supreme Answer in Jesus Christ."

Richard J. Mouw, president, Fuller Theological Seminary

"Questions make some Christians nervous. Not Douglas Rumford, who realizes that real people have real questions that deserve real answers. This book explores important questions asked in the Bible . . . and offers us question-askers insight, admonition, and great encouragement."

Daniel Taylor, author of *Letters to My Children* and *The Healing Power of Stories*

"Doug Rumford uses the probing questions of Scripture to shake us out of our complacency. Reading this book will prod you toward a more intimate relationship with God. I recommend it highly."

Tremper Longman III, professor of Old Testament, Westminster Theological Seminary and coauthor (with Dan Allender) of *Intimate Allies* and *Bold Purpose*

"If you ask profound questions, you get profound answers. . . . If you ask no questions, you get no answers at all. If you're looking for answers, here are the profound questions."

Bobb Biehl, author of *Asking to Win* and president, Masterplanning Group, International

"For years I have been asking my children questions, like 'If you could be an animal, which one would you be, and why?' . . . They thought the questions were fun. Little did they know that I used their answers to understand what was in their hearts. After a while they began to see patterns in their answers that showed *them* what was in their hearts. As Douglas points out, God already knows what's in our hearts. His questions are designed to help *us* know, for the purpose of change."

Ron DiCianni, artist, author of *Beyond Words*

"In this thought-provoking book, Doug Rumford challenges Christian attitudes and action in applied lifestyle values based on God's timeless Word."

C. John Nill, Walk Thru the Bible Ministries

"In addition to being the omnipotent creator of all mankind, the God of the Bible is also personally interested in our lives. Doug Rumford makes that clear as he carefully examines the very personal questions God has asked men and women throughout history. None of the pagan gods are ever presented as even remotely interested in their subjects. It is easy to love and is a joy to serve the God that is presented in this book!"

Tim LaHaye, author of *Left Behind*

QUESTIONS GOD ASKS

QUESTIONS SATAN ASKS

Douglas J. Rumford

Tyndale House Publishers, Inc.
WHEATON, ILLINOIS

The personal stories in this book are true. Many are told with the permission of the people involved. In some cases, names and identifying details have been altered to preserve anonymity.

Visit Tyndale's exciting Web site at www.tyndale.com

Published in association with the literary agency of Alive Communications, Inc., 1465 Kelly Johnson Blvd., Suite 320, Colorado Springs, CO 80920.

Designed by Catherine Bergstrom
Edited by Vinita Hampton Wright

Library of Congress Cataloging-in-Publication Data

Rumford, Douglas J.
Questions God asks, questions Satan asks / Douglas J. Rumford.
p. Cm.
ISBN 0-8423-5119-1 (alk. Paper)
1. Christian life—Presbyterian authors. I. Title.
BV4501.2.R817 1998
248.4—dc21 98-6793

ISBN 0-8423-5119-1

Printed in the United States of America

06 05 04 03 02 01 00 99 98
10 9 8 7 6 5 4 3 2 1

To my family

Sarah

Kristen, Matthew, Timothy, and Peter

and to our partners in ministry at

First Presbyterian Church, Fresno, California,

who have encouraged me in every way.

Together we are learning to hear life's questions

and answer with faith and faithfulness.

Contents

INTRODUCTION

How to Get the Most from This Book

Some books are read for relaxation, others for information. Some people read for content, while others look for the action. This book is written for transformation and re-creation. The goal is insight into who we are spiritually.

In my book *SoulShaping: Taking Care of Your Spiritual Life,* I explained the value of spiritual reading in maintaining our spiritual vitality. This discipline could also be called prayerful reading. We read as a means of meeting the Lord. To understand how this differs from ordinary reading, think of the difference between reading a newspaper and a love letter. We read the newspaper quickly, scanning the headlines, skimming the ads, perusing the comics and box scores—then discard it. A brief love letter, however, is read over and over again, not for the sense of content, but for the sense of presence and emotional connection it inspires. It is saved and reread often.

This book is meant to be a type of love letter for your soul. Of course, the Bible is the ultimate love letter—and a Bible passage provides the focus for every chapter of this book. You will get the most from *Questions God Asks/ Questions Satan Asks* if you read it prayerfully, ready to stop and reflect along the way. When you start to read each time, don't worry about finishing the chapter; think instead about reading for that one idea that God wants to share with you at that time. That thought may come directly from the Scripture passage, the sentences on the page, or from the thoughts that are triggered as you read. The point is, savor the thought. Take time to reflect and even to journal on it. If you do, this book will lead you into new adventures of spiritual growth.

This may be a more interactive type of reading than you've ever done before. Why? Because this is a book of questions.

Life is a series of questions and answers.

- What will you do when you grow up?
- Will you get married?
- Do you know where you're going to school?
- Will you drink or use drugs?
- Will you take the job offer or stay with your present one?
- When should you start your family?
- Should you adopt a child?
- How do you help solve the problems in the community?
- Do you want the medical personnel to take extraordinary measures to prolong your life?

The toughest questions are never on paper. They are asked and answered in flesh and blood, laughter and tears. We are often tempted to ignore the questions, failing to realize that such an approach simply answers them in less-than-satisfying ways. We try the Scarlett O'Hara technique. This heroine from the classic novel *Gone with the Wind* was part of a Southern plantation family living through the turmoil of the American Civil War. When faced with questions, she would respond, "I'll think about that tomorrow." When tomorrow came, she had few appealing options because circumstances answered the questions for her.

I have often thought about the questions we have for God. Why is there suffering and evil? What is God's will? How do science and Scripture relate? Some excellent books deal with these questions. But this book grew out of a thought I had one day as I was writing in my journal. I wrote:

> Lord, we are always asking you questions—though we rarely stop long enough to listen to your answer. But what questions do you have for us? What do you care about?

This led to a time of study and reflection as I searched God's Word for the questions that are asked of us. I found that both God and Jesus asked a number of questions. I also learned that some of the best questions come from the dark side. The evil one challenges us many times. He asked the first question in the Bible and changed human life and destiny forever. We may try to ignore or deny his questions, but they persist. It is only when we really understand the questions that we can discover the answers that set us free from the questions' seductive power.

We all know the value of questions in learning. The Socratic method of leading students to discovery through questions has guided teachers for more than two millennia. But few realize that God used the Socratic method long before Socrates was born! Questions move us from being spectators to participants. They cause us to stop and take stock of what we believe and how we behave. Questions push us to challenge our assumptions, to assess our needs, to clarify our thinking, and to confront our imposed limitations. They prod us to analyze, criticize, and synthesize. They shake us up!

> As you master the art of asking profound questions you'll be able to unlock information, insight and wisdom within a friend in any situation. You'll be able to open doors to inner motivation and dreams which no one has ever been able to unlock. You'll be able to solve problems, analyze risks and take leadership you've never before dreamed possible. For questions are like intricate, brass keys which unlock the lock boxes of people's minds and hearts, their hopes and their dreams.[1]

As I have considered God's questions, my study and reflection have led me deeper into both self-understanding and experiencing God. More than any other exercise thus far, these questions have helped me delve into God's priceless character, eternal wisdom, boundless grace, righteous expectations, and expansive love. I have also uncovered many of my unexamined assumptions and seen how often I have supposed things that just aren't true.

The right question is like a jeweler's chisel that shatters an uncut, dull-looking stone into a precious treasure with gleaming facets of beauty and value. While the wrong questions take us on senseless detours, the right questions take us to the very heart of life.

This book, then, provides a series of soul-searching questions. These chapters need not be read in order since they do not build on each other. You may want to skim the table of contents and see what topic stirs your interest. You might even jot a few thoughts in your journal on the topic before you start reading. To encourage the process of spiritual reading, I have provided questions and thoughts in the margin. These will help you interact with the text in a way that will make the material apply to your unique spiritual journey.

Notes

1. *Asking to Win,* self-published by Bobb Biehl (Lake Mary, Fla.: Masterplanning Group, International), 4. Avialable only through Master planning 1-800-443-1976.

CHAPTER 1

"What did God really say?" Looking for Loopholes

Genesis 3:1

YOU KNOW THE story. A story of forbidden love. The parents hated each other. But these star-crossed lovers couldn't resist the magnetic attraction. Even when they discovered they were from rival families, they clung to their love and plotted for its fulfillment. When Romeo was sent into exile for killing Tibalt, Juliet and the friar made plans to feign Juliet's death and provide a way for a reunion with Romeo until the families could be reconciled. But word reached Romeo through a friend that Juliet had died. The friar's messenger, who had been sent to tell Romeo the truth, hadn't gotten to Romeo in time. So Romeo went to Juliet's burial vault. He broke into it and saw Juliet's body. He saw with his own eyes that she was dead. Of course, he thought he could trust his senses, so in his despair he killed himself. And Juliet awakened to her worst nightmare and took her own life.

The irony of this gripping tragedy stirs us. And no matter how often the story is told or what new form it takes, it still makes our heart cry out. But think about it. Romeo killed himself because he lacked the truth. With his senses he thought he saw the truth, he thought he'd heard the truth, and he staked his life on it. But he was dead wrong. People are doing that every day. They are dying for lies. And they are starving for the truth.

> **Now the serpent was more subtle than any other wild creature that the Lord God had made. He**

said to the woman, "Did God say, 'You shall not eat of any tree of the garden'?" And the woman said to the serpent, "We may eat of the fruit of the trees of the garden; but God said, 'You shall not eat of the fruit of the tree which is in the midst of the garden, neither shall you touch it, lest you die.'" But the serpent said to the woman, "You will not die. For God knows that when you eat of it your eyes will be opened, and you will be like God, knowing good and evil." So when the woman saw that the tree was good for food, and that it was a delight to the eyes, and that the tree was to be desired to make one wise, she took of its fruit and ate; and she also gave some to her husband, and he ate. Then the eyes of both were opened, and they knew that they were naked; and they sewed fig leaves together and made themselves aprons. (Genesis 3:1-7, RSV)

The Voice You Trust Will Determine Your destiny

From the beginning of human history, people have been subject to the dangers of lying and deception. Jesus warned of this when he rebuked the unbelieving crowds: "You belong to your father, the devil, and you want to carry out your father's desire. He was a murderer from the beginning, not holding to the truth, for there is no truth in him. When he lies, he speaks his native language, for he is a liar and the father of lies" (John 8:44, NIV).

When we reject God's Word, we forfeit the truth and fall victim to Satan's deceptions. Nowhere is this more clear than in the first question ever posed in the Bible. The serpent in the Garden of Eden asked our first parents a question that is asked of every single one of us: "Did God say . . . ?" And how you answer that question is how you determine your destiny. Some people ask, "Did God say anything?" They start that far back—questioning that God even reveals himself in the Bible or otherwise. Other people ask, "Well, what did God *really* say? What did he really mean?"

We are all faced with a choice concerning whom we will believe. A lot of people think the story of Adam and Eve in the Garden of Eden is simply about apples and trees and making fig-leaf aprons. It's not. The story in the Garden of Eden is about thoughts and words and how they shape our deeds. It's about love and loyalty. It's about freedom and responsibility. And unfortunately many of us fail to see the truth for the trees!

When we look at this passage, we have to ask the question, What was this serpent character, really? Is there actually a devil? In his *Index of Leading Spiritual Indicators,* George Barna says that most Americans do not believe in Satan or the devil. Six out of ten adults surveyed believe Satan is not a living being but a symbol of evil. He is simply a principle of evil.

C. S. Lewis poses the issue to us in clear terms. In the preface to his classic book *Screwtape Letters,* he wrote: "There are two equal and opposite errors into which our race can fall about the devils. One is to disbelieve in their existence. The other is to believe and to feel an excessive and unhealthy interest in them. They themselves are equally pleased by both errors and hail a materialist or a magician with the same delight."[1]

What do I believe about the devil?

What does the Bible and Jesus teach about the devil?

How does my understanding of the devil affect my spiritual life?

The Bible clearly teaches that Satan is an individual being with personality and power. Jesus believed and taught in terms of a literal Satan. And that is what I believe. If you have not reached a place of such certainty, don't let that deter you from continuing to read and reflect.

Satan is not God's equal.

The mistake we often make is to think of Satan as the exact opposite of—and equal to—God. But Satan is not equal with God in any way. Satan started out as an angel, a creation of God. Satan is not omniscient, knowing everything, and he is not omnipotent, all powerful. He is not omnipresent; he cannot be everywhere. He is not God. The Bible doesn't teach the dualism that is present in other cultures and religions, in which evil and good are on an equal plane and are battling one another for supremacy. Satan undoubtedly has power, and he rules over a host of angels—the principalities and powers of the air, as the apostle Paul referred to them. But Satan is not God's equal.

Satan attempts to usurp God's authority, as he attempted to usurp it in the Garden of Eden. As we look at the serpent's questions to Adam and Eve, it's clear that the goal is to coax them away from the authority of God so that they will question that authority and, ultimately, disobey it.

Who is your authority?

The Bible teaches us that God is our authority and that he has established a gracious covenant with us in which we have freedom with responsibility. This freedom comes, however, as we submit to God. But Satan would have you believe you're your own boss. Culture encourages that posture: There is no ultimate authority to which we must answer. No matter what is going on in the universe, all that matters is what the individual thinks and says and believes and decides.

Who is my authority, on a day-to-day basis?

On what do I base my decisions and attitudes?

At what point did I choose this authority?

Whom will you trust? Who will guide and direct your life? Now, this passage shows us the process that I call the road to deception. How do people fall into deception? How do they fall into not trusting in God's Word and believing that they are the judge of all things? It's a process of five steps.

Five Steps to Deception

Subtle questioning of God's Word

"Did God say . . . ?" The tempter begins with suggestion rather than argument. Have you ever been going along very happily and suddenly someone makes a suggestion that throws you off? Someone who hasn't been nice to you before sends you a nice letter. You think, wow, that's really neat. And you share that with someone who says, "I wonder why he sent you that." The person may not know of anything actually wrong, but just the suggestion awakens all sorts of suspicions: "Yeah . . . why did he send me this? I bet I can't trust him—he's just trying to get on my good side. . . .” Suddenly you’re going down another path, and you have no idea what the truth is.

That’s the tempter’s way. The incredulous tone. “Did God say that you shouldn’t eat of all the trees in the Garden?” In the tone is the answer. Just like when people say to you, “Are you done yet?” They aren’t really asking a question. Or, “Are you doing that again?” The tone says it all. Rather than launch a frontal assault, the tempter arouses doubts and sows seeds of suspicion. This way Satan doesn’t have to take the blame; he just gets things going. If he were interrogated, he’d simply shrug and say, “I just asked the question. *You’re* the one who drew the conclusion.”

With this question, Eve began to think consciously about God’s word for the first time. To this point, she’d simply enjoyed free conversation and took all statements at their face value. She’d never even thought of double entendres and mixed messages and verbal games.

The same thing often happens when a student begins college and encounters her first class that uses “higher criticism” (honest, that’s the term they use for it) of the Bible, which questions things, such as the veracity, the authorship, and the actual text of biblical books. The young student who has simply read the Bible in full trust suddenly finds herself caught up in a maelstrom of intellectual questions that can rattle her faith. It’s like awakening from a pleasant dream to a real nightmare.

How have I been tempted to question God’s Word?

Has my intellectual confidence in the Bible ever been shaken?

How has my level of confidence in God’s Word affected my spiritual vitality?

Innuendo and exaggeration

The serpent said to the woman, “Did God really say, you must not eat of *any* tree in the Garden?” Now look in your Bible at Genesis 2:15-17. Let’s see what God really said. There we read, “The Lord God took the man and put him in the Garden of Eden to work it and take care of it. And the Lord God commanded the man, ‘You are free . . .’ [Note: Those are God’s first words!] ‘You are free to eat from any tree in the garden; but you must not eat from the tree of the knowledge of good and evil, for when you eat of it you will surely die’ ” (NIV).

God was saying, "You are free to eat from any tree in the Garden except this one." God gives expansive, gracious provision for his people. But the evil one, the tempter, turns that on its head and reformulates it with a negative emphasis.

We know all about this, don't we? A parent says to his teenager, "You may take the car tonight; I trust you to get home at the time we have agreed upon. I have filled it with gas so you can go wherever you need to go. The only thing I don't want you to do is go over to the Materialism Mall, where that huge bar is. You know about all these problems that are going on there. Just stay away from that area, but you can do anything you want the rest of the night. I trust you to use good judgment. Have a great time!" But during the evening, a "friend" says to this teenager, "What do you mean you can't go anywhere you want to go? You mean you can't do anything you want to do? Your parents are setting all these boundaries and restrictions on you. What's the deal with you? Are you going to listen to them?" And the teenager suddenly begins to think, *Yeah . . . what* is *the deal with my parents? Don't they trust me?*

What started out to be a gift of freedom and affirmation by the parent—who was intending to say, "Hey, I love you. I trust you. Do what you want. My assets are at your disposal"—suddenly becomes a restrictive prohibition. What was meant to be a gracious, generous opportunity is turned into what seems like a niggling, restrictive rule. Innuendo and exaggeration. Satan misrepresents the truth. He says, "You can't eat of any tree in the Garden?" No, God said, "You may eat of any tree except one." Satan says, "God won't let you have any?" Satan makes that good commandment of God seem oppressive and restrictive.

What could Eve have done at this point? First of all, she could have remembered her position. God created man, male and female, to exercise dominion over creation. We read in Genesis 2:15 that the Lord put Adam in the Garden and said that he was "to dress, till and keep" (KJV). That means: "You are to take care of the Garden, develop it, and make the most come out of it. But I also want you to keep it holy, to protect it from intruders." Does that surprise you? God says, "I need you to protect the Garden and keep it holy. Keep it because there is someone out there who wants to get in here and undo all of this good thing." With that rulership comes responsibility. The freedom that comes from owning a car entails the responsibility to keep it filled with gas and maintained, or soon it will let you down. With authority and freedom come responsibility. So they should have been paying attention to what was going on around them. Right off the bat, when the serpent showed up and started questioning God's word, Eve could have exercised her "keeping responsibility" and given the serpent the ol' heave-ho! She could have remembered her position of authority and her duty in responsibility. But she wasn't paying attention. And as it turns out, Adam was paying even less attention.

Do I appreciate my authority and responsibility in Christ?

Matthew 10:1-8 and Ephesians 6:10-18 give me a glimpse into my spiritual authority. How can I cultivate this awareness and confidence in the midst of moment-by-moment living?

The first way to deal with temptation is to recognize the lie and silence it. That's where it all starts. Recognize the lie. You're being told something that isn't true here. Silence it. Because if you don't, you will stumble into the third step on the road to deception, which is debate.

Debate

Debate is often a sign that you are looking for loopholes. That's when the battle is usually lost. Whenever you and I accept the questioning of God's authority as the legitimate basis for debate, we give the enemy the high ground. I learned about the importance of high ground when I played paint ball at our men's conference. It was a painful lesson. I learned that those who have the high ground (and, naturally, I didn't!) have the advantage of being able not only to look down on you but also to move more easily. And their paint balls fly more quickly. Shooting uphill doesn't seem to have the same impact. Likewise, when you open yourself to debating on the legitimacy of God's authority, you're giving the enemy the high ground.

You may be thinking, *Wait a minute, Doug, we're not robots, are we? I mean, we can ask God questions. We can try to understand what the Bible says.* Absolutely. But there is a difference between an honest question and a question disguised as an accusation. There is a difference between honestly exploring a subject from the perspective of faith, which is seeking to understand, and saying, "There is really nothing to this." The tone makes all the difference.

In this passage Eve begins to debate with the evil one. And she says, "No, we may eat of the trees of the Garden, except we may not eat of the central tree nor may we touch it." Note that a careful reading of Genesis 2:17 reveals that God didn't say anything about not touching the tree. It seems that Eve was on the defensive here. Instead of calmly correcting the serpent and rebuking its presumption, Eve overcorrects, and in that overcorrecting she makes God sound more harsh than he is. People will do that. In a sense we wonder if Eve herself had suddenly begun to feel that God was *not* very fair for setting limits. We don't know. We do know this: As she began to debate, she herself began to take the tempter's side in the process.

As I grow in my faith, I face many tough questions. What are some of the ones I'm dealing with now?

What is my attitude as I explore those questions?

Do I ask questions from a place of honest, humble exploration? Or do cynicism and criticism flavor my search? Why?

Denial

Debate leads to denial. When you get into denial, the evil one takes off his disguise and makes a direct attack. Following Eve's "correction," the serpent says to her, "You will not surely die. For God knows that when you eat of it your eyes will be opened, and you will be like God, knowing good and evil." We look at Genesis 2:17, and it says: "For when you eat of it you will surely die" (NIV). But in Genesis 3:4 we read: "You will not surely die." Now, somebody's lying. Somebody's wrong!

At this point Eve should have heard the alarms sounding and seen the red flags waving: Warning! Warning! It's like my computer; there is this little red *x* that comes up and says, "You have performed an illegal function, and you will be shut down." And suddenly, *bang,* it's gone, and you're looking at a blank screen! Now with my computer, I keep asking myself, *What did I do?* I keep repenting of the illegal thing I've done! In my state of limited computer literacy, I don't even know when I'm performing an illegal function! I have no idea what I've done. But Eve should have known. Yet the serpent was permitted to continue his demonic dissertation. And he called God a liar.

We might translate it something like this: "Eve," the serpent says, "God lied to you. You're not going to die. Furthermore, you know why he told you that? Because he didn't want you to be like him, knowing good and evil. He wants to keep all this God stuff for himself, and he doesn't want to share with you. Isn't he a creep? So you go ahead, and you eat of that tree! You'll be just like God!" The tempter presents God as a petty, jealous God, who is trying to keep us from what is rightfully ours. He misrepresents God and God's intent. Satan creates competition and rivalry between humanity and God. And he says, "You will learn good from evil."

There are two ways to learn good from evil. One is by doing what we know is appropriate and experiencing the benefits of that goodness. The other is by going against what we know is right and receiving the bad consequences and punishment for our wrongdoing. You can learn that it's good not to steal. One way is by not stealing and then seeing someone get caught in public, be humiliated, and taken away by the authorities. Suddenly, you realize that you can walk around with a clear conscience. It feels good not to steal. So when you get a letter from the IRS, you don't get nervous! When you open it, you find your forms for next year's estimated payments or a refund check because you were so honest.

Everybody will learn good from evil. The question is, How will we learn? The evil one says, "Eat of the tree, and you'll learn about good and evil." But that will lead to becoming like the serpent (the devil) himself. Now the truth is, God does want us to be like him. But it will not happen by the serpent's methods!

Well, at this point the tempter's work is done. He began with the subtle questioning of God's word. "Did he really say that?" From there he went to innuendo and exaggeration: "You mean you can't eat from one of these trees?" The

Are there times when I deliberately do what I know is wrong? What are some of the factors that lead to this?

Are there problems such as fatigue, discouragement, lack of support from others that make wrongdoing more tempting?

What can I do to better "keep" or guard myself?

third step is debate—looking for the loopholes. And the fourth step is outright denial: "No, you won't die."

Enticement

At this point the serpentine con game is almost over. All he has to do now is step back and watch it work. He allows Eve to wrestle with the fifth step, which is enticement. With Eve's attention diverted from God and his command, she is focused on this gorgeous tree with its beautiful fruit that was right there for the taking. And the blame for the temptation rests squarely on Eve's (and later Adam's) shoulders. Likewise, it rests squarely on our shoulders.

How can that be? The devil tempts us, but the blame rests on us? James 1:14 says, "Each person is tempted when he [or she] is lured and enticed by his [or her] own desire" (RSV). We usually say that the fault lies "out there" somewhere. I got angry because somebody out there pushed my buttons. It's the fault of worldly culture; it's the fault of the government. We always want to put the blame "out there."

But the Bible teaches us that we sin when we are enticed and lured by our own desire. Think of a radio and radio waves. Out in our atmosphere are hundreds of radio waves. But when you're listening to the radio, you're only tuned in to one radio wave, and that's the only one you hear.

Likewise, no temptation will affect you unless you are tuned in to it. I have had people get angry at me, and I realized there was no legitimate basis for their anger. I can love them through it because I am not tuned in to the anger response. But if I am tuned in—if I'm tired, for instance, I might tune right in to that anger and respond with my own anger. But I have to recognize that my anger is my fault, not theirs.

What are you tuned in to? Satan had tuned in to exactly where Eve was. It's ironic isn't it? He went after her thirst for knowledge and her thirst for godliness. And he turned those on their heads and made them the occasion for sin and destruction. Eve followed her impressions rather than the

Creator's instructions. When we reject God's Word, we forfeit the truth, and we fall into Satan's deceptions.

What are my desires that Satan could turn into enticements?

What are my weak spots?

Standing against Satan's Questions

I want to close by talking about three principles that help us stand firm in God's truth.

Question the questioner.

Not every question deserves an answer. That's very hard for us to realize and understand. But when questions come out of the pit, like this one did, they don't deserve an answer. They deserve to be silenced and dismissed. Question the questioner. What's the motive? Remember, there is a difference between an honest question asked with humility, seeking information and understanding, and an accusation disguised as a question.

Remember the person who said, "Aren't you finished yet?" It wasn't a question. Questions can lead us forward when we approach them with the humility of an explorer rather than the caustic arrogance of a critic. Question the questioner. Always look at where these questions are coming from. College students who are faced with intense faith-testing questions need consider not only the legitimacy of the question but also the character and attitude of the questioner. See where it's coming from. And then answer it accordingly—with integrity and grace, but with wisdom.

Know God's Word.

Eve misquoted God's command. Remember God said, "You are free to eat from any tree in the garden; but you must not eat from the tree of the knowledge of good and evil" (NIV). Eve added, "And you must not touch it." God never said that. Ignorance of God's Word will lead to the rejection of God's Word. That may sound harsh, but it's absolutely the truth.

Polls frequently reveal that the Bible is revered but not read. I read of a Gallup poll finding that 89 percent of us won't read the Bible today. Daily Bible reading was reported by only 11 percent of the 1,559 adults polled.

That's down slightly from a peak of 15 percent in 1982 and up slightly from 10 percent in 1944, says George Gallup Jr. "Our frequency of Bible reading had remained virtually unchanged over the years. . . . People revere the Bible, but they don't read it—that's what it comes down to," he says. The poll also showed that 22 percent never read the Bible—down from 24 percent in 1982. Women, African Americans, older people, Protestants, evangelicals, southerners, and the less educated are more likely to read the Bible and read it more often than other groups. Gallup also asked people about the role of religion in public schools. Most favored activities that have been found legally permissible by the Supreme Court. Some findings:

- Seventy-five percent approved of using the Bible in literature, history, and social studies classes.
- Seventy-nine percent approved of teaching students about the world's major religions.
- Seventy-five percent approved of offering elective courses in Bible studies.[2]

In many ways we are like the two on the road to Emmaus following Jesus' crucifixion. They were discouraged. Then Jesus, unrecognized by them, joined them. We read:

> Then Jesus said to them, "You are such foolish people! You find it so hard to believe all that the prophets wrote in the Scriptures. Wasn't it clearly predicted by the prophets that the Messiah would have to suffer all these things before entering his time of glory?" Then Jesus quoted passages from the writings of Moses and all the prophets, explaining what all the Scriptures said about himself." (Luke 24:25-27)

After Jesus left them, the story continues: "They said to each other, 'Didn't our hearts feel strangely warm as he talked with us on the road and explained the Scriptures to us?'" (Luke 24:32, NLT).

Like the disciples, we are discouraged because we don't know God's Word. When we study, he opens our eyes and warms our heart. The devil then finds it much harder to pull the wool over open eyes!

How well do I know the Bible?

What realistic commitment can I make to regular Bible reading and study?

Trust God's wisdom.

Eve relied on her senses instead of her holy common sense. And when that happened, she got carried away. Likewise, Romeo relied on his senses, and he died for a lie. Too often we learn the hard way that God really knows best. There are a lot of things in this life that don't make sense. They just don't make sense. We wonder why God won't let us do certain things or go certain places. We wonder why certain things couldn't happen. We are frustrated with God, but we just have to draw back and trust God's wisdom.

There once was a wise man. Many, many people would come to his door daily to discuss their problems with him. One day, after listening to many people for many years, he decided to gather together the people who had come to him for that day, and he gave them each a bag of rocks. He had them paint on each of their rocks what their problems were. Some would write, "money," "anxiety"—whatever—on a rock, and then they would fill their burlap bag with their own problems. They wrote their name on the outside of the bag, and then he had them all put their bags in the center of the room. Finally, when everyone had done so, he had them all circle around, and he said, "OK, now I would like you to pick up any bag you want, and those will be your problems." After a long time it turned out that they all ended up picking up their own bag with their own problems.

Isn't it interesting that God has given each of us the problems that only we are able to bear. Although we may sometimes covet others' experiences, we are better able to trust God to solve our own problems.

Those who observe life find themselves more and more likely to agree with God's counsel. They see that abusing

If I were to evaluate my level of trust in God between one and ten, how would I rate? (One signifies no trust whatsoever, and ten puts me right up there with the apostle Paul or Mary, the mother of Jesus.)

In what ways can I cultivate greater trust in God's Word and will?

their bodies and relationships leads to pain, regret, even death. They see that following God's counsel leads to health and joy and life. They see God's faithfulness. Unlike the devil, God really keeps his word.

What about You?

When we reject God's Word, we forfeit the truth and fall to Satan's deceptions. And the greatest tragedy is not that one person like Romeo occasionally dies for a lie but that all humanity came under the sentence of death through believing the serpent's lie. He tempts us with deadly fruit.

The fruit that God offers us will open our eyes to good and evil by nourishing us on the good and guarding us against evil. This is the fruit of the Spirit described in Galatians 5:22-23. "But when the Holy Spirit controls our lives, he will produce this kind of fruit in us: love, joy, peace, patience, kindness, goodness, faithfulness, gentleness, and self-control. Here there is no conflict with the law."

When you are asked the question "Did God really say . . . ?" learn to question the questioner. Soak in God's Word, and let his wisdom seep into every dimension of your life. Remember the disciples' experience with Jesus. He had said some very hard things, and nearly everybody left him. He turned to his disciples and said, "Are you going to leave, too?" And Peter responded with these words: "Lord, to whom would we go? You alone have the words that give eternal life" (John 6:67-68). That's what we, too, have been given: not the words of death, but the words of life.

Notes

1. C. S. Lewis, *Screwtape Letters* (New York: The Macmillan Company, 1961), 3.
2. Kim Painter, *USA Today,* 1986.

CHAPTER 2

"Where are you?" The Hiding Reflex

Genesis 3:9

There is virtuous fear which is the effect of faith, and a vicious fear which is the product of doubt and distrust. The former leads to hope as relying on God, in whom we believe; the latter inclines to despair, as not relying upon God, in whom we don't believe. Persons of the one character fear to lose God; those of the other character fear to find him. BLAISE PASCAL

"AW, COME ON. No one can see us."

It did sound like fun. And I didn't see how we could get caught. It was dark and cold. Over a foot of wet snow had fallen. We had been sledding for most of the afternoon. Now it was dark, and soon we'd go in for dinner. My friend Ryan (not his real name) and I were in a wooded lot behind his house, which overlooked Jessup Road. We made a batch of snowballs and waited.

"Here comes a car," he whispered loudly.

"Target approaching!" I said, picking up a firmly packed snowball.

"Wait . . . hold it . . . just a little longer . . . NOW!" said Ryan.

We both let our snowballs fly. One landed right in front of the car, while the other hit the roof. We heard the metallic *thud,* and it sounded so loud!

Our gleeful smiles froze as we heard the screech of brakes and the car door open.

"Hey!" called an angry voice. "I'm coming to get you!"

He sounded high school age—*and he was running across the street right into the woods where we were.*

Ryan and I took off in different directions. We ran—slipping and sliding, pushing through the wet bushes, dodging trees. I cut across a number of yards and kept running until I was in another wooded lot a long way from the road. I stopped running and stooped down behind a tree and listened. All I could hear was my heavy breathing. I tried to hold my breath and listen. But it was hard to concentrate because I really had to go to the bathroom!

I didn't move for at least ten minutes. Until that moment, I don't think I knew how scared I could get or how bad I could feel. It was like being cold and dark and wet *inside.* I remember praying, "Dear God, get me out of this, and I'll never throw snowballs at cars again!"

Hiding. For some it's a game, but for most of us it's a way of life. We all have a hiding reflex. We all want to cover up what we're doing wrong. A group of boys is looking at a dirty magazine in the bedroom, and Mom suddenly opens the door. What happens to the magazine? It's hidden behind someone's back. Some girls are writing an unkind note about one of their classmates, and suddenly that girl walks right around the corner! They hide the note. A man is traveling and goes to a place that he would never visit in his own town because he would never want to be seen there. Just as he comes out the door, he sees an old friend coming down the other side of the street. What does he do? He hides.

Our hiding reflex is inherited. It appeared at the dawn of human life. Hiding immediately followed Eve and Adam taking fruit from the tree of the knowledge of good and evil. Their knowledge did not set them free.

Let me set the stage. What was going on in the Garden of Eden as the taste of the fruit was still on their lips?

At that moment, their eyes were opened, and they suddenly felt shame at their nakedness. So they strung fig leaves together around their hips to cover themselves. (Genesis 3:7)

The silence was awkward. Suddenly they had become conscious of every word, every move, every sound. Each was lost in thought—strange thoughts. Thoughts they had never had before. Their conversation had always been so light and easy before. But now it seemed a strange intrusion. Out of habit they stayed close to each other—but facing away from each other most of the time. Their newly made covering felt so uncomfortable, so unnatural against their bodies.

Then each of them heard a sound. Just the day before, that sound had been welcome. They had been resting quietly after the day's activities. When they heard him coming, they had eagerly run to meet him. They had talked and talked, savoring the serene leisure of the close of the day. It had been that way every day.

Have I ever experienced such a time of rest and peace in God's presence?

But this time was different. This time, a strange tingle shot through each of them. With a start they looked at each other, amazed at what they saw in each other's eyes. It was a new look—a startled, frightened look. Instantly, each of them wanted to run *from,* not toward, the sound. They couldn't bear to look in God's eyes. The laughter and freedom of yesterday were now dim memories. Now there was simply one desire: to get away. So they hid themselves. And the Lord called out, "Where are you?"

What was that time of peace like?

What would it be like?

When have I wanted to run from God and others?

That was more than a request for their location. It was an invitation. And it's the invitation God has been calling out to humankind ever since. "Where are you?" But it's an invitation we've often refused.

Where did I hide?

"Where Are You?"

The real purpose of this question is to probe our spiritual condition. It asks us to explore the landscape of the heart and assess our direction and our destination. It's uncanny how the experience of our first parents is imprinted on our spiritual genes. What drove them to hide still drives us. The most powerful forces are those of fear and shame.

Shame and fear motivate our hiding.

Adam said, "I was naked," and God said, "Who told you that you were naked?" At first this, too, seems to be a ridiculous question. Was God trying to keep the fact that they had no clothes a secret? Such a conclusion demeans God and humanity. Perhaps we'd understand it better if we phrased it this way: "Who made you self-conscious about your body? Why do you suddenly feel compelled to hide?"

God's question indicates to us that the knowledge of evil comes at the price of shame. This is the difference, theologically, between being unclothed and being naked. To be unclothed simply meant that Adam and Eve had no clothes. They were comfortable not only physically but emotionally and spiritually. No self-consciousness interfered with their relationship with God or with each other.

But sin brought a new—and upsetting—sense of self. This is described as nakedness. Nakedness is more than just physical exposure of the body. It describes being vulnerable in heart, mind, and soul as well. Nakedness refers to being open, being seen for who you really are in your whole person. And that can be extremely threatening and put us on the defensive.

Evil distorts how we see ourself and others. We no longer look with pure eyes of appreciation. Now we see each other through the lenses of lust and judgmentalism. We no longer walk in freedom, carefree and accepting of who we are. Haunted by the threat of nakedness, we want to cover up and posture so that others will be impressed. Or at least they won't see our faults.

Adam was ashamed. Shame is a sense of lowered self-worth. It's the sense of knowing that you haven't been the person you want to be. You haven't lived up to the standards you have for yourself. And so you want to hide that from people. You don't want people to see that you're not quite what they think you are. You don't want people to know what you're really like. You're afraid—of rejection, of punishment. When you slip, you try to cover it up. You play the hypocrite, the actor, hiding behind a mask.

When we become aware of our weaknesses, we want to hide. When we fail, we want to hide. When we are hurt, we want to hide. When we fear that too much is expected of us, we want to hide. And when we hear God approaching, most of us want to hide.

We hide in many ways.

AVOIDANCE. This was Adam and Eve's strategy. They hid themselves and hoped that God would go away.

Avoidance is a primary coping strategy. We avoid going to the doctor so we don't have to face the truth about our physical condition. We avoid starting exercise so we won't have to face how out of shape we are. I have often seen people go through periods of time when they won't come to church because they want to avoid considering God's call on their lives. Some people will avoid you when they are struggling, especially if you've been a spiritual friend to them. They don't want to be reminded of that part of their life that is in need.

Avoidance is simply another term for delay. Problems don't go away when we avoid them. They come around at the most inconvenient times! And usually with greater intensity. God flushed Adam and Eve out of the bushes so that they could deal with reality in the most effective way. His directness resulted in appropriate coverings, natural consequences, and the promise of salvation.

BUSYNESS. We hide behind our activities. We keep so busy with the outer world of schoolwork, family, sports, business deals, or church work, that we are deaf to the inner cries of the soul. People who have an opportunity to sit and rest will often keep going at a frantic pace because they don't want to face up to what the quiet would bring.

But constant motion will not bring us to maturity. As we rush about, we are less and less satisfied. The time comes when we are forced to stop, through illness, a family or rela-

Are there times I hide behind a mask?

What kinds of masks do I use?

Busyness?

Competency?

Overwork?

Neediness?

There are innumerable masks. What are my favorites?

How often is avoidance a problem for me? In what circumstances and relationships?

How can I respond differently?

tional crisis, or an emotional overload. Then nothing will remain hidden.

Does my pace of life encourage hiding from God?

What activities are especially distracting and time consuming?

ACCOMPLISHMENT. We often live as if success in one or two areas could make up for our failures or shortcomings in other areas. Remember the parable of the rich fool? When his barns were full to overflowing, he decided to tear them down and build bigger ones. "'And I'll sit back and say to myself, My friend, you have enough stored away for years to come. Now take it easy! Eat, drink, and be merry!'

"But God said to him, 'You fool! You will die this very night. Then who will get it all?" (Luke 12:19-20).

What good is your performance? What good is your success? What good are bigger barns, bigger houses, bigger cars, a bigger name, a bigger reputation, a bigger impact? What good is it? It is not your worldly success but your eternal soul that is required of you.

Plaques on the wall cannot substitute for piety in the heart. Commendations from the world cannot excuse a lack of consecration in our life. Assets in the bank cannot atone for resistance to God's call.

Do I try to impress God and others with my accomplishments?

Do I use accomplishments to excuse my lack of obedience or responsibility in other areas?

PURSUIT OF PLEASURE. Several years ago Neil Postman wrote a book called *Amusing Ourselves to Death.* What a vivid description of our society! And that's what many of us try to do. We hide behind entertainment and pleasure. Pleasure can be either a distraction that diverts us or a drug that numbs us. We feed our body and our desires while we ignore some of the most urgent needs of our heart.

Pleasure has its place in life. God has given us many good gifts for re-creation—which we usually spell recreation. When pleasure keeps us from spiritual priorities, however, it becomes a problem. One man had a hobby that was innocent in itself, but he ended up selling all his equipment related to the hobby. When he looked closely at his calendar and his budget, he felt he had allowed his hobby to control too much of both.

GOING THROUGH THE MOTIONS. Revelation 3:16 describes this as being lukewarm. The church in Laodicea was religious but not genuine. They were religiously active but not authentic. There was no congruence between what they said and how they behaved. Jesus said, in effect, "I wish that you were hot or cold. I could deal with it if you absolutely despised me for certain reasons, or if you loved me with a passion. But because you are just lukewarm, I'm going to spit you out of my mouth."

Lukewarmness describes outward involvement that keeps our heart insulated and isolated from the touch of God. We just go through the motions. We hide through being close enough to think it makes a difference to God but far enough to keep God from making a difference in our life.

Hiding doesn't work for long. It isn't effective. It robs us of what we most need in life. But more important, why hide when we can live in freedom and joy? The amazing grace in this story is that hiding is based on the wrong idea of God. God isn't as we expect him to be, ready to condemn, punish, abandon, and reject. When you hide, you become your own prisoner. God is the one who seeks to set you free.

The God Who Questions Us

We can learn a lot about a person by the questions he asks. Other religions do not portray a God who asks us questions. They do not portray a searching God. When God asks, "Where are you?" he gives away his own location. He reveals his character. He shows his heart. And what we learn draws us out of hiding.

God will always find us.

Hiding is based on the premise that God can't see us unless we want to be seen. That's one of the big lies that most people believe. When I was a little boy, I sucked my thumb. I remember discovering at some point that if I put my hand up over my eyes (like a person shading himself from the sun), I couldn't see anybody. I assumed that they couldn't see me. One day I came home from kindergarten and went into our family room to watch television. I put my thumb in my mouth and my hand up to shade my eyes. (Of course,

What amusements interfere with my relationship with God?

Why am I drawn to these amusements? What do I need to do about them?

In what ways do I simply go through the motions of my faith?

Am I really engaged in Bible study, prayer, giving, service, or worship?

starting kindergarten is a traumatic experience!) My mom walked into the room and said, "Get your thumb out of your mouth. You're starting school now." I thought, *How did she know? I had my hand up!*

I have a friend who leads worship. He knows that many people are self-conscious about raising their hands as they worship the Lord, so he says, "If you want to raise your hands but are worried that others might see you, just close your eyes." That comment always gets a good laugh. But many people live as if they can hide, when, in fact, they are always in God's sight.

Psalm 139 describes how there is no way to hide from God. Because God is God, nothing in all creation escapes his knowledge. We use the great *omni-* words to describe these characteristics of God. *Omni* is a prefix that means "all." God is omniscient; he knows everything. The psalmist says, "O Lord, you have examined my heart and know everything about me. . . . You know what I am going to say even before I say it, Lord" (Psalm 139:1, 4, NLT). Omnipresent means that God is present everywhere. "I can never escape from your spirit! I can never get away from your presence!" (Psalm 139:7). God is omnipotent, having all power. He made our body and formed our destiny (see Psalm 139:13-16). Now, if all these characteristics are true, what sense does it make to hide?

What assumptions have I made about God?

How do I respond to the fact that God is everywhere and knows everything?

What, then, am I really hiding from?

There is a soul-chilling passage in Romans 2:16 that says this: "The day will surely come when God, by Jesus Christ, will judge everyone's secret life." It is absurd to deceive ourself and think that we can hide from God. Guilt triggers the hiding reflex, but it's really an absurd reflex. Yet we hide.

God longs for our redemption, not our punishment.

To come out of hiding into fellowship with God—even if it means chastisement—is to be redeemed.

God could have had a different approach to Adam and Eve. He could have come with threatening force. Picture God as a five-star general. He crashes into the Garden and sounds the charge. The angelic troops muster and surround the Garden of Eden. God calls out on the megaphone, "All right, flush 'em out!" The angelic hosts start their search. They get closer and closer. Suddenly, Adam and Eve are forced into the open. They are tried, sentenced, and executed before a firing squad right then and there.

God could have done that. It would have been appropriate. He had said, "If you eat of its fruit, you will die." In other words, "If you break my rules, there will be terminal consequences!" But God didn't do that.

God could have ignored them. We learn from the Scriptures that God met with them every evening in the cool of the day when the evening breezes kicked up through the Garden. Can you imagine how beautiful that was? So imagine the first day after they've sinned. Adam and Eve are hoping God doesn't come. And God doesn't come. And God doesn't come the next day either. I'm guessing that by the fourth or fifth evening, Adam and Eve look at each other and finally say, "So where did he go?"

"I don't know."

"Do you miss him?"

"Yeah, I really do."

God could have ignored them, giving them the cold shoulder. People do that, don't they? Have you ever received the silent treatment as punishment? Have you ever known someone who had such vindictive parents that they just ignored the child to demonstrate their disappointment or disgust? God could have just walked away and left it at that. But he didn't. He's after redemption and fellowship, not condemnation and separation.

When we sin, God comes looking for us.

Here is the point we need to understand. This truth will transform our life. When we sin, God comes looking for us. When we fail, God seeks us out. When our reflex is to hide, God's response is to find.

When Adam and Eve deliberately disobeyed God, did God desert them? No. He came to them. Their sin did not separate them from God. God came to them. Yes, their disobedience affected their relationship with God, but God still pursued them. God came after them. Our guilt does not cut us off from God. Only our refusal to come out of hiding separates us from God. God is a seeking and finding God.

In Ezekiel 34:11, God says, "I myself will search and find my sheep." In Luke 15 Jesus uses three parables to describe the seeking and finding God. He tells us that God is like a shepherd who seeks the lost lamb. God is like the woman who loses one of her ten coins. (I think that parable would make a lot more sense if we talked about a lost credit card! Have any of you ever searched high and low for a lost credit card? Then you understand the searching God!) God is like a father who welcomes his rebellious children.

Our God is a searching God. We read in 1 John 1:7, "If we walk in the light, as he is in the light, we have fellowship with one another, and the blood of Jesus, his Son, purifies us from all sin" (NIV). In contemporary evangelism we refer to people who are looking for God as "seekers." But what we have to understand is that God is the first seeker. Jesus said, "And I, the Son of Man, have come to seek and save those [like Zacchaeus] who are lost" (Luke 19:10).

Our refusal to come out of hiding, to acknowledge and confess our sin, and to repent disrupts our relationship with God. We aren't held at bay by God's rejection of us. When we violate God's standards, he still calls out to us, "Where are you? I want you back!"

"Where are you?" This question exposes our anxious guilt and our hiding reflex. But it also reveals the very character of God. Our God is the God who seeks and finds. Our God is the God who doesn't desert us when we fail him. We learn that he is a God who doesn't degrade us or devalue us when we fall. We learn that he is a God who doesn't threaten or intimidate us.

At the end of World War II, a Japanese soldier by the name of Shoichi Yokoi went into hiding. He lived in a cave on the island of Guam. Yokoi later said that he knew the war was over because of the leaflets that were scattered throughout the jungles of Guam. But he was afraid that if he came out of hiding, he would be executed. This man stayed in hiding for twenty-eight years in his jungle cave, coming out only at night. During this long period of time, he lived on frogs, rats, snails, shrimp, nuts, and mangoes. Finally, two hunters came upon him and told him that he need not hide any longer. At last he was free, and with new clothes to wear and food to eat, he was taken by plane to his home, to his family.[1]

You see, God asks us where we are in order to draw us into a relationship. He doesn't intimidate us with his righteous wrath. He draws us. God is looking for us, inviting us to come out of the hiding caused by our shame, guilt, or fear.

What about You?

Have you seen your hiding place described in this chapter? How have you been hiding from God? Why have you wanted to hide? Has it worked? Are you happier now to be out of fellowship?

Did you know that God is right here today, asking, "Where are you?" He's after you, but in a loving way. He's coming after you with that soul-searching question to help you understand why you're hiding and to help you come out and be reunited with him.

Notes

1. Paul Lee Tan, *Encyclopedia of 7700 Illustrations* (Rockville, Md.: Assurance Publishers, 1979), 1651.

CHAPTER 3

"What have you done?" Drifting toward Destruction

Genesis 4:10

TWO MEN WERE riding on a railroad train across country. One of the men predicted that within a few years the little white churches they could see dotting the countryside would be only a memory buried in the ruins of all religion.

The other replied, "Still, the life of Christ is fascinating. I think an interesting romance could be written about him."

"And you're just the man to write it," replied the other. "Go ahead. Tear down the prevailing sentiment about his deity, and paint him as a man—a man among men."

The man took the challenge. He was a first-rate lawyer and military general, and he felt he could build an indisputable case against Christ. For two years he studied in the best libraries of Europe and the United States, seeking information that would enable him to write the book that would destroy Jesus as the Christ.

While writing the second chapter of his volume, however, he found himself on his knees, crying out in faith to Jesus Christ, saying, "My Lord, my God." The evidence for the deity of Christ was overwhelmingly conclusive. He could no longer deny that Jesus Christ was the Son of God. The one he had determined to expose as a fraud had captured him.

"After six years given to the impartial investigation of Christianity," he wrote, "as to its truth or falsity, I have come to the deliberate conclusion that Jesus Christ was the

Messiah of the Jews, the Savior of the world, and my personal Savior."

The man? Lew Wallace. The book? *Ben Hur.* Published in 1880, it remains possibly the greatest novel ever written concerning the time of Christ.[1]

But what about the other man? His name was Robert Green Ingersoll, the foremost orator and political speechmaker of late nineteenth-century America—perhaps the best-known American of the post–Civil War era. He bitterly opposed the religious right of his day. He was an early popularizer of Charles Darwin and a tireless advocate of science and reason.

The mystery of Ingersoll was that he was raised in a Christian home. His father was a Presbyterian and Congregational minister. Robert was brought up on the Bible and the Westminster Shorter Catechism and taught a strict observance of the Sabbath day. He was admonished to search the Scriptures, but he continually questioned them. They did not solve his childish doubts or answer his many questions. "Something wrong, somewhere," was his frequent comment, even as a boy, as he read the Bible. His father was troubled. He could not comprehend such skepticism in such a young child. He would never, in his wildest dreams, have imagined this boy would one day become the most famous agnostic of the nineteenth century. Ingersoll's friend I. Newton Baker reported:

> The simple truth is that Mr. Ingersoll was an unbeliever from his childhood. He has said to me as to others, that he never remembered the time when his mind did not reject and his heart resent what he believed to be the cruelties and falsehoods of many of the Bible doctrines and narratives, and when he did not hate with all his soul the injustice and savagery of the man-made God of the Scriptures.[2]

Folk wisdom tells us that if you have a nightmare of falling, you will wake up before you hit bottom. Life experience teaches us, however, that many people who are falling into terrible self-destruction do not wake up.

The road from God often begins on a gradual slope. People don't necessarily plunge over the cliff of apostasy, blasphemy, or gross disobedience in a single step. In fact, the separation from God can begin in the midst of religious activity, as it did with Ingersoll. Two people can react very differently to the same material. Wallace's study of God's Word broke his heart open. Ingersoll simply walked farther and farther from his initial religious training. The small steps added up to a widening distance.

The story of Cain presents such a journey away from God. But it also reveals the checkpoints of grace that God provides along the way. It is not only a warning to those who are picking up speed on the downslope of unbelief, but it is for all of us who wrestle with dark desires. This story shows us a number of opportunities Cain had to turn back to God. It reminds us of the warning from Hebrews 3:7: "That is why the Holy Spirit says, 'Today you must listen to his voice. Don't harden your hearts against him.' "

Now Adam slept with his wife, Eve, and she became pregnant. When the time came, she gave birth to Cain, and she said, "With the Lord's help, I have brought forth a man!" Later she gave birth to a second son and named him Abel.

When they grew up, Abel became a shepherd, while Cain was a farmer. At harvesttime Cain brought to the Lord a gift of his farm produce, while Abel brought several choice lambs from the best of his flock. The Lord accepted Abel and his offering, but he did not accept Cain and his offering. This made Cain very angry and dejected.

"Why are you so angry?" the Lord asked him. "Why do you look so dejected? You will be accepted if you respond in the right way. But if you refuse to respond correctly, then watch out!

> **Sin is waiting to attack and destroy you, and you must subdue it."**
>
> **Later Cain suggested to his brother, Abel, "Let's go out into the fields." And while they were there, Cain attacked and killed his brother. (Genesis 4:1-8)**

The First Step Away from God: The Wrong Focus

The process of becoming distant from God happens one step at a time. The first step is described in God's first interaction with Cain.

Cain and Abel brought their offering to God. But when God did not look on Cain's offering with favor, Cain became angry. Cain looked dejected. As some translations say, his face was downcast. The reactions of anger and dejection are the first clues into Cain's spiritual condition.

Duty or devotion?

Many scholars say that Abel's offering was acceptable over Cain's because of the nature of the offering. They say that Abel's was more acceptable because it involved a blood sacrifice from the choice lambs of his flock. Cain's was simply grain. But Hebrews 11:4 points us to another reason, a more compelling reason:

> It was by faith that Abel brought a more acceptable offering to God than Cain did. God accepted Abel's offering to show that he was a righteous man. And although Abel is long dead, he still speaks to us because of his faith.

It is the nature of the *offerer,* not the offering, that matters most to God. This was a point God often made to his people. The Lord says in Isaiah 1:14-16:

> I hate all your festivals and sacrifices. I cannot stand the sight of them! From now on, when you lift up

> your hands in prayer, I will refuse to look. Even though you offer many prayers, I will not listen. For your hands are covered with the blood of your innocent victims. Wash yourselves and be clean! Let me no longer see your evil deeds. Give up your wicked ways.

What does the Lord require of us? Not the ritual offerings of ceremonies, but the genuine offering of ourself. God looks at the heart. God was showing Cain that he was performing his religious acts as a duty, rather than as a devotion. Cain was trying to get by with fulfilling the minimum obligation when God wanted the maximum devotion.

Cain came to sacrifice the way too many of us go to church. Do you find yourself asking, *What am* I *going to get out of this?* People go to church to hear a particular preacher or because they enjoy the music or want to participate in a particular program. Naturally we seek personal benefits to nurture our faith, but there must also be a clear commitment to express our devotion to the Lord. When we perform our spiritual actions as obligations, we focus on what we want to get out of them, not on what we give God. The real question is not, What's in this for me? but How am I going to honor and worship the living Lord?

Cain was trying to get ahead on his own. We know this because of his reaction to God's chastisement. When God told Cain that his offering was unacceptable, Cain could have responded differently. He could have bowed in repentance and humility, saying, "Lord, what do I need to do to please you? Search me, O God, and know my heart. Test my thoughts and motives. Cleanse me from any wickedness. I just want to please you, Lord." That's how Cain *could* have responded. Instead, he was angry. His face was downcast. His concern was not with God's honor but with his own gain. Such offerings are not acceptable to God. What arrogance! He was not coming to God with a genuine heart. So God came to him with a warning.

In what ways do I try to use my faith for my own advancement at the expense of honoring God?

Notice in this passage how often God comes to Cain.

Cain only comes to God once—to bring his sacrifice—and even then he is just going through the motions. But now God comes to Cain. In spite of an unacceptable offering, God seeks out Cain. Listen to what he says in verses 6-7:

> "Why are you so angry?" the Lord asked him. "Why do you look so dejected? You will be accepted if you respond in the right way. But if you refuse to respond correctly, then watch out! Sin is waiting to attack and destroy you, and you must subdue it."

Being honest is frightening—and not easy.

God's warning was also an invitation, but Cain would refuse to accept it. That which we least want to do may in the long run bring us the most benefit. But we refuse to do it. That which we find most frightening may in the long run bring us the most peace and security. But still we refuse to do it. I know of suburban drug users, successful by worldly criteria, who have refused to get help and have suffered increasing losses. First they miss a few days of work, then they have to sell their vacation home. Soon their business begins going backward due to a lack of attention. Creditors lose patience, and financial ruin looms. All this is happening while marriage and family are crumbling and often breaking under the pressure.

We see the same tendency in ourself when we refuse to submit to God's commands for spiritual discipline, for ethical integrity, for social responsibility, for respect, and for kindness in all relationships. We all know how we resist doing what we know we need to do. C. S. Lewis brings the high cost of such behavior to light:

> Teachers will tell you that the laziest boy in the class is the one who works the hardest in the end. They mean this. If you give two boys, say, a proposition in geometry to do, the one who is prepared to take trouble will try to understand it. The lazy boy will learn it by heart because, for the

> moment, that needs less effort. But six months later, when they are preparing for the exam, that lazy boy is doing hours and hours of miserable drudgery over things the other boy understands, and positively enjoys, in a few minutes.
>
> Laziness means more work in the long run. Or look at it this way. In a battle, or in mountain climbing, there is often one thing which it takes a lot of pluck to do; but it is also, in the long run, the safest thing to do. If you funk it, you will find yourself, hours later, in far worse danger. The cowardly thing is also the most dangerous thing.[3]

There is a cowardice in not being honest, especially with ourself. The cowardice stems from the fear of seeing what we're really like. We're afraid to consider what God is calling us to do in our life. In the long run that cowardice is more costly than we may ever imagine. When God didn't accept Cain's offering, this should have given Cain pause to think about the reasons. That should have been a soul-searching time for Cain. Instead, the only sacrifice Cain would make would be the sacrifices of his conscience and soul.

Am I honest with myself?

Are there areas I hold back from the Lord and myself?

How might my holding back cost me—spiritually, emotionally, relationally, practically?

Facing up to who we really are can be absolutely frightening. At the same time, once we break through the resistance it can be totally invigorating. If you've ever come to the point of confession, you know the incredible freedom it brings. You come to a point where you finally confess your own wrongdoing; you come clean in that moment, and you may feel almost giddy.

There's a vivid picture of this kind of confession in the book *Dead Man Walking* by Sister Helen Prejean, about the trial and execution of a man who, with a partner, brutally attacked a teenage couple, raping the girl and then murdering both the boy and the girl. It is an unpleasant story to read, but a redemptive thread runs through it. Matthew Ponselette, who is on death row for the crime, denies his role in it until the very end. Sister Helen continually visits him, encouraging him to tell the truth. "The truth will set you free," she says, quoting Jesus. Ponselette continues to deny his guilt. Finally, he is taken to the execution chamber and strapped to the table, where the needles for the lethal injection are put in place. He asks to be lifted to face the witnesses. As he does this, strapped to the execution table in a cruciform manner, he confesses and asks forgiveness. And in the midst of that wrenching situation, you can feel the serenity wash over him as he surrenders to justice—and to the mercy promised to those who seek it.

Cain was like Matthew Ponselette, only he never reached the point of breaking. Maybe there was no Sister Helen Prejean in his life who would drive him to understand that the truth will set you free. But Cain was one who persistently denied and distanced himself from God. Remember Genesis 3 when God went looking for Adam and Eve in the Garden? They were hiding. Well, the story of Cain is a bit different. Cain doesn't hide; he simply defies God.

The Second Step: Rejecting God's Correction

> You will be accepted if you respond in the right way. But if you refuse to respond correctly, then watch out! Sin is waiting to attack and destroy you, and you must subdue it. (Genesis 4:7)

Here we see the second step in growing distant from God: rejecting God's correction. When we do this, we become more vulnerable to dark desires. And Cain is being given a warning here by God. First God says, "Cain, if you do what is right you will be acceptable." God is always saying that to you and me. I love the New Living Translation's version of this: "You will be accepted if you respond in the right way." It's as if God is saying, "Cain, we have to work through some things here. You need to grow, you need to change, but the end result will be your acceptance. If you don't do what is right, sin is crouching at the door." This is a vivid picture.

The picture of sin waiting to attack is actually an image of a beast ready to pounce. Those who camp in the mountains often experience bears coming through their campsite. There are also occasional reports of mountain lions. Now picture this: You are in your tent asleep, and you are startled awake by a rustling outside your tent. You hear a low growl right at your door. Something is crouching there. Its desire is to have you! Are you going to throw open the tent flaps and say, "Here, kitty"? I don't think so!

The Lord gives Cain warning—and hope. Most people miss the hope, but it is clearly stated: "You will be accepted." A lot of times we think that, once we've been tempted, we're just going to fall into sin, as if we can't stop the process. But God appeals to us to stop that process, just as he appealed to Cain. The Lord says, "No, Cain, you can master this. You can stand against this." And the way we do that, of course, is the picture of Jesus in Gethsemane. Pray, lest you fall into temptation. (See chapter 19 on Jesus and the disciples in Gethsemane.)

Are there signs of sin crouching at the door of your heart? Are there any areas in your life where you know there is a mountain lion out there ready to spring on you? Maybe it's anger that somebody wounded you. Maybe you have been dealt with very unfairly, and by all objective standards you have an absolute right to be bitter and angry. What are you going to do with it? It's crouching at the door.

Maybe discontent is on the prowl. You see many friends and acquaintances getting ahead in life. They seem to be making their way in life, and things aren't going quite right for you—or you think you should be farther along. You're somewhat angry at God and resentful of others when they share their own good news. Sin is crouching at the door.

Maybe physical temptations are stalking. Desires that are gnawing at the door, scratching at the frame, threatening to

What beasts are crouching at my door?

What is required to subdue or avoid those beasts?

What one step can I take right now?

break through. Whatever it is, will you hear the warning, or will you allow it to take you one step farther from God?

The Third Step: Welcoming Sin

As we consider the mystery of God's grace reaching out continually to Cain, we also find here the mystery of iniquity. Cain welcomes the sin. He opens the door and embraces the charging beast, and it devours him. It consumes him in such a way that he becomes a beast himself, stalking his brother. And in his raging appetite of bitterness he pounces upon his righteous brother and devours him without remorse. Sin crouching at the door consumed Cain, and he then consumed an innocent person.

Cain refused the discipline of the Lord. We have an explanation of this in Hebrews 12:7-11, where it talks about being disciplined. When God first came to Cain, he disciplined him. Now, none of us like discipline. As a child, I didn't like being disciplined by my parents, my coaches, or my teachers. And I see that carrying on to the next generation. None of us like being disciplined in our work or anything else. But discipline, the Bible tells us, is a sign of love.

> As you endure this divine discipline, remember that God is treating you as his own children. Whoever heard of a child who was never disciplined? If God doesn't discipline you as he does all of his children, it means that you are illegitimate and are not really his children after all. Since we respect our earthly fathers who disciplined us, should we not all the more cheerfully submit to the discipline of our heavenly Father and live forever? For our earthly fathers disciplined us for a few years, doing the best they knew how. But God's discipline is always right and good for us because it means we will share in his holiness. No discipline is enjoyable while it is happening—it is painful! But afterward there will be a quiet harvest of right living for those who are trained in this way.

Cain was meant to be trained when God gave him that warning. But he refused it. Why? I think Hebrews 12:14-15 helps us understand that.

> Try to live in peace with everyone, and seek to live a clean and holy life, for those who are not holy will not see the Lord. Look after each other so that none of you will miss out on the special favor of God. Watch out that no bitter root of unbelief rises up among you, for whenever it springs up, many are corrupted by its poison.

Cain was a farmer, but the plants he tended most grew from the seeds of bitterness in his own heart. He was angry with his brother, Abel. We don't know why. Maybe because his little brother was a pest. Maybe because the younger one always has it easier, and the older one has it tougher. We don't know why. But he was bitter toward his brother. And he allowed that bitterness to germinate into envy, competition, and resentment. He is like the bitter servant in the parable of the talents. Remember the parable in which the servants were given five talents and three talents, and one was given one talent? The one-talent servant went and hid it, and when he was asked why he hid it, he said, "I knew you were a hard master so I hid the talent." His image of the Lord was resentful and bitter, so he reacted foolishly.

Don't underestimate the power of sin. It is wicked, and it is swift. There is no gradual evolution into sin. The extreme expression of sin's entrance into the world comes immediately, in the second generation. In the opening chapters of Genesis, sin breaks into the Creation. It speeds like a deadly virus through the entire human system and the created order. Sin contaminates every aspect of life: between a person and God, between a person and him- or herself, between a person and others, and between a person and the created order. Although God pronounced a curse on sin, we see here that the real curse is sin itself, destroying creation from within.

Are there any seeds of bitterness in my life?

Am I bitter about my past?

Am I bitter about my current situation?

Am I likely to uproot my seeds of bitterness or cultivate them a little longer? Why?

In fact, that's the theme of Genesis 4–11. God shows us how sin destroys the human race. Even after the cleansing flood, history immediately begins its downward spiral to the Tower of Babel, when God's judgment broke forth again. Only the continuing expressions of God's grace and mercy could break the cycle of sin and its consequences.

Cain was jealous of his brother's relationship with God. He thought that by getting rid of his brother, who was a mirror of his failure, he would get rid of his problem. But God held up the mirror of holiness, and Cain was forced to see himself as he was.

The Fourth Step: Missed Repentance

Cain murdered his brother and buried him in the field. But he couldn't hide that fact from God. "Where's your brother?" What we often see as an accusation is another opportunity for grace and repentance. Again we ask ourself, what could Cain have done? He could have said, "I killed him. I don't know why—I wish I hadn't. I would do anything to have him back." And he could have fallen into the arms of God and received forgiveness.

But Cain responded, "I don't know. Am I my brother's keeper?" (NIV. The word *keeper* reveals Cain's burning animosity. This word denotes a condescending care for one who can't take care of himself. It's as if Cain were saying, "Am I supposed to take care of 'little Abel' all the time?")

When Adam and Eve sinned against God and heard God coming into the Garden, what did they do? They hid. They were ashamed. How does Cain react? Certainly not with shame. He is arrogant. He struts with a casual bravado in the presence of God Almighty—and all the time with blood on his hands. There is a nonchalance about him that shows a hard, cold heart.

If you are ashamed because of your sin, God bless you! But God pity the person who doesn't care. Of course, we don't want to be locked in shame; we want to be set free from it. And when we confess, God forgives our sins and cleanses us from unrighteousness. But when we refuse to repent, when we refuse to speak the truth, when we deliberately defy God—then we should pray because we are in mortal danger. I'm not being melodramatic.

Cain doesn't get it. He looks God in the eye and says, "Am I my brother's keeper?" Not only is this the obvious expression of hatred toward his family, but it is in direct defiance of God.

Then God says, "What have you done?" It's not a request for information. Whenever God asks questions in Scripture, it's never because he lacks information. It's a soul-searching question, a question for self-examination. This is the last opportunity for Cain to come right with God.

God is finally ready to speak in judgment against Cain. Even at this point, I believe, Cain can repent. But he refuses to repent. So God pronounces his judgment. And do you know what God gives Cain? He gives Cain what Cain wants. God sends Cain from God's presence. God says, in effect, "You are going to be a restless wanderer. You don't want anything that I can give you. You don't want my presence, so go. If you want to go, go and live in the land of Nod." (Isn't that a great word? It's not meant to describe the dreamland of many congregations at sermon time!) The land of Nod is a rich Hebrew concept for the desolate realm of those who wander in lostness. It's a pathetic image. It's a sad, frightening, chilling image.

What does Cain say to that? "My punishment is too great for me to bear." He complains—but he does not repent. What's with this man? He might have said, "Lord, your punishment is more than I can bear. I'm broken; forgive me, I want to change." What would God have said? "Welcome home, my son! Kill the fatted calf! My son was lost, and now he is found!" God would have done that, as hard as you and I find that to believe. That is the depth of God's grace and God's pursuit. But Cain says, "They will kill me out there." God says, "No, they won't. I'll put a mark on you and let you live." The mercy of God is astounding. Letting Cain live.

Of course, now we can see that there is judgment in this scene, too. Mercy with judgment is part of how God does things sometimes. Cain could have changed. Have you watched throughout this passage what God did constantly as he pursued? And yet we also see here the mystery of iniquity. The mystery of human beings, in which there is a cycle of self-destruction. The cycle began when Cain brought his offering—and he brought his first—out of a sense of religious obligation. He went through the formality and then learned that God was looking at the heart and not just the action. But he rejected divine correction. He became resentful, antagonistic, and bitter. That bitterness bore fruit in murder. Then Cain was rebuked by God, and his heart was hardened, and finally he was driven into exile.

It is difficult for many to accept and affirm the judgment of God. How does this account of God's dealing with Cain help me understand God's grace and justice?

Here's the process in a nutshell. When we deny our problems and sins, we grow to resent God. When we are defiant in the face of God's warning, our resentment turns into resistance. And finally, deliberate disobedience leads to defying God and being driven from God's presence.

What about You?

How does Cain's story affect my view of God?

Sometimes it's really tough to do the hardest thing. To be honest and let God's Word come through to your heart and say, "Hey, pal, you've got to deal with this." Sometimes what you're dealing with is so hard that you wonder if you will come out of it alive. But we're much worse off when we keep drifting away from God. We may be avoiding judgment, yes, but also avoiding the love that can restore us.

Facing ourself can be very hard. Confessing our wrongdoing is hard. One thing to keep in mind is that we need only to confess to those people who have been affected. The circle of confession extends only to the circle of offense. So if you've done something wrong between you and God, you need to confess to God only. If you need a counselor or pastor, that's fine, too. If you've offended one person, it's just between you and that one person. God doesn't want us to rehearse our sins to an audience; he's not out to hurt us in some humiliating, vengeful way. But he requires that we face our sins and confess our faults so that he can help us.

Just like Cain, we fear humiliation, rejection, being seen for what we are. But we should be more afraid of becoming hard in our heart as Cain did. Beware of those steps that will take you away from God's grace, love, and restoration.

God pursues us. The message of grace in this passage is one of mercy in verse 7: "If you do what is right, will you not be accepted?" (NIV). Or as the New Living Translation says, "You will be accepted if you respond in the right way."

God comes to each of us and says, "What have you done?" The only question that really matters now is, "Then what will you do?" What will you do?

Notes

1. This information was compiled by Doug Rumford from the following sources: Frank S. Mead, ed., *The Encyclopedia of Religious Quotations* (Old Tappan, N.J.: Fleming H. Revell, 1965), 59; introduction to *10 Basic Steps* (Campus Crusade for Christ, 1970); Josh McDowell, *Evidence That Demands a Verdict* (Campus Crusade for Christ, 1972), 367–368; Paul Lee Tan, *Encyclopedia of 7700 Illustrations* (Rockville, Md.: Assurance Publishers, 1979), 850.
2. I. Newton Baker, "Robert G. Ingersoll: An Intimate View," (http://www.infidels.org/library/historical/newton_baker/intimate_view.html).
3. Richard J. Foster and James Bryan Smith, eds., *Devotional Classics* (San Francisco: HarperCollins, 1993), 8.

CHAPTER 4

"Do you fear God for nothing?" Attacking Our Motives

Job 1:9

Even so, I love Thee and will love
and in Thy praise will sing,
solely because Thou art my God
and my Eternal King. ANONYMOUS

THERE ONCE WAS a minister—an evangelist and church planter. He was energetic and incredibly focused, and because of this, he got a lot done. He worked hard, passionately, and God blessed his efforts.

As so often happens with such people, others began to resent him. They resented his reputation for being a wonderful servant of God. They resented the authority that had come to rest on him in the Christian community. They resented how feeble their own efforts appeared compared to his.

Well, eventually these resentful Christians made the man's life miserable. Rumors began to follow him: He was an egomaniac. He took money from people. He was out to build his own little empire. Things got so bad and so confused, that the minister finally had to circulate a letter to the churches, explaining in detail how he worked and why. He was undoubtedly hurt the most over people accusing him of wanting to be the big shot and of profiting off others' trust—when his true heart's desire was to proclaim God's love and human redemption through Christ. That letter to the churches is heartbreaking to read. But if you'd like to read it, turn to 2 Corinthians. The minister I speak of was the apostle Paul.

Have your motives ever been questioned? When you've worked hard at something, and it's a success, and you've finally settled back to rest and enjoy the fruit of your labor, somebody murmurs something about your real agenda. Maybe you've been involved in a parent-teacher organization—your contribution to the community and to the future of the younger generation—and people wonder if you're in it so you can have more say over which teachers your children get. Or maybe you make a significant donation to some organization, and word gets around. "What was that for?" people are asking. If you get into politics at any level, your motives are automatically suspect.

And sometimes we question our own motives. We do something good and then interrogate ourself later: Was I really doing that for unselfish reasons? You do something that puts you in the spotlight, and people start whispering. One teenager, shy by nature, asked permission to put posters up at her high school. These posters had positive faith messages in them, and some of the kids really seemed to notice them. The girl felt pretty good; here she could communicate the gospel in a nonconfrontive, positive way. But later she heard people accusing her of trying "to act like God or something." She had consciously put up those posters to share the Good News. But now even she wondered if her schoolmates were right. Maybe she couldn't trust herself to know why she did what she did. Sometimes it seems that you can't win.

The issue of motives is real for all of us. And it's a matter of the heart. And when it's a matter of the heart, it's a matter of faith. It can become a battleground of faith. In fact, in the story of Job the question of his motives was the catalyst for the whole story.

> **One day the angels came to present themselves before the Lord, and Satan the Accuser came with them. "Where have you come from?" the Lord asked Satan.**
>
> **And Satan answered the Lord, "I have been**

> **going back and forth across the earth, watching everything that's going on."**
> **Then the Lord asked Satan, "Have you noticed my servant Job? He is the finest man in all the earth—a man of complete integrity. He fears God and will have nothing to do with evil."**
> **Satan replied to the Lord, "Yes, Job fears God, but not without good reason! You have always protected him and his home and his property from harm. You have made him prosperous in everything he does. Look how rich he is! But take away everything he has, and he will surely curse you to your face!"**
> **"All right, you may test him," the Lord said to Satan. "Do whatever you want with everything he possesses, but don't harm him physically." So Satan left the Lord's presence. (Job 1:6-12)**

Satan Attacks Job's Motives

Does Job serve God for nothing or for what he's going to get out of it? That's the basic question here. Satan attacks our motives, and he emphasizes the fact that they are mixed. There are noble elements but also some selfish elements to all of our words and actions. Satan accuses us of looking primarily for what we are going to get out of it. And he tries to take us out of the action in that way.

Accusing us before ourself and God

Two words are frequently used to designate the evil one. The first one is *devil,* which is the English translation of a Greek word *diabolos* meaning "slanderer." As a slanderer, his purpose is to expose, embarrass, and malign people in order to set them in opposition to each other or to God. The second word we use for the evil one is *Satan. Satan* is the Hebrew word meaning "the accuser." Satan was like the prosecuting attorney in a courtroom. The prosecuting attorney would stand on the right-hand side of the accused and bring charges against the accused. In the book of Job, it's as if Satan is on the right-hand side of Job, bringing charges against him.

This same picture is in Zechariah 3:1-2. Jeshua, the high priest, is standing before the angels of the Lord, with Satan standing at his right side to accuse him.

> Then the angel showed me Jeshua the high priest standing before the angel of the Lord. Satan was there at the angel's right hand, accusing Jeshua of many things. And the Lord said to Satan, "I, the Lord, reject your accusations, Satan. Yes, the Lord, who has chosen Jerusalem, rebukes you. This man is like a burning stick that has been snatched from a fire."

In other words, God is saying, "Don't hassle this man. I have snatched him out of the fires of judgment. So you don't have anything to say about it." The Lord acknowledges the fact that Jeshua looks like one who has been snatched out of the fire. He's a mess! But instead of condemnation, the Lord cleans him up and gives him a whole new set of clothes! This is a beautiful picture of what it means to be a believer in Christ. God overrules Satan's accusations in the book of Zechariah.

When I feel dirtiest, I expect to be accused. It's hard to believe that God is willing to clean me up! What dirty clothes do I want God to remove now?

But in the book of Job we see the story of what Satan can do to a person. He is our accuser. And he accuses us for at least three reasons in his diabolical strategy.

SATAN ACCUSES US TO SEPARATE US FROM GOD. Satan believes that if he can bring charges against us, he will separate us from God. When he brings charges against Job, he begins by calling Job's character into question. With a cynical smirk, Satan argues that Job's righteousness simply makes good sense—or should I say good *cents*. Job, according to Satan, serves God because it brings prosperity. It's a pretty good deal. Take all that stuff away, and what would Job be like?

Satan is not only accusing Job of mixed motives, but he's even calling God into question. He is implying that the only way God can get people to believe in him is through "blessing bribery." He attempts to drive a wedge between Job and God by calling both of them into question.

SATAN ACCUSES US TO UNDERMINE OUR CONFIDENCE IN OURSELF. If Satan can get us to question ourself, we may become self-suspicious and hesitate to do what we originally intended to do. I was talking with a friend several years ago who was interested in writing articles and books. He shared some really neat ideas with me. So I said, "So what are you planning to do with these?"

"I feel ambivalent about trying to get published. I want to, but then I'm not sure."

"Why?"

"Because I think it's really an ego thing. If I got something published, I think I would become so proud that I wouldn't be able to honor the Lord."

That's a genuine dilemma. As we talked, the subject of mixed motives emerged. Should a Christian singer wait until she has her ego under control? Should a Christian musician be silent until there's no vestige of pride in the performance? What if all authors had such qualms? We may well have no books! If authors, performers, or teachers (the list could go on and on) hadn't used their gifts because they were afraid of mixed motives, they never would have blessed the millions of people whose lives they have touched. Using our gifts is a matter of obedience. Let God take care of the ego. Satan wants to put us out of the game by undermining our confidence.

Wouldn't it be odd if we did things—but didn't want to get anything out of them? If we spent our life doing things that gave us no satisfaction? Doesn't it make more sense that God would give us the ability and the desire to do things that would be helpful to others? That way, we all benefit. I help you because I'm motivated, and doing good things is rewarding for me. Sounds like an effective system to me. Yet Satan wants to throw it out of balance by condemning us for wanting to feel good or be satisfied in some way. Are you beginning to see how imbalanced that is? If we respond to Satan the way he wants us to respond, then

Have I held back in exercising my gifts because I fear the sense of personal pride that may come or the recognition I may receive?

Is my hesitation (regarding my gifts) from God?

our attention is turned away from God, we don't use the gifts God has given us, and no one benefits.

SATAN ACCUSES US TO GET US CAUGHT UP IN THE PARALYSIS OF ANALYSIS. Ultimately, the devil is pleased when we waste our energy on analyzing ourself and our possibilities rather than actually doing anything. If I did that, would it make me proud? Do I really want to get involved to help, or so I can impress so-and-so? What would people think if I took this position—that I'm a favorite of our pastor? We can ponder possibilities for weeks and months. The devil doesn't care how he keeps us from acting, keeps us out of the game, as long as we're out.

Sometimes we get so obsessed with fear that we miss God's will. Rather than making a decision, we go back and forth about it. *Is this really what God wants me to do?* The paralysis of analysis. Satan uses it any time he can: Keep thinking, keep meditating, keep questioning. Just don't do anything.

Dealing with Satan's Accusing Questions

Now, how do we deal with these attacks? It's difficult because, to be honest, the devil's questions hit a sore spot. We are vulnerable when they come up. Our motives *are* mixed. We *do* struggle with pride. It's easy to be overwhelmed by accusations because there is often some truth there. Our freedom comes when we get beyond the accusation.

Don't equate your conscience with God's voice.

The conscience is an inner voice of the heart, but it must not be equated with God's voice. The conscience may be informed by godly values and standards. So when your conscience makes you feel bad because you told a lie or makes you feel bad because you thought about stealing, it's responding out of God's standards and values.

But the conscience can be misinformed. It can be dulled, even numbed. There is a cultural Novocain being injected into the consciences of people today. People are doing things that are absolutely wrong, and they have no conscience about them whatsoever. We call that sociopathic. And yet we are seeing more and more of it at every level.

Our conscience is inadequate. Listen to the apostle Paul. In 1 Corinthians 4, Paul was being accused by his congregation of having mixed motives. And he was being judged by his congregation. There were some super apostles who were showing up and saying that because Paul didn't charge enough, he was trying to gain their sympathy. They were saying a lot of unusual things. But Paul describes how he deals with that in 1 Corinthians 4:1-5. Listen to this:

> So then, men ought to regard us as servants of Christ and as those entrusted with the secret things of God. Now it is required that those who have been given a trust must prove faithful. I care very little if I am judged by you or by any human court; indeed, I do not even judge myself. My conscience is clear, but that does not make me innocent. It is the Lord who judges me. Therefore judge nothing before the appointed time; wait till the Lord comes. He will bring to light what is hidden in darkness and will expose the motives of men's hearts. At that time each will receive his praise from God. (NIV)

What is the difference between evaluating myself and judging myself?

Which am I most likely to do?

What does Paul's advice mean to me?

Paul was saying, "Even though my conscience is clean, it doesn't mean I'm not condemned." He was exhorting believers to get on with living and not be distracted by sifting through motives.

Don't be too preoccupied with self.

There was a man who was in the court of Louis XIV in France. He was a noble and therefore was expected to attend the magnificent parties and social events of the court. As he began to grow in his Christian faith, however, he was having a very hard time justifying his involvement in such extravagant activities. He began to write for guidance to a spiritual director named Fénelon. Fénelon gave this advice to this nobleman in France.

> I conclude, when God places us in certain positions which obligate us to take part in everything, as in the place where you are, the only thing to do is live in peace, without constantly quibbling about the secret motives which can unconsciously slip into the heart. We should never finish if we want to constantly sound the bottom of our heart. And in wanting to escape from self in the search for God, we should be too preoccupied with self in frequent examinations. Let us go on in simplicity of heart.[1]

Has God put me in places that need to be viewed, not as detriments and distractions, but as places of special opportunity?

How can I be involved in situations "in simplicity of heart," as Fénelon counsels?

That's rather mature advice. Basically Fénelon is saying, "Look, God's put you where he's put you. He understands you are going to have to be involved, not in immoral activities, but in activities that may just seem to you like poor stewardship or a waste of time or will put you on display where you may get proud and believe some of the stuff they say about you. Just leave all that aside and focus on God in the midst of all that."

Sound your heart.

Now, sounding our heart has a place. Samuel Langhorne Clemens loved life on the Mississippi River. He received his pilot's license to navigate the great river, but the outbreak of the Civil War ended his chances of fulfilling his ambition. But he preserved his love in his pseudonym "Mark Twain." Because of the fluctuating waters, river navigators had to continually measure the depth (sound) of the river to prevent the riverboat from running aground. "Mark twain" was the leadman's call, meaning a two-fathom (twelve-feet-deep) sounding, or safe water. They were sounding the water to see if they could keep going. We are to sound our heart and to check the depth of it. But it should lead to two things.

First of all, sounding our heart should lead us to humility.

When we realize how much we wrestle with pride and mixed motives, we can humble ourself before God and say, "O Lord, have mercy."

Second, sounding our heart makes us more dependent on God. We realize that we're lost without some help. When we use our gifts, we should become more, not less, dependent on the Lord's guidance.

Keeping in Mind God's Motives

The evil one really is trying to condemn us and block our progress. When we fall, he wants us to stay down. When we're ashamed, he wants that shame to devastate us. When we begin to doubt ourself, he does everything he can to use that doubt to cripple and stop our forward movement.

But God's purposes are nothing like that. God is not trying to condemn us or to block our progress. God searches our heart for correction, not for condemnation. God searches our heart for growth, not stagnation. God searches our heart for dependence, not despair.

Therefore, you and I need to learn to listen for God's approval instead of Satan's accusations. Whenever you hear the voice of accusations you need to train yourself to listen for God's voice—because God will be speaking. Hear the truth of God instead of Satan's lies.

Don't confuse Satan's accusation with the Holy Spirit's conviction.

The Holy Spirit's conviction brings a godly sorrow that makes you humble and dependent. Satan's accusations make you discouraged, desperate, and willing to give up on God. That's his whole strategy.

Romans 8:1 says, "Therefore, there is now no condemnation for those who are in Christ Jesus" (NIV). You do something really stupid. If you haven't yet, you will. You know it's really wrong, and Satan shows up and says, "You are scum. You are not worth anything. God hates you for doing that. You call yourself a Christian?" You need to hold up that verse and say, "Wait a minute, I know it was stupid,

When have I felt the conviction of the Holy Spirit?

If I can't name a time, what would I expect the Spirit's conviction to be like?

How is the Spirit's conviction different from Satan's accusations?

What are some of Satan's most frequent accusations against me?

but there is no condemnation for those who are in Christ Jesus."

Remember that Jesus has taken all the brunt of Satan's accusations.

First John 1:8-10 says: "If we claim to be without sin" [which is what Satan sometimes tries to make us think we should be], "we deceive ourselves and the truth is not in us. If we confess our sins, he is faithful and just and will forgive us our sins and purify us from all unrighteousness" (NIV). Then John continues, repeating the same point again to make sure we've got it. "If we claim we have not sinned, we make him out to be a liar, and his word has no place in our lives." Then John presents a courtroom scene:

> My dear children, I write this to you so that you will not sin. But if anybody does sin, we have one who speaks to the Father in our defense—Jesus Christ, the Righteous One. He is the atoning sacrifice for our sins, and not only for ours but also for the sins of the whole world. (1 John 2:1-2, NIV)

Remember how we saw Satan the accuser on the right hand of the accused? God is on his bench ready to judge. But as Satan begins to level his accusations against us, one steps in front of us. It is Jesus Christ. He is our advocate. He is our defense. He answers all charges against us saying, "I've already paid the fine, I've already served the time. I've already taken this person's sin upon myself. It is finished." Satan is silenced, and God says, "Case dismissed." The case is dismissed every time because you have put your faith and trust in Jesus Christ.

What Do We Do with Blessings?

The story of Job poses one more issue that is often overlooked. But it is a primary avenue for Satan's accusations. Job's trouble began because Satan was questioning Job's blessings. We talk about trials all the time, but what is our theology of blessings?

What do you do with blessings? What do you do when God does good things in your life? I realize most of the time we are used to hearing about suffering and pain and sorrow. But a lot of us have been richly blessed by God, and we don't feel worthy of it. We may ask the question of ourself: So, am I a Christian because it honors God or because it brings me blessings?

We need to think very clearly about what to do with the blessings that come from service to God. Clear thinking on this question helps us understand God's love and our responsibility.

Blessing is a natural consequence of obedience.

Many people have drawn simplistic conclusions that have nothing to do with biblical truth. My friend, the aspiring author, didn't want to write primarily for the blessing. He just wanted to get into it to serve people. I can understand that. That's a noble motive, and it is the godly motivation behind our service. Certainly if you don't have something to say to help people and to honor God, you had better be silent.

But at the same time we must understand that God promises blessings not simply as a bribe to invite our obedience but as the natural consequence of following his ways. Doesn't that make sense? A blessing can be the natural consequence of obedience—even as a person who eats healthy foods and exercises will naturally experience physical vitality, or an athlete who conditions and practices diligently experiences a measure of success. Even as a musician who rehearses consistently experiences increasing virtuosity, so following God's way often brings blessings as a natural consequence.

That should not be mistaken for serving in a way that obligates God to do something for us. God is never in our debt. But he blesses us as we follow his ways.

Missiologist Donald McGavran coined the phrase "redemption and lift." He noticed that when a group of people would come to know Christ as Lord and Savior, everything in their lives would improve. They would have better marriages and family life. They would be better citizens. They would actually make more money and move up in social standing. He noticed this pattern in other countries as well as America. Once you are redeemed you are lifted up. So the question is, Were people accepting Christ so they could be lifted up? No. But because they accepted Christ, they became more responsible in the stewardship of their gifts and had financial success. Because they had more integrity in their relationships, they had better relationships. Because they had a greater sense of following God's priorities, they stayed away from things that destroyed their lives and then experienced blessing. You see the picture? When you follow God's ways, often—as a natural consequence—you will experience his blessing and goodness. Always? No. Is everybody who is following God's way blessed with prosperity? No. But many times God's blessings will come along.

> *John Hutton used to tell how once, at a great gathering in Yorkshire, he had hardly started on his sermon when a miner leaped to his feet and led the congregation in the Doxology. Hutton, as he put it, "sank like a punctured tyre" and took some time to get upon his way again. Scot preachers do not like such interruptions. At the close the man apologized, explaining he had only been a Christian for some months.*
>
> *"I used to drink, to knock the wife about, to pawn the furniture, and now it is all so gloriously different. I can't sit still—want to get up and sing about it." Asked how he fared down the pit, the man said that, of his particular lot, only he and one other professed Christianity, "and the others quiz us daily."*
>
> *"What do they ask?"*
>
> *"Oh, well, yesterday they said to us, 'You don't really believe that yarn about Jesus turning the water into wine, now, do you?'"*
>
> *"And what did you say?"*
>
> *"I said, 'I am an ignorant man; I know nothing*

about water and wine. But I know this—that in my house Jesus Christ has turned beer into furniture! And that is a good enough miracle for me!' " [2]

What he meant, of course, was that the money he had been wasting on beer before Christ touched his heart was now being invested in furniture and ways of blessing his family. That redemption and lift, when God changes nothing into something, is the work of God's grace and goodness.

Are there areas in my life where I have experienced a "lift" because of my faith?

"Solely because thou art my God . . ."

One of the most powerful expressions of selfless devotion is an anthem our choir often sings called "My Eternal King." Reflect on these words of one whose motives have been purified by God's love:

My God, I love Thee,
not because I hope for heaven thereby,
nor yet because who loved Thee not
must die eternally.
Thou, O my Jesus, thou didst me
upon the cross embrace.
For me didst bear the nails and spear
and manifold disgrace.
Why, then why, O blessed Jesus Christ,
should I not love Thee well,
not with the hope of winning heaven,
nor of escaping hell.
Not with the hope of gaining ought,
not seeking a reward,
but as thyself has loved me
O ever loving Lord.
Even so, I love Thee and will love
and in Thy praise will sing,
solely because Thou art my God
and my Eternal King.

ANONYMOUS, SEVENTEENTH-CENTURY LATIN,
TRANSLATED BY REV. EDWARD CASWALL

When Satan accuses us, there is a sense in which we could say we understand his accusations because Paul says in Romans 3:23, "All have sinned; all fall short of God's glorious standard." And you can say to Satan, "Tell me something new. This is no surprise to me!" But then we can speak the words of Romans 8:1 with joyful confidence, "So now there is no condemnation for those who belong to Christ Jesus." Or you can turn to Psalm 139:14, which says: "I am fearfully and wonderfully made" (NIV). Or Psalm 8:4-6:

> **What are mortals that you should think of us,**
> **mere humans that you should care for us?**
> **For you made us only a little lower than God,**
> **and you crowned us with glory and honor.**
> **You put us in charge of everything you made,**
> **giving us authority over all things.**

What about You?

Don't believe the evil one's lies. Search your heart, and when somebody challenges your motives, take a look at that and say, "You know, there is too much of *me* in this thing. Thanks for reminding me of that." Then go forward freely. Let yourself become more dependent upon God and say, "God, unless you change me I'm this kind of a person."

When you feel the sting of the lash, know that God is not holding the whip. God does not lash you. God searches our heart for correction, not condemnation. God searches our heart for growth, not stagnation. God searches our heart for dependence, not despair. Listen for God's approval whenever you hear Satan's accusations.

Notes

1. Fénelon, *Christian Perfection* (Minneapolis: Bethany House, 1947), 7–8.
2. Arthur John Gossip, "What Religion Does for One Who Really Tried It," in *Experience Worketh Hope* (Edinburgh: T. & T. Clark, 1945), 38–39.

CHAPTER 5

"Where were you when I laid the foundations of the earth?" An Answer to the Suffering

Job 38:4

While Earth wears wounds, still must Christ's
Wounds remain,
Whom Love made Life, and of Whom Life
made Pain,
And of whom Pain made Death.
L. D. LAURENCE HOUSMAN[1]

CENTURIES AGO RABBI Akieba, an itinerant Jewish scholar, came to a town and wanted to spend the night there. The townspeople hated Jews and refused him lodging. The rabbi went into the nearby woods to spend the night with his donkey, his rooster, and his lamp. He lit his lamp and opened up the holy scroll so he could study. As he was studying, the wind blew fiercely and knocked the lamp over, breaking it. He couldn't study anymore, but Rabbi Akieba said, "All that God does, he does well," and he went to bed. That night he slept soundly. But while he was sleeping, thieves stole his rooster and his donkey. When he awakened in the morning and saw his losses, he said easily, "All that God does, he does well." Then he went back to the village. When he arrived there, he was horrified by what he saw. In the middle of the night soldiers had attacked the village, killing all the inhabitants and plundering it completely. He also learned that the soldiers had passed through the same part of the woods where he had slept. "If my lamp had been burning, the soldiers would have seen me. If my rooster would have crowed, or my donkey would have brayed, they would have gotten me." And he bowed his head and said, "All that God does, he does well."[2]

The problem of suffering poses one of the eternal questions of the soul. It has caused the failure of many a faith. Those who are maturing in their faith have learned how to respond to trials and suffering. How do we gain the perspective seen in the rabbi? How can we reach the place of trusting in the midst of pain and suffering? How can we ever learn to say, no matter the circumstances, "All that God does, he does well"?

Suffering stirs the deepest feelings in people. It stirs the most profound questions. Consider the fact that we have rarely, if ever, heard a sermon on what Phil Yancey has called the "problem of pleasure."[3] Why is life so good?" Think about it: Why does ice cream taste so great? Where did chocolate syrup come from? Why did God give us raspberry tarts? Why is a kiss so sweet? Why is conversation so interesting? Why is music so inspiring? Why is beauty so pleasing? Why is there all this pleasure in the world? I don't understand it. How can there be so much pleasure in a world where people act the way they do?

When has pain and suffering touched my life in a way that stirred a questioning of God?

What did I do with my questions?

But we've all found pain driving us to ask the toughest questions. What is the meaning of life? What is the nature of God? How could he allow this to happen? Pain strips us, opens us, and gets us down to the basics. Suffering opens it all—from the immediate experience of pain to the deeper philosophical questions.

Any exploration of this subject requires a study of Job. In this story God gives us insight that pushes us to the limits of faith. While we see there are no easy answers, there are principles that equip us for life's most difficult challenges.

No One Is Exempt from Suffering

Many of us assume that suffering should be based on some sort of mathematical formula of cause and effect that governs the universe. We seek a reason for suffering with the same kind of compulsion that a flower seeks the light or a compass seeks magnetic north. We know that some suffering is merely the consequence of certain situations and behaviors. But the first truth about suffering is that it is mysterious. Part of the mystery is that it comes to all people in ways that are by no means proportionate to any human calculation of cause and effect.

The story of Job confronts us with this mystery from the start. Job is a model of faith and parental love. From the opening verses of this magnificent story we see a man of integrity, a man of faith. Job was a man who had enjoyed God immensely. He was a man we would have liked to be with. The book of Job begins with a description of a godly man and his family.

> **There was a man named Job who lived in the land of Uz. He was blameless, a man of complete integrity. He feared God and stayed away from evil. He had seven sons and three daughters. He owned seven thousand sheep, three thousand camels, five hundred teams of oxen, and five hundred female donkeys, and he employed many servants. He was, in fact, the richest person in that entire area.**
>
> **Every year when Job's sons had birthdays, they invited their brothers and sisters to join them for a celebration. On these occasions they would get together to eat and drink. When these celebrations ended—and sometimes they lasted several days—Job would purify his children. He would get up early in the morning and offer a burnt offering for each of them. For Job said to himself, "Perhaps my children have sinned and**

> **have cursed God in their hearts." This was Job's regular practice. (Job 1:1-5)**

Job has all that life can offer. He has a vital faith. He has immense prosperity. He has a wife and children that love him and each other. He has their spiritual concerns on his heart. This is a picture of the good life. Without knowing what is to come, we see no reason to expect bad things to happen to this good man.

Then one day disaster strikes, like four hammer blows. The first three servants bring devastating reports of Job's financial ruin. He no longer has farm animals to provide their milk and their meat and their daily sustenance. He no longer has sheep to provide food and wool for clothing and materials for trading. He no longer has camels to carry his goods to the far corners of the world. Bankruptcy won't even describe Job's situation; this is total liquidation. Job has no material assets left to his name.

But before this news can even register, the worst news comes. A fourth servant arrives and says, "Your sons and daughters were feasting in their oldest brother's home." Job no doubt smiles faintly at the thought of his family. Of course, he knows they were together for their regular custom. *At least I still have them,* he thinks. But the servant continues, "Suddenly, a powerful wind swept in from the desert [like a tornado] and hit the house on all sides. The house collapsed, and all your children are dead" (Job 1:18-19).

Stunned silence. What would you expect Job to do? How would you respond? What we read has left generations in awe.

> **Job stood up and tore his robe in grief. Then he shaved his head and fell to the ground before God. He said,**
>
> **"I came naked from my mother's womb,**
> **and I will be stripped of everything when I die.**
> **The Lord gave me everything I had,**

and the Lord has taken it away.
Praise the name of the Lord!"

In all of this, Job did not sin by blaming God.
(Job 1:20-22)

Honestly, most of us don't understand Job's reaction. We would have expected any number of reactions, but not worship. I would have expected anger, weeping, rage, despair. But not worship.

If the book of Job ended at this point, it would be the kind of message you might expect. You might expect a self-righteous preacher to shake a finger in your face and say, "Now, you should be like Job. You should never get mad at God, and even if everything in the world goes wrong, you just worship God. Just swallow your pain and take it." That's what we would expect.

But the story of Job does not stop here. The story *starts* here. And thus begins one of the most profound and challenging books in all of human literature. It deals with this difficult issue: Why do the *righteous* suffer? We need to highlight that word *righteous,* because the book of Job is not solely about evil and suffering in the world. The book of Job is not solely about why evil happens. It really focuses on the tougher question: Why does evil happen to people like Job?

We should keep in mind that *righteous* in this context doesn't mean that a person is without sin. The Bible clearly teaches that *all* of us have sinned and fallen short of God's glory (see Romans 3:23). But we must consider the fact that those who trust in God through Jesus Christ, those who follow him as faithfully as they know how, those who truly love God suffer. And we can be considered righteous in Christ. Why this suffering? It's one thing when a criminal is gunned down after killing a person in a hostage crisis. But what do we make of the pastor and his wife who are beaten to death in their home on Christmas? The causes for the suffering of God's people cannot be calculated by any formulas known to us.

What does Job's response teach me about his view of his prosperity?

What is my attitude toward my worldly goods?

How does my attitude toward possessions affect my spiritual vitality?

In order to understand this, we have to go back to the second scene in the book of Job (1:6-12). While we were still savoring the idyllic picture of Job in verses one through five, the scene shifted to another drama, described in verses six through twelve. This section sounds a caution to all who wonder about suffering.

Suffering cannot be understood from a natural, earthly perspective.

The scene shifts from Job's earthly estate to an unusual scene in heaven.

> **One day the angels came to present themselves before the Lord, and Satan the Accuser came with them. "Where have you come from?" the Lord asked Satan.**
>
> **And Satan answered the Lord, "I have been going back and forth across the earth, watching everything that's going on."**
>
> **Then the Lord asked Satan, "Have you noticed my servant Job? He is the finest man in all the earth—a man of complete integrity. He fears God and will have nothing to do with evil."**
>
> **Satan replied to the Lord, "Yes, Job fears God, but not without good reason! You have always protected him and his home and his property from harm. You have made him prosperous in everything he does. Look how rich he is! But take away everything he has, and he will surely curse you to your face!"**
>
> **"All right, you may test him," the Lord said to Satan. "Do whatever you want with everything he possesses, but don't harm him physically." So Satan left the Lord's presence. (Job 1:6-12)**

This is truly one of the most fascinating, puzzling, unsettling accounts in the Bible. We cannot fully understand it, but we can draw at least two lessons from this scene.

First, *there is much going on in life that we can never know from our finite perspective.* We have no idea what is going on in the heavenly council of God. How Satan has access to God is something we don't understand. Why God would point out Job is beyond our comprehension. From the outset of this story, we are shown the fact that there's much more to suffering than simple cause-and-effect equations. Whenever there is suffering, we are taught that there may be things going on in the heavens that must be taken into account. These are things we may never know—even as we wouldn't know Job's situation apart from God's revelation.

When we suffer, we often jump to conclusions that cause more pain.

The scene in God's heavenly council shows us that there's more to Job's situation than he or any other human beings know. But they try to make sense of things as if they knew it all. The drama of the book of Job hinges on what our literature teachers call dramatic irony. Irony describes the situation in which the reader knows something about the situation or the characters that the characters don't know about themselves. As we watch them, we have more information than they have. If they knew what we know, they would act or speak differently. This is the second lesson to be drawn from the heavenly council: When we fail to understand that there are spiritual dynamics in process that we cannot perceive, *we draw hasty conclusions and make accusations that cause even greater suffering.*

When have I been tempted to jump to conclusions that may have nothing to do with the problem?

Did I learn more later that changed my interpretation of the situation?

How can I respond differently in the future?

This is what makes the speeches of Job's friends in later chapters so inappropriate. They assume that Job is being punished. When Job fails to confess to sin, they then chide him for self-righteousness. In fact, they have no idea about what happened in the heavenly council between God and Satan.

Have you ever had an experience with Job's "comforters"? I know a family whose child was brain damaged at birth. Members of the extended family urged the parents to

Have I ever had an experience with Job's "comforters"?

How did it affect my faith and the situation?

Have I ever sounded like one of Job's comforters?

have a healing service for the child, which they did gladly. The parents have a rich and mature faith. When the child didn't improve, however, the extended family accused the parents of harboring sin and unbelief. "If you had faith, your child wouldn't be suffering." I cannot put into words the grief such accusations have caused.

Our expressions of hurt and confusion may prepare us for God's touch in the midst of our suffering.

Job's initial response to his calamity is truly inspiring. But as his suffering continues, including an extremely painful attack of boils (which may have been similar to what modern medicine calls shingles), Job moves into expressions of deep dismay and questioning of God.

> **"I cannot keep from speaking. I must express my anguish. I must complain in my bitterness. Am I a sea monster that you place a guard on me? If I think, 'My bed will comfort me, and I will try to forget my misery with sleep,' you shatter me with dreams. You terrify me with visions. I would rather die of strangulation than go on and on like this. I hate my life. I do not want to go on living. Oh, leave me alone for these few remaining days.**
>
> **"What are mere mortals, that you should make so much of us? For you examine us every morning and test us every moment. Why won't you leave me alone—even for a moment? Have I sinned? What have I done to you, O watcher of all humanity? Why have you made me your target? Am I a burden to you? Why not just pardon my sin and take away my guilt? For soon I will lie down in the dust and die. When you look for me, I will be gone." (Job 7:11-21)**

We can relate much more readily to this type of reaction. Job is so tired. He says, in effect, "I just want to go to sleep and get away from the pain for a while." But when he lies down, he has a nightmare. "Thanks a lot God! I can't even get away from you in my sleep." Then he goes on to say, "I prefer strangling and death, rather than staying in this body of mine. I despise my life; I don't want to live anymore." And then he says this. "Leave me alone. My days have no meaning."

Job's honesty reminds us that even as a parent can hold a crying child who is saying terrible things, God can embrace us in the midst of our soul-cries. We are not rejected for struggling, for expressing our pain. God even tolerates many of the foolish things we say. Somehow, the very expression of our grief makes way for God's healing touch.

C. S. Lewis was married in 1956 and suffered the loss of his wife just four years later. In his classic *A Grief Observed,* he writes:

> Meanwhile, where is God? This is one of the most disquieting symptoms. When you are happy, so happy that you have no sense of needing Him, so happy that you are tempted to feel His claims upon you as an interruption, if you remember yourself and turn to Him with gratitude and praise, you will be—or so it feels—welcomed with open arms. But go to Him when your need is desperate, when all other help is vain, and what do you find? A door slammed in your face, and a sound of bolting and double bolting on the inside. After that, silence. You may as well turn away.[4]

We can imagine few more discouraging images for God's response in our time of greatest need than having the doors of heaven bolted and double bolted against us. We can almost hear the sound of footsteps walking away! This is where Lewis began—but it is not where he concluded. At the end of the book, as he nears the resolution of his grief, he reflects on the many questions a sufferer lays before God.

> When I lay these questions before God I get no answer. But a rather special sort of "No answer." It is not the locked door. It is more like a silent, certainly not uncompassionate, gaze. As though he shook His head not in refusal but waiving the question. Like, "Peace, child; you don't understand."
>
> Can a mortal ask a question which God finds unanswerable? Quite easily, I should think. All nonsense questions are unanswerable. How many hours are there in a mile? Is yellow square or round? Probably half the questions we ask—half our great theological and metaphysical problems—are like that.[5]

When all is said and done, we will not have all the answers.

We may catch a glimpse behind the curtain of mystery. There are times when God gives his special touch to those in the midst of pain. And there are other times when his purposes become clear. Rabbi Akieba saw almost immediately the hand of God by which small losses prevented a much greater loss.

Have I ever lost something that helped me find something much more important?

I don't know if there has ever been any time in your life when you have been able to look back and see that the lamp that broke and got blown out turned out to be something that protected you. Have you looked back over your life and seen that something you lost helped you find something much richer? I don't know if you have reached that point yet. But you may.

God Answered Job–with Questions

We cannot count on answers in this life. We cannot count on answers from God—as much as we may think God owes that to us. In fact, God never really answers Job's questions. Beginning in chapter 38, God addresses Job. But it is not what we would call an answer.

> **Then the Lord answered Job from the whirlwind:**
> **"Who is this that questions my wisdom with such ignorant words? Brace yourself, because I have some questions for you, and you must answer them.**
> **"Where were you when I laid the foundations of the earth? Tell me, if you know so much. Do you know how its dimensions were determined and who did the surveying? What supports its foundations, and who laid its cornerstone as the morning stars sang together and all the angels shouted for joy? (vv. 1-7)**

After no less than fifty questions in a row, the Lord challenges Job:

> **"Do you still want to argue with the Almighty? You are God's critic, but do you have the answers?"**
> **Then Job replied to the Lord, "I am nothing—how could I ever find the answers? I will put my hand over my mouth in silence. I have said too much already. I have nothing more to say." (Job 40:1-5)**

Then God proceeds with another barrage of questions. Never once does God speak of Satan, nor of Job's guilt or innocence, nor of the misunderstanding of Job's friends. God never tells Job why he suffers. Job is not given information concerning his circumstances. Instead, he is given a revelation of God's character. These questions are, in fact, God's answer to Job. They all serve to remind Job that God is God, that God is ruler over the microcosm and macrocosm, and that surely God is ruler over Job and his circumstances.

One of the most powerful testimonies to God's presence in the midst of seemingly senseless suffering comes from

Sir Arthur John Gossip. The following account is from one of his sermons. The man he describes is himself.

> I know a man who had to pass through an experience even more suddenly devastating than that which befell Ezekiel. "'Son of man, behold I take away the desire of thine eyes with a stroke.' So I preached unto the people in the morning. And in the evening my wife died." A bleak message! Yet the prophet was at least granted one full day's warning. But this poor soul had not even a second's. In a twinkling she was gone. And that grim night amid the tumbled ruins of what, ten minutes before, had been a home, he tried to give her, not of compulsion, but as a free gift; and asked that, since he had to bear the pain, he might not miss or lose what it was sent to teach him.
>
> The years slipped past, and many letters reached him all of a kind; one from two missionaries in the wilds of Africa. The one had lost her husband, drowned on their honeymoon in the United States, and with that, faith went out, until somebody sent her what that man had written in the dark to steady his own soul. And faith revived in her, and she went to the foreign field. The husband of the second, too, was drowned in Africa; and her faith also went to pieces. Until the one, who had been through it all herself, read to the other what had brought her back. And that other, too, came home. And, together, they wrote to the man, whom they will never see, "You can be absolutely sure that it was not for nothing that your heart was broken. It had to be, in order that two lost souls might be found again."
>
> So it was not chance-blown, did not just happen. It had meaning in it: was a plan thought out by God. And the man is content.

"Father, what shall I say? Save me from this hour? But for this cause came I unto this hour. Father, glorify Thy name."

We had better remember that, and hold to it. For, if the dark does fall around us, it will help to bring us through.[6]

Suffering Is Not Answered by Understanding, But by Trust

We will not have all the answers to our suffering, but we will have God. Suffering is not answered by understanding but by trust. That's what it's all about. You and I may never understand why things happen as they do. Only trust will sustain us. We'll never understand why suffering happens, but we can know God is with us through it all. That doesn't trivialize it, but that deepens it.

Job understood this righteousness at the beginning, and he responded with a deep righteousness. But then he learned it in a whole other way. You may know the ending of the book of Job. He gets everything back. Not the same people—obviously, the children were gone. But he gets a new family, he gets a new home, a new this and that and the other. And it's a real anticlimax. It's only told in a few sentences because the real riches that Job has received are those of knowing God more fully.

What about You?

Have you been stopped cold by suffering? Have you questioned God? Has someone questioned *you* while you were in great pain and confusion? Where are you now in the process of accepting that you won't always receive an answer? Is God enough—even without answers? What has God said to you lately, if anything?

If you haven't asked yourself these questions yet, you will eventually. Remember that Job brought all his anger and disappointment to God. Those were not pretty prayers! God is big enough for our questions and all the emotions that go with them. Please, don't silence your heart in the midst of suffering. Allow your faith to learn and grow during life's painful processes.

We can never "justify the ways of God to men," to use the phrase of John Milton. But when all is said and done, we will not have all the answers—but we will have God. And God *is* enough. Enough for our comfort when we mourn, our peace when we fear, our assurance when we doubt, our courage when we face the unknown. God himself is the answer to our suffering.

Notes

1. "A Prayer for the Healing of the Wounds of Christ," in *Masterpieces of Religious Verse,* ed. James D. Morrison (Grand Rapids: Baker Book House, 1948), 199.
2. Based on material from William J. Bausch, *Storytelling* (Mystic, Conn.: Twenty-Third Publications, 1984), 72.
3. Philip Yancey, "The Problem of Pain," *Christianity Today* (17 June 1988), 80.
4. C. S. Lewis, *A Grief Observed* (New York: Bantam Books, 1961), 4–5.
5. Ibid., 80–81.
6. Arthur John Gossip, *Experience Worketh Hope* (Edinburgh: T. & T. Clark, 1945), 19–20.

CHAPTER 6

"Why did you laugh?" Examining Our Assumptions

Genesis 18:13

In faith we have just enough light to follow the right way, but on either side is the abyss.
ABBE HUVELIN

The natural mind is ever prone to reason when it ought to believe; to work when [it] ought to be quiet; to go our own way, when we ought steadily to walk on in God's ways, however trying to nature. GEORGE MÜLLER

MANY TIMES GOD calls his people to do something the world and human instinct call foolish, even laughable. A man with no money feels led by God to open an orphanage. Ridiculous, most people say, to take responsibility for a group of children without proof of assets and without the assurance of daily provision. Some would even call it cruel, getting the children's hopes up when they could so quickly be disappointed. Yet George Müller of Bristol (England) began such an undertaking in the 1830s when he had the equivalent of only fifty cents to his name. Refusing to make his needs known to anyone, he prayed. In time, over $7 million came in for the orphanage. Müller constructed a building able to house over two thousand children at any one time. Although Müller never made his needs known to anyone but God, the children never missed a meal in all the years of Müller's ministry.

At one point, when asked in a letter about the specific needs of the orphanage, Müller replied, "While I thank you for your love, and whilst I agree with you that, in general, there is a difference between *asking for money* and *answering when asked,* nevertheless, in our case, I feel not at liberty to speak about the state of our funds, as the primary object of the work in my hands is to lead those who are weak in faith to see that there is *reality* in dealing with God *alone."*[1] George Müller was taunted at first by many, but in the end, he had the last laugh—the laugh of joy!

Our God is a God of comedy. I don't mean the situation comedy of television nor the slapstick style of Charlie Chaplin. Don't mistake the term *comedy* for great punch lines or pies in the face. Theological comedy is comedy at its highest. It is the comedy that expresses the confidence that things will turn out for the best, even though there's very rough going for a while. In the comic process, the pompous presumptions of evil are exposed and torn down.

Professor Leland Ryken writes: "A story in which the action descends from romance [which Ryken describes as "an idealized picture of human experience"] to catastrophe is a tragedy, and an upward movement from bondage to freedom is comedy."[2] We see examples of the comic in the stories of Joseph in Genesis, and in the stories of Ruth and Esther, where tragedies are resolved with happy conclusions.

The problem for most of us is that we have forgotten this fundamental characteristic of God. We have made a number of assumptions that rule out the improbable. Consequently, we fall prey to discouragement and despair when God is about to do the laughable in our life.

God is constantly surprising us with outlandish, unpredictable strategies for accomplishing his work of judgment and redemption in the world. We often describe God as all-powerful, all-knowing, and present everywhere. We describe him as wise and loving and faithful. But there are other attributes that escape our attention because we have become accustomed—and numb—to the incredible stories in the Bible. While the familiar may not breed contempt, it can breed inappreciation. God's creativity and "light touch" are amazing.

Who would have thought of

- using Noah and his family to preserve humankind and the creatures of the earth on an ark through the Flood?
- using a dejected, rejected man guilty of manslaughter, Moses, to lead his people to freedom?
- causing plagues of frogs and other creatures that represented the very gods the Egyptians worshiped?
- causing the Red Sea to split open for the Israelites to pass through and then close in to drown the armies of Pharaoh?
- giving the people a diet of manna from heaven?
- choosing a foreign woman, Rahab, to provide security for Israel's spies in the Promised Land?
- choosing another foreign woman, a Moabitess named Ruth, to be in the lineage of David, the king of Israel, and of the Messiah himself?
- using Gideon's three hundred men to defeat thousands?
- sending a young boy against a giant?
- using a choir at the front of an army to sing praises to God while the three armies that had come to attack Israel turn on themselves in self-destruction?
- asking a Syrian leper named Naaman to go dunk in the Jordan River seven times to be healed of leprosy?

- planning for a virgin to give birth to the Messiah and that Messiah using the least in the eyes of the world to shape his destiny ever since?
- using a small band of ordinary people to change the world?

What other stories from the Bible show us the creative, comic side of God?

When have I seen God's "light touch" in my life? in others' lives?

What is God really like if he does these kinds of things? What attributes would you use to describe God in light of these circumstances? One of our problems is that we are too familiar with Scripture narratives. They don't catch us by surprise as they do people who encounter them for the first time.

The comedy of Scripture is rich because it is rooted in the harshest realities of life. God's ways are not for the amusement of the idle nor for the fascination of the curious. God works wonders for people who wonder how they will survive. But he does so in unexpected ways. In the process, he challenges our common assumptions. We are of dour disposition when God wants us to lighten up in every way.

In Genesis 17 and 18 we see this comic side of God break through in one of its most vivid presentations.

> **Then God added, "Regarding Sarai, your wife—her name will no longer be Sarai; from now on you will call her Sarah. And I will bless her and give you a son from her! Yes, I will bless her richly, and she will become the mother of many nations. Kings will be among her descendants!"**
>
> **Then Abraham bowed down to the ground, but he laughed to himself in disbelief. "How could I become a father at the age of one hundred?" he wondered. "Besides, Sarah is ninety; how could she have a baby?" And Abraham said to God, "Yes, may Ishmael enjoy your special blessing!"**
>
> **But God replied, "Sarah, your wife, will bear you a son. You will name him Isaac, and I will**

> **confirm my everlasting covenant with him and his descendants. As for Ishmael, I will bless him also, just as you have asked. I will cause him to multiply and become a great nation. Twelve princes will be among his descendants. But my covenant is with Isaac, who will be born to you and Sarah about this time next year." (Genesis 17:15-21)**

Continuing in Genesis 18, we read that the Lord appeared to Abraham with his angels.

> **"Where is Sarah, your wife?" they asked him.**
>
> **"In the tent," Abraham replied.**
>
> **Then one of them said, "About this time next year I will return, and your wife Sarah will have a son."**
>
> **Now Sarah was listening to this conversation from the tent nearby. And since Abraham and Sarah were both very old, and Sarah was long past the age of having children, she laughed silently to herself. "How could a worn-out woman like me have a baby?" she thought. "And when my master—my husband—is also so old?"**
>
> **Then the Lord said to Abraham, "Why did Sarah laugh? Why did she say, 'Can an old woman like me have a baby?' Is anything too hard for the Lord? About a year from now, just as I told you, I will return, and Sarah will have a son." Sarah was afraid, so she denied that she had laughed. But he said, "That is not true. You did laugh." (vv. 9-15)**

All laughter in Scripture is not jovial laughter. Sarah's response in this passage is an example of that. Often our laughter is dark, laced with sarcasm and cynicism. It springs from human pain and disappointment and unbelief. This was the nature of Sarah's laugh. But God would change all that. He wants to transform our dark, cynical, despairing laughter into the bright laughter of belief and hope.

"Why Did You Laugh?"

Most of us react to circumstances so quickly that we rarely consider or understand the reasons for our reaction. There are times, however, when it's important to stop and consider the why. Our reaction may be the tip of the iceberg—the evidence of a cold and dangerous wound or sin or a barrier between us and God that could threaten our future. The time spent searching our soul could release us from the icy grip of bitterness, disappointment, and disillusionment. Rather than the iceberg sinking us, the truth and healing touch of God can break it up so it will no longer be a threat.

God's question forced Sarah to consider her reaction. Were Sarah to have answered God's question, we can postulate at least four reasons behind her laughter. These reasons reveal many assumptions we hold concerning God and ourself:

What alarms have I set for God?

We assume that God will work within a certain time frame.

When God gives us a promise (or we make a commitment to God), a clock starts ticking. We may not even be aware that we wound it up and set an alarm, but a clock started ticking. And there's a certain amount of time we're willing to wait for God to fulfill his promises. We wait for a family member to come to know Christ as Lord and Savior. We wait for God to heal one we so dearly love. We pray for a job or for financial relief. We pray for direction in life. No matter what we're praying about, we've set an alarm, and when it reaches a certain point and that alarm goes off, the bitterness sets in. Bitterness believes that delays indicate either God's indifference or impotence. This produces the sardonic laugh of disappointment, the guffaw of cynicism. This could well have been behind Sarah's response.

When have I experienced disappointing delays in areas such as my personal life, family, education, vocation, or church life?

How have these delays affected my spiritual life?

Remember that God's promise was first given to Abram when Abram was seventy-five years old. God came again after twenty-four years, when Abram was ninety-nine. Twenty-four years of waiting for a child to be conceived!

Now imagine entering into dialogue with Sarah. You ask her, "Why did you laugh?"

"Who wouldn't laugh?" she might respond. "It was laugh or cry. I confess I had been anxious for years, each month wondering. Then the anxiety became, dare I breathe it, anger. This was no careless anger, mind you; I know the awesome nature of God! I had seen the Lord work, bringing us to a new land, prospering us in every way—every way but one. But waiting for a child was too much. He raised my expectations so high, but then I had to live with the grief month after month after month. Twenty-four years! When I was eavesdropping that day and heard God say that I would have a child in the next year, I had almost forgotten the promise. After all, for years I no longer had that monthly reminder. The laugh escaped my lips before I knew it."

Sarah's laughter had sprung out of pain—pain at God's delay. What she could not know was that God's delay was aimed at revealing that nothing is impossible for God. God's delay was to teach that apart from him, we can do nothing (see John 15:5). When we set a schedule for God, we will learn that his watch is set to a different standard. In the life of discipleship, we learn that faith may not see the hands of the clock, but it can hear the ticking.

We assume that God's work is limited to our own abilities.

One of our most common assumptions is that God's work is limited to our resources and abilities. Genesis 18:11-12 says: "Since Abraham and Sarah were both very old, and Sarah was long past the age of having children, she laughed silently to herself. 'How could a worn-out woman like me have a baby?' she thought. 'And when my master—my husband—is also so old?' "

Old and worn out. Sarah couldn't imagine God working again. In our imaginary conversation with Sarah, we might hear her say, "I have often wondered why we had to wait so long. God knows I was faithful and hopeful as long as I could stand it, but after ten years I gave Hagar to Abram. I was weary with waiting. I was afraid God had forgotten me. I thought the end of my fertility meant the end of God's possibility."

John Newton, the fiery converted slave trader and composer of "Amazing Grace," was writing a letter of counsel to a young ministerial candidate. This candidate was impatient, expressing the concern that his gifts were being "wasted" in his current situation. Newton cautioned him on overconfidence in our abilities:

> That which finally evidences a proper call, is a correspondent opening in providence, by a gradual train of circumstances pointing out the means, the time, the place, of actually entering upon the work. And until this coincidence arrives, you must not expect to be always clear from hesitation in your own mind. The principal caution on this head is, not to be too hasty in catching at first appearances. If it be the Lord's will to bring you into his ministry, he has already appointed your place and service, and though you know it not at present, you shall at a proper time. *If you had the talents of an angel, you could do no good with them till his hour is come, and till he leads you to the people whom he has determined to bless by your means* [emphasis added]. It is very difficult to restrain ourself within the bounds of prudence here, when our zeal is warm: a sense of the love of Christ upon our hearts, and a tender compassion for poor sinners, is ready to prompt us to break out too soon; but he that believeth shall not make haste. I was about five years under this constraint; sometimes I thought I must preach, though it was in the streets. I listened to everything that seemed plausible, and to many things which were not so. But the Lord graciously, and as it were insensibly, hedged up my way with

> thorns; otherwise, if I had been left to my own spirit, I should have put it quite out of my power to have been brought into such a sphere of usefulness, as he in his good time has been pleased to lead me to. And I can now see clearly, that at the time I would first have gone out, though my intention was, I hope, good in the main, yet I overrated myself, and had not that spiritual judgment and experience which are requisite for so great a service.[3]

Whether we are discouraged by our lack of abilities or overconfident because of our sense of ability, we are making the wrong assumption if we think ability is the determining or limiting factor in life. If God can make a donkey talk or make stones cry out, "Hosanna!" he can surely do what he wants with his willing disciples.

We often walk by evidence, not by faith.

Our faith is most often based on the evidence we see in this world, rather than on the promises we have heard from God's Word. We are looking for human and worldly support to stimulate faith. This is especially true when all the human and worldly factors point in the opposite direction.

In what ways am I tempted to limit my life to what I can do or to possibilities I can see?

How are my abilities limited when it comes to God's work?

Many people had assumed that the Christian faith was all but extinguished from China under communist rule. There was little evidence of God's presence and much evidence of the oppressive forces of communist ideology. But when China began to be open to the rest of the world, we saw that Christianity had not only survived but thrived. The following account shows us the persistent work of God when it appears that "nothing" is happening:

> Pastor Chen was in for a shock when the doors of his Chinese prison finally swung open. As he stood on the threshold of freedom, anticipation mixed with dread. It had been 18 years since the Communists had wrenched him from the church he loved and the

300 people he had faithfully served. Since then, a violent revolution had ravaged the church. Perhaps only a few members remained.

Chen, however, stepped into the sunlight of a new, more liberal day for China—and into the arms of a church that in his absence had grown to 5,000 (through house churches). Today, some 20,000 believers meet in homes throughout the area.

Chen's experience is not unique. "The first thing I had to do was repent," said a pastor from Yenan Province, who was released in 1981 after more than 20 years in confinement. In prison, he had mourned for his church, imagining it scattered and frightened. On his release, he found a vital, growing, witnessing church that had multiplied in size many times. Today, his church serves as a base of outreach to the entire countryside.[4]

Has God ever surprised me in this way?

When has it seemed that God has forgotten and then I've seen him move?

What similar stories have I heard from others?

We assume that God's work is limited to those who never fail him.

Sarah might have laughed because she knew—deep within—that she was not worthy of receiving God's blessing. Like Abraham, who had lied (see Genesis 12:10-20), she too, had fallen into disobedience. Sarah doubted God and gave Hagar to Abram to be a surrogate mother for Sarah. Sarah's first struggle was doubting God. But second, Sarah in bitterness drove Hagar and her son, Ishmael, into the wilderness.

You see, Sarah was just like us. We call her an Old Testament saint, not because she was perfect, but because she was redeemed from her imperfections by faith. Bright laughter breaks out when God overcomes the limitation of our failure.

Listen to these words in Genesis 21:1: "Now the Lord was gracious to Sarah as he had said, and the Lord did for Sarah what he had promised" (NIV). It is interesting to me that this chapter does not talk about Abraham and what we often call the patristic, dominating, male-oriented perspective of the Scriptures. You haven't read the Scriptures carefully if that's all you see. Because here they are talking about the tenderness of God toward a woman. God uses a woman to create a generation—a dynasty. The Lord was gracious to Sarah. His work is always personal, even if it goes far beyond you. His work is always gracious toward you. Even with what you have done.

> Sarah became pregnant and bore a son to Abraham in his old age, at the very time God had promised him. Abraham gave the name Isaac to the son Sarah bore him. When his son Isaac was eight days old, Abraham circumcised him, as God commanded him. Abraham was a hundred years old when his son Isaac was born to him.
>
> Sarah said, "God has brought me laughter, and everyone who hears about this will laugh with me." And she added, "Who would have said to Abraham [or who would have thought] that Sarah would nurse children? Yet I have borne him a son in his old age." (Genesis 21:2-7, NIV)

We see something beautiful about Sarah here. And she says, "Everyone who hears about this will laugh with me." She joined in the joke.

God Is a God of Laughter

God's laughter is not ironic or jeering or bitter. It is not the laughter of scoffing disbelief. It's not even the self-depreciating laugh of the all-too-aware-of-their-own-unworthiness types. God's laughter is the laughter of the God who is always on time, though maybe by surprise. It's the laughter of God, whose power overcomes our limitations. It's the laughter of God whose grace overcomes our failures. For nothing is impossible with the Lord. To remind us of these glorious truths, Abraham and Sarah named their son Laughter. We believe in the God of Abraham, Laughter, and Jacob!

What reversals has God shown me?

Are there things in my past that looked hopeless—but God overcame?

What stories of God's overcoming have I heard from others?

God will often turn things on their head.

I was reading recently about Richard Wurmbrand. He was a Romanian Christian who wrote *Tortured for Christ.* In that book he talks about the beatings he received in Romania at the hands of the Communist dictators. He was imprisoned for his Christian faith in communist jail cells thirty feet beneath the ground. After his release many years later, when he spoke to groups, he would apologize for having to sit while speaking. He would explain that fourteen years of beatings had taken a toll on his feet. He could not stand in one place for more than a few moments. He told how he and his comrades had languished, forgotten—or so they thought—in those deep gray, underground cells, illuminated by a single lightbulb that dangled from the ceiling. They had forgotten what color was; they couldn't remember the faces and voices of loved ones. Wurmbrand described only the mildest of indignities that were inflicted upon them by Communist torturers, refusing to reveal the full scale of their torture. Still, every night he joined with other prisoners to kneel and pray for America, for America's churches, for America's children.

Back in 1992 Wurmbrand was asked to return to Romania, which was joining all of Eastern Europe in breaking free from the communist stronghold. He was asked to visit his Christian countrymen, who had been locked behind that iron curtain as it was rusting into dust. He went to the city in which the first Christian bookstore in the nation had opened. He was asked if he would like to see the warehouse. He was led downstairs into a small room that was stuffed with books. He took one look and froze in surprise. Wurmbrand spun around and took his wife into his arms. Then in view of everyone present, this elderly saint whose feet required him to sit while lecturing began to dance with joy. Do you know why? That warehouse was his old cell! The very place where he had knelt and prayed and endured torture was now becoming a beacon of light to the world. God's reversal. And the laughter that broke out from Richard's lips was God's laughter! Everyone there laughed in joy and praise to the God of great surprises.[5]

Nothing is too hard for God.

The Lord wants to give us the eyes of faith to see beyond the human possibility. Our hope is not in human possibilities but in the divine, infinite power behind God's promise. Bright laughter breaks out when God overcomes human limitation and human abilities. The Lord said to Abraham (and of course he knew that Sarah was eavesdropping!), "Is anything too hard for the Lord?" The same principle was given to another childless woman who is about to experience an even greater miracle. "For nothing is impossible with God" (Luke 1:37).

I believe that you and I each have a list of things that we believe are too hard for God. We think that God cannot

- change the hardened heart of a loved one who is uninterested in Christ;
- bring reconciliation in a broken relationship;
- open the doors to fulfill our heart's dream;
- provide the financial resources we need;
- release us from pain or anxiety or fear; or
- release us from the lingering pain of heartbreak, jealousy, or anger.

Then we hear a story such as that of Richard Wurmbrand, and our heart stirs with hope.

"Is anything too hard for the Lord?" Take that question with you into your day. As you face every circumstance, ask yourself: Is *this* too hard for the Lord? As you take time to reflect, you will be greatly encouraged. Experiment with turning these circumstances over to the Lord, trusting him to work. You may find yourself laughing much more!

What are at least three things I think are too hard for God?

Why do I think this?

What will I do with these things now?

What about You?

So my question to you is this: Are you listening for God's promises in your life right now? His promises aren't limited to Abraham and Sarah, Isaac and Rebekah, Jacob and Rachel, and the others. His promises are for each of us. Are you listening?

Are you trusting his timing? Have you set a bitterness alarm that you need to turn off today? Trust his timing.

Have you limited God's powers in your life because you say, "I don't see the resources around here to do this"? Base your dream and your faith on belief without evidence. I believe the evidence will arise to substantiate what God has given.

Lastly, have you surrendered your desires and your failures to the Lord? Release your bitterness and let in his joy.

Notes

1. Arthur T. Pierson, *George Müller of Bristol* (Old Tappan, N.J.: Fleming H. Revell, n.d.), 167.
2. Leland Ryken, *The Literature of the Bible* (Grand Rapids, Mich.: The Zondervan Publishing House, 1974), 23.
3. C. H. Spurgeon, *Lecture to My Students,* quoting John Newton (Grand Rapids, Mich.: Baker Book House, 1977), 32.
4. Sharon E. Mumper, "The Church the Gang of Four Built," *Christianity Today,* 15 May 1987, 17.
5. Adapted from Steve Halliday, *No Night Too Dark* (Sisters, Oreg.: Multnomah, 1993), 89–91.

CHAPTER 7

"Shall I hide my plan?" The Audacity of Prayer

Genesis 18:17

You pay God a compliment by asking great things of him. St. Teresa of Avila

IT HAPPENED IN early December 1934 in a little town in China. Betty Blackstone, her husband, Bill, and their twenty-month-old son, Bobby, had returned to their village after leaving it to escape the onrush of Mao Tse-tung's army. The army had passed by, but the area was still full of Communists. Their house was the only one outside the city walls the Communists had not completely destroyed.

At about 2:30 one morning, they were awakened by shots from a repeating weapon. It sounded as though it were at their front gate. It meant Communists; local bandits had no such modern weapons. They jumped from bed and dressed in silence. They grabbed the small suitcase of diapers, milk powder, and other essentials for the baby, went to his bed on the sleeping porch and looked down at him. What to do next? If they woke Bobby, he might cry and give them away to the soldiers outside.

Betty sank to the floor with no strength. Bill stooped down, kissed her, and prayed in a whisper—a prayer thanking God for his presence, affirming that he had called them to China and that he would give them strength and be with them whatever happened. After the prayer, they had such perfect peace that they went back to bed and to sleep.

At an early morning prayer meeting, the Chinese Christians asked, "Why didn't they get you? We heard them go by, marching down the road that leads to your house." The Blackstones could not answer that question.

In the next airmail letter from Bill's mother she asked, "Did anything special happen out there on December 3? Many of the women here at Hollywood Presbyterian Church felt a deep burden to pray for you. They phoned around and found that many felt the same burden, so they met at the church. (It was the day of Hollywood Women's Club, and some even missed the meeting!) They knelt and prayed until the burden was lifted. Then they got up, wondering what in the world all this meant, and went home. We are all anxious to know what happened."

Betty looked in her diary. At the very hour the Communists were going along the path to their house, the women at Hollywood Presbyterian were on their knees in prayer. "According to the people who lived along the street, the Communists had gotten as far as our house but then changed their minds and retraced their steps, shooting their weapons."

Writing of her experience, Betty said, "There are many things I do not understand about prayer; for instance why we were spared and other missionary families were not. But one thing I do know—our lives were saved because we had friends back home who were obediently and fervently interceding for us."[1]

It's easy for us to doubt that we matter much to God, especially in the area of prayer. Who would have the audacity to think that their paltry words and desires could have any affect on the outcome of events? Who are we compared with the forces at work in the world? Who are we compared with the power and will of the Lord God Almighty? According to human reason, trying to change things through prayer makes as much sense as trying to rewrite history. It just can't be done.

Yet God's Word exhorts us to prayer again and again.

Through prayer, God promises to reveal his truth to us. As we read in Jeremiah 33:2-3:

> Thus says the Lord who made the earth, the Lord who formed it to establish it—the Lord is his name: "Call to me and I will answer you, and will tell you great and hidden things which you have not known." (RSV)

What is my attitude toward prayer?

God promises to deliver us through prayer. As he says through the psalmist: "Trust me in your times of trouble, and I will rescue you, and you will give me glory" (Psalm 50:15).

Is prayer central or secondary in my life? Why?

We Think Far Too Little of Prayer's Importance

God seeks to engage us in prayer continually. God's question to himself in Genesis 18:17 shows this clearly. It's an amazing revelation of God's desire to involve us actively in his work.

> **Then the men [this is referring to the three angels who had come to visit Abraham and Sarah] got up from their meal and started on toward Sodom. Abraham went with them part of the way.**
>
> **"Should I hide my plan from Abraham?" the Lord asked. "For Abraham will become a great and mighty nation, and all the nations of the earth will be blessed through him. I have singled him out so that he will direct his sons and their families to keep the way of the Lord and do what is right and just. Then I will do for him all that I have promised." So the Lord told Abraham, "I have heard that the people of Sodom and Gomorrah are extremely evil, and that everything they do is wicked. I am going down to see whether or not these reports are true. Then I will know."**

The two other men went on toward Sodom, but the Lord remained with Abraham for a while. (Genesis 18:16-22)

This question that God poses to himself reveals a profound truth about prayer. The very fact that God asks this question gives us an essential insight into prayer: Prayer makes a difference. The exact nature and scope of that difference will become clear as we proceed.

The way we approach prayer tells us a great deal about ourself and our theology. Some people are fatalists, viewing their destiny as set, with little confidence in the effectiveness of prayer. They think of prayer as a psychological comfort but not as a spiritual force that creates change. Others are theoretical believers but practical atheists: They believe that prayer can make a difference but fail to practice it. Then there are those who have seen a "history of wonders" (to use the phrase of E. M. Bounds) through their diligent prayer.

What strikes me most about this explanation of prayer?

How does it differ from or confirm my conception of the purpose of prayer?

How does this affect the way I pray?

What is prayer all about? E. M. Bounds, who was a great preacher and teacher of prayer around the time of the mid-nineteenth century, said this:

> Prayer has everything to do with molding the soul into the image of God and everything to do with enhancing and enlarging the measure of God's grace in our life. Prayer has everything to do with bringing the soul into complete fellowship or communion with God. It has everything to do with enriching, broadening and maturing the soul's experience with God.[2]

What a grand and glorious vision! Yet it's not much of a reality in most of our life. Is there a way to awaken our heart so that we long for prayer and experience its benefits? Is there a way to experience prayer more as a conversation with God rather than a monologue with ourself? Abraham's experience shows us that prayer begins, not with our requests, but with our relationship with God.

We Are Meant to Intercede as Partners with God

To intercede means to stand with God on behalf of others. What does that look like? Abraham gives us a vivid picture of intercession in this encounter. "The men turned away and went toward Sodom, but Abraham remained standing before the Lord" (Genesis 18:22, NIV). Perhaps Abraham stood literally between the Lord and Sodom. If so, that's a powerful picture of intercession. We shouldn't interpret this as Abraham trying to overcome God's antagonism. This is *not* a picture of Abraham blocking God's way, as if God were bent on Sodom's destruction. It is a portrait of partnership.

A key passage that sheds light on this is Ezekiel 22:30. The Lord is about to move in judgment against Jerusalem and says, "I looked for a man among them who would build up the wall and stand before me in the gap on behalf of the land so I would not have to destroy it, but I found none. So I will pour out my wrath on them" (NIV). The phrase "I looked for a man among them who would . . . stand before me in the gap" expresses God's desire for an earthly partner. It's as if God is saying, "Is there one human partner who will join with me so I can funnel my divine resources through that human person into the situation? Isn't there anyone who will join me?"

Where do I see some gaps at this time? In my family? School? Friendships? Neighborhood? Community? Workplace? Church? Lord, where do you want me to stand?

This is a profound picture. When you pray for another person, you see, you stand *with* God and not against him. Together you seek God's love and grace for this person.

"We must not conceive of prayer," said Archbishop Trench, "as overcoming God's reluctance, but laying hold of his highest willingness."

Somewhere we have the picture of a stingy God who resents doing good things for his children. If you are really good, according to this distorted thinking, God may give you something good once in a while. But you have to pester him. You have to overcome his resistance, his antagonism, because he'd really just as soon not share at all.

This picture is all wrong.

> "Keep on asking, and you will be given what you ask for. Keep on looking, and you will find. Keep on knocking, and the door will be opened. For everyone who asks, receives. Everyone who seeks, finds. And the door is opened to everyone who knocks. You parents—if your children ask for a loaf of bread, do you give them a stone instead? Or if they ask for a fish, do you give them a snake? Of course not! If you sinful people know how to give good gifts to your children, how much more will your heavenly Father give good gifts to those who ask him." (Matthew 7:7-11)

God is ready to give. He is looking for a person to stand in the gap. What happens with the person who fills the gap? That person completes the connection between God and the situation. This is a mystery, indeed, but it is a principle God has woven into the fabric of creation. God uses us to proclaim the Good News—for how can people hear without one who will proclaim? He uses us to feed the hungry—for inasmuch as we serve the least, we serve him. *We matter!*

And when you fill the gap, you enter more fully into the heart of God. If you want to know God, pray for someone. Be still first, and then pray. If you want to know God, you will then know his tenderness as you have never known it before. When I quiet my heart before the Lord and pray for people, I'm often moved with a tenderness that is not naturally mine. In prayer you will taste God's compassion. You will experience his power and see the abundance of his grace and mercy. You will see that he is strong to save, and you will fall in worship before him. He is an awesome God.

And when you pray for another person, you do not stand against God, but you are given the privilege of standing with him on behalf of others. As we learn the Lord's heart, we can call upon his love and resources and begin to carry the Lord's burdens as well as experience his benefits.

If you intercede for other people, you will begin to experience a burden and a care you have never felt before. So you might want to prepare yourself when you pray for someone. And please, don't just toss off the phrase "Well, we will pray for you." This is a key role in the coming kingdom. Remember Moses' interceding for the people when God was about to judge them for their sin with the golden calf? God is looking for that compassion that fuels active involvement through passion and prayer.

Have I ever been burdened to pray for someone? If not, does this mean that I have to feel something as I pray? What does this idea mean to me?

When We Pray, We See God's Nature and Character in New Ways

What do we learn about God as he comes to us in this time of prayer? We learn to avoid caricatures about him. We learn that he wants us to stand with him. But perhaps the most intriguing lesson of all is what we learn as Abraham pours out his heart, seeking God's mercy: Pray persistently, and you will see God's nature in new ways.

The following passage in Genesis 18:22-33 is a vivid example of holy boldness that reveals the extent of God's love and grace:

> **The two other men went on toward Sodom, but the Lord remained with Abraham for a while. Abraham approached him and said, "Will you destroy both innocent and guilty alike? Suppose you find fifty innocent people there within the city—will you still destroy it, and not spare it for their sakes? Surely you wouldn't do such a thing, destroying the innocent with the guilty. Why, you would be treating the innocent and the guilty exactly the same! Surely you wouldn't do that! Should not the Judge of all the earth do what is right?"**
>
> **And the Lord replied, "If I find fifty innocent**

people in Sodom, I will spare the entire city for their sake."

Then Abraham spoke again. "Since I have begun, let me go on and speak further to my Lord, even though I am but dust and ashes. Suppose there are only forty-five? Will you destroy the city for lack of five?"

And the Lord said, "I will not destroy it if I find forty-five."

Then Abraham pressed his request further. "Suppose there are only forty?"

And the Lord replied, "I will not destroy it if there are forty."

"Please don't be angry, my Lord," Abraham pleaded. "Let me speak—suppose only thirty are found?"

And the Lord replied, "I will not destroy it if there are thirty."

Then Abraham said, "Since I have dared to speak to the Lord, let me continue—suppose there are only twenty?"

And the Lord said, "Then I will not destroy it for the sake of the twenty."

Finally, Abraham said, "Lord, please do not get angry; I will speak but once more! Suppose only ten are found there?"

And the Lord said, "Then, for the sake of the ten, I will not destroy it."

The Lord went on his way when he had finished his conversation with Abraham, and Abraham returned to his tent.

I have a confession to make. Were you to go back in my sermon archives and listen to tapes of when I read this maybe ten years ago, I read it sort of like this:

"Lord, if there are fifty people there would you hold back?"

"I'll hold back."

"How about forty-five, huh? Can I get you down to forty-five? How about forty—forty once, forty twice, forty going three times." And so on.

I thought Abraham was like an auctioneer or a shopper haggling at a bazaar. Was Abraham getting God to "lower his price"? Is that what this exchange was all about? That's what I used to think.

But I've since come to believe that Abraham was not haggling with God. No, Abraham was appealing to God's virtue. Abraham believed that God is merciful. And he asked the question, "Lord God Almighty, just how merciful are you?" Sodom and Gomorrah together could have well contained thousands of people. There is no reason to think of these as tiny villages. These could have been rather large settlements. They weren't little, and they weren't necessarily poor and impoverished. And so when God came down to investigate, Abraham explored God's mercy.

It is encouraging to discover the depths of God's mercy. We are encouraged by Hebrews 4:16: "Let us then approach the throne of grace with confidence ["boldly" in some translations], so that we may receive mercy and find grace to help us in our time of need" (NIV). We come boldly before the throne of God.

Notice how Abraham comes before God. He says, "I am dust and ashes, I don't even have a right to be here, you can silence me at any time," but in the midst of admitting his limitations he claims his privilege as a son of God, as a friend of God.

Read Psalm 103. What does this psalm tell me about God's mercy for me and for all his creatures?

God fulfills his promises.

God makes promises—and then he fulfills them. In Genesis 17 the Lord had first come to Abraham and Sarah in order to announce the fulfillment of his promise to them. They would have a son, Isaac, as God had promised twenty-four years earlier.

Prayer is rooted in the promises. These very promises give us the audacity to ask boldly of God. Jesus Christ came to make God's promises real to us. This is about the "Yes," the fulfilling of God's promises. It says this:

> For the Son of God, Jesus Christ, who was preached among you by me and Silas and Timothy, was not "Yes" and "No," but in him it has always been "Yes." For no matter how many promises God has made, they are "Yes" in Christ. And so through him the "Amen" is spoken by us to the glory of God. Now it is God who makes both us and you stand firm in Christ. He anointed us, set his seal of ownership on us, and put his Spirit in our hearts as a deposit, guaranteeing what is to come.
> (2 Corinthians 1:19-22, NIV)

As you and I come to prayer, we have God's promises. And those promises are made "Yes" in Jesus Christ. So our confidence builds as we know that he is already here, he's already come to us, he has given us promises, and he intends to fulfill them.

This kind of hope inspires prayers, the impact of which may never be measurable. In 1727, under the leadership of Count Zinzendorf, the Moravians established a round-the-clock prayer meeting for the revival and spread of Christianity. They organized two bands for prayer—one for men and one for women. Each had twenty-four members. Each person would pray for one hour every day, so that there was continuous prayer each day. This prayer was maintained unbroken for one hundred years! The fruit?

- The Moravian missions church grew three times as large as the home church.
- A Moravian witness to John and Charles Wesley led to their conversions and to the revival that became known as Methodism.
- The beginning of worldwide missions was

> launched with great blessing and would continue for over a century.[3]

What promises from God's Word inspire my hope in prayer?

What one can I use for a particular situation right now?

Who are some of the hard people I could be praying for?

Some people reading this may see only coincidences, not answered prayer. But I can testify with those who say, "All I know is that when I pray, 'coincidences' happen. When I don't, they don't!"

God is a just God.

This incident with Abraham and the three visitors also gives us insight into God's justice and mercy—into his judgment and redemption—to inform our prayers.

We may fear praying for someone because we know that he is "out of line" with God. I was counseling with a man whose stepparent claimed to be a Christian but was living a life inconsistent with Christ's standards. One of his questions was how to pray for her. "She seems to be a long way from God. And it's sad," he continued, "because she led me to Christ."

Abraham could have had similar questions about Lot. He and Lot had been close. Lot must have known much about Abraham's God. But Lot was captured by the culture. Still, Abraham would intercede boldly, fervently, for his loved one. In the process, however, Abraham learned some things that are very hard to hear about God's judgment. Why was this important? Because God wanted Abraham and his descendants to understand clearly the nature of God's compassion and the reality of God's justice.

God's inquiry into Sodom demonstrated God's meticulous fairness and his boundless patience. The Lord said, "A complaint has come up against Sodom and Gomorrah." These three visitors were sort of a white-paper committee, going down to investigate that situation and see if it really was as bad as they'd heard.

This word *outcry* in the Hebrew could mean either of two things. It could have been the outcry of those who had been treated unjustly, who cried out, "Lord, have mercy, the abuse and perversion of Sodom is so great!" Or it could simply have been the outcry of the evil itself—the obscene noise of vulgar, unrighteous living. Either way, God went to investigate. Judgment is always preceded by warning—and usually by multiple warnings.

Here we have redemption and judgment set side by side. The Lord came to Abraham and said, "The promise is going to be fulfilled. You are going to have a son now. He will carry on the covenant. I will be faithful to you. I will bless the world because of you." And at the same time the Lord was on that mission of bringing a new baby, he was on the mission of bringing judgment.

After the angels had delivered their message in verse 16, "They looked down toward Sodom" (NIV). Catch that dramatic contrast. The promise is fulfilled before the judgment is executed, lest Abraham fall into abject despair. Abraham sees God's love and his justice, God's blessing and God's curse. Often we see only one dimension of God and miss the glory of his fullness.

It's like a surgeon who cuts into a body in order to heal. It's like a counselor who leads a person through a journey of pain to the past in order to reveal the road to freedom for the rest of that person's life. Like the coach who exercises the athletes to the point of exhaustion so that they can triumph in the day of the contest. Like the judge who demands restitution in the name of justice. These and many more examples show us that God's ways are complex and multifaceted, and they comprise countless factors that, if taken in isolation, would give a caricature of God's true nature. When we see only one or two aspects of God's character, we get an unfair and distorted picture of God's being.

You see, if fire and brimstone were the only things that rained down from heaven, we would fall into despair. But what else rained down that day? A promise. Faithfulness in a covenant and the expression of mercy. The judgment is set in the framework of the miraculous fulfillment of God's promises and the overwhelming revelation of mercy that comes through his dialogue with Abraham.

Many people accuse God of being short-tempered and irritable, especially in the Old Testament. But there is only one God of the Scriptures. The God who came to Abraham came also to us in Christ. People who read the Old Testament and accuse God of being unjust and quick to judge do not understand the biblical records, and they do not know him. God is rich and complex, and even his justice is set in the context of incredible mercy. He calls us his friends. He fulfills his promises. He reveals himself to us. So with those revelations in mind, we are moved to stand with God on behalf of others. This is the meaning of intercession.

God remembers others because of our prayers.

So what happens? It seems that there was probably only one righteous person in Sodom—Abraham's nephew, Lot. Behind Abraham's passion was his desire to save his own family. But as Lot shared with his children and his sons-in-law and sons-in-law-to-be, they all mocked and reviled him. They made fun of the threat that God would come. You know the rest of the story. Lot escaped with his wife and his two unmarried daughters, but Lot's wife looked back and became a pillar of salt, encrusted in the debris. And then Lot's two rather unrighteous daughters seduced him so they could have children by him. So even Lot has a rather questionable record here. But notice what the Scriptures say. Following the destruction of Sodom and Gomorrah, the story switches back to Abraham:

> **The next morning Abraham was up early and hurried out to the place where he had stood in the Lord's presence. He looked out across the plain to Sodom and Gomorrah and saw columns of smoke and fumes, as from a furnace, rising from the cities there. But God had listened to Abraham's request and kept Lot safe, removing him from the disaster that engulfed the cities on the plain. (Genesis 19:27-29)**

Abraham was a man of habit. After he prayed for someone, he went back to see what God had done. That's a crucial follow-up. And though Sodom was destroyed, Lot was not. God remembered Abraham, the one who had stood with him. Look again at that phrase: God remembered Abraham, and saved Lot! Lot wasn't saved because of his virtue but because of Abraham's intercession.

What about You?

We pray because that's what friends do. I don't simply mean that's what human friends do for each other but what *friends of God* do. In Isaiah 41:8 God calls Abraham "my friend." But this privilege is not reserved for Abraham alone. In the upper room, Jesus says,

> I no longer call you servants, because a master doesn't confide in his servants. Now you are my friends, since I have told you everything the Father told me. You didn't choose me. I chose you. I appointed you to go and produce fruit that will last, so that the Father will give you whatever you ask for, using my name. (John 15:15-16)

That's the audacity of prayer and the gospel—that we are made friends with God, even to the extent that we learn what's on his heart. We learn it not only through what is revealed in God's Word but also through the nudges of the Holy Spirit, as the Blackstones' friends experienced. And as we pray, we become like him. Incredible!

Notes

1. Betty Blackstone, "Mission Update," *Prayer/Action* 22, no. 2 (April/June 1993). Betty Blackstone is a retired Presbyterian missionary.
2. E. M. Bounds, *The Necessity of Prayer* (Grand Rapids, Mich.: Baker Book House, 1978), 64.
3. Richard Lovelace, *Dynamics of Spiritual Life* (Downers Grove, Ill.: InterVarsity Press, 1979), 152.

CHAPTER 8

"What do you have there in your hand?" Releasing Our Heart Desire

Exodus 4:2

TIMOTHY BOTTS AND his wife, Nancy, left for Japan right after college to teach conversational English with Brethren in Christ Missions. In spite of three good years, Tim began to feel that he was spinning his wheels because he wasn't using his artistic gifts.

So Tim and Nancy returned to the United States, where Tim began working as a staff artist designing books for Tyndale House Publishers in Wheaton, Illinois.

"I felt guilty that I wasn't doing the harder thing of being a missionary. I thought that being a book designer might be second best as a career, but it was what God seemed to be leading me to do."

Then, as the new year of 1984 approached, Tim made a resolution to read through the whole Bible. Because he is a visual person, Tim kept a sketchbook journal of what he'd read. He would copy the verses in his unique style of calligraphy, trying to picture through the words what the verses were saying. He found this to be a powerful, energizing devotional exercise. During the two years he spent doing this, Tim would occasionally share a verse-sketch with colleagues at work. One day he was invited to present his sketches at one of Tyndale's weekly chapel services. He showed slides of his favorite verses, explaining how he had tried to make the words look like what they mean.

"Most calligraphers decorate or embellish the words, but

my style is to make the words look as relevant as they are," Tim told the Tyndale employees at chapel that morning.

Following the presentation, Wendell Hawley, Tyndale's acquisitions director, asked Tim if he would be interested in compiling the sketches into a book. Tim was pleasantly surprised. It had never crossed his mind that these sketches were anything more than a means to feed his own soul.

"When they said the first printing would be fifteen thousand copies, I panicked," said Tim with a laugh. "I don't even have a thousand friends!" But Tim greatly underestimated the power of his gift. That first book by Timothy R. Botts, *Doorposts,* won the Gold Medallion Award in its category from the Evangelical Christian Publishing Association, the annual award from the Type Directors' Club of New York, and to date has sold over one hundred thousand copies. Since then, Tim has produced four other books and a number of inspirational calligraphy products that have been distributed all over the world.

"I am learning that my artwork is cross-cultural as I receive letters from places such as Japan, Nigeria, and France. What I couldn't do as a missionary, God is allowing me to do as a graphic artist."

One of the most discouraging misconceptions about following the Lord is that we are usually called to do what we don't want to do with gifts we don't have. While there is some truth to the fact that God calls us to do challenging things in full dependence upon him, we are mistaken if we generalize this as the whole of discipleship. The truth is: God calls us to do what we love in order to show others God's love. Tim's story shows us that when we use our gifts, we may do even better than we could imagine—and we may do something different from what we first thought God wanted us to do.

Moses was a man who had given up on his dream. He had hoped to use his gifts of leadership to save his people, but everything went wrong. Then one day God came to Moses and asked him a question. Certainly God's interaction with

Moses at the burning bush is one of the Bible's most enlightening and delightful descriptions of God's call. As you read a portion of it, look for a touch of what I call "holy humor" as God speaks with Moses. We'll look at Exodus 4:1-5 as Moses is considering his call from God. He has already posed a number of objections, each carefully answered by the Lord. The story continues:

> **But Moses protested again, "Look, they won't believe me! They won't do what I tell them. They'll just say, 'The Lord never appeared to you.'"**
>
> **Then the Lord asked him, "What do you have there in your hand?"**
>
> **"A shepherd's staff," Moses replied.**
>
> **"Throw it down on the ground," the Lord told him. So Moses threw it down, and it became a snake! Moses was terrified, so he turned and ran away.**
>
> **Then the Lord told him, "Take hold of its tail." So Moses reached out and grabbed it, and it became a shepherd's staff again.**
>
> **"Perform this sign, and they will believe you," the Lord told him. "Then they will realize that the Lord, the God of their ancestors—the God of Abraham, the God of Isaac, and the God of Jacob—really has appeared to you."**

What does this passage have to do with our heart desire? And how did God use this incident to get at the heart of Moses' desires? Many of us haven't yet realized that our desires are sparks from God's fire. Moses didn't seem to realize it either. But God took some time—in a humorous way—to reveal to Moses a lot about himself and about God's purposes for him.

Moses' Reluctance and God's Persuasion

Most of us are familiar with this story. Moses had been born in Egypt at a time when Pharaoh commanded the midwives to slay all male children born to the Jews. Moses was safely delivered and put in a waterproof basket on the river, where he was rescued by one of Pharaoh's daughters. He was raised in the Egyptian court with all the privileges and honors accorded to one of Pharaoh's own. But he risked trying to help Hebrew slaves. As a consequence of murdering an Egyptian taskmaster, Moses fled to Midian. After forty years God came to Moses as he was tending flocks. When a bush burst into flames, Moses went to examine it and encountered the living God.

God instructed Moses to go back to Egypt and set the Israelites free. But Moses was a reluctant volunteer, to say the least. He did not want to go back. Instead, he listed excuse after excuse as to why he couldn't return.

In this scene God and Moses are trying to work through to a resolution. In Exodus 3 Moses began by asking, "Who are you, God?" And God made clear that he is the God who hears and delivers his people. He is God of the present moment and is able to respond to people.

Then Moses proceeded to question who he, Moses, was that he should even attempt such a thing. Why would they ever listen to him? Moses was going to learn that God uses the ordinary things he has given us to serve his highest purposes and fulfill our deepest desires.

God's methods are fascinating. His words to Moses lead him through a soul-searching process in which he comes not only to understand God more fully but to understand himself more deeply. That soul-searching process begins when Moses asks God, "Why would they listen to me?" And God says, "What do you have there in your hand?"

Moses is asked to look at the staff. Now, we have to understand the significance of the staff before we get the full impact of this question. Remember, Moses was raised in Pharaoh's court. Now do you know what Pharaoh and the Egyptians thought about shepherds? They despised them. That's why when Joseph's family left Israel and came back into Egypt, they were given the land of Goshen, which was far away from most normal Egyptian settlements. The Egyptians didn't want shepherds to be near them.

What have you given up?

Moses would never have held a shepherd's staff when he was in Pharaoh's court. He would have held writing implements as he gained the finest education Pharaoh could provide. He would have eaten the finest foods and worn the finest clothing. But he never would have held the despised tool of a shepherd.

The staff Moses held when God spoke through the burning bush must have held great significance for Moses. First, it must have reminded him of what he had given up. It was as if God said, "Look at that staff, and think about what you gave up when you fled Egypt. Think of what it led you to." I think Moses had some mixed feelings as he looked at that staff. He remembered what his little hands had held in those days of growing up in Pharaoh's court. They contrasted sharply with what his big, weathered hands held now.

That staff represented the whole new life that Moses was leading in Midian, far different from the life he had led in Egypt. He was on the far side of the desert. That's a fascinating little description that is given to us earlier in this passage. Think of the most unsophisticated little town in your part of the country; that's where Moses lived. The far side of the desert is a fascinating description of nowhere.

Moses was alone; he was feeling isolated. There were no executive search firms that visited the far side of the desert. There were no talent scouts who were scouting on the far side of the desert. There is only one person watching you on the far side of the desert. That is God. And as Moses looked at his staff, it reminded him that he had fled from where he was known, where he would have been cared for.

What is your heart desire?

Remember that Moses was rescued as an infant. Time and again he heard his "mother," Pharaoh's daughter, tell the story. Every birthday he may have heard it again. "Oh, my

Have I ever sensed God urging me to do something, such as talk to a friend about his faith? write a special letter? give someone a gift that would encourage his faith? take leadership responsibility?

How did I respond?

What sort of excuses am I most likely to make?

Is there any object in my life that reminds me of a difficult period of time I have gone through?

If I were to look at it and reflect on it, what thoughts would come to mind?

How does this affect me spiritually?

son, remember when I found you in a basket on the river? You were wrapped in blankets so that you wouldn't wiggle out of your basket or get wet. And right after I found you, how that young girl, Miriam, offered the Hebrew family to assist in nursing you?" From the moment he was born, the idea of being rescued, of being saved from death, was deeply embedded into Moses. It permeated his heart, his bones, his very being. Deep within his soul, he knew what it felt like to be threatened. While he was grateful for the miracle of being taken from the river, it must have left an indelible imprint because he had a real dislike for bullies.

We read in Hebrews 11:23-25: "By faith Moses' parents hid him for three months after he was born, because they saw he was no ordinary child, and they were not afraid of the king's edict. By faith Moses, when he had grown up, refused to be known as the son of Pharaoh's daughter. He chose to be mistreated along with the people of God rather than to enjoy the pleasures of sin for a short time" (NIV).

First of all, Moses left bully Pharaoh. He didn't see how he could fight bully Pharaoh directly, but he could refuse to be a part of his household. He also couldn't stand to see an Egyptian beating a Hebrew, one of his own people. Glancing this way and that, seeing no one watching, Moses killed the Egyptian and hid him in the sand. He was a rescuer. He killed a bully Egyptian.

But the Israelites turned against him, so he fled into the wilderness. In the wilderness he encountered seven women who were daughters of the priest at Midian. They had come to draw water for their father's flocks. Some other shepherds, however, came along and began to drive the women away. But Moses came to their rescue. He drove the bully shepherds away and watered the flocks of the Midianite women.

Bully Pharaoh, bully Egyptians, bully shepherds—Moses resisted them all. His heart desire was to be a deliverer.

Moses' experience in Egypt had taught him that he couldn't rescue people on his own in his own way. Still, that heart desire attracted the attention of the heavenly Father. In fact, I believe it was the spark and the flint of the heavenly Father. That heart desire was to do good for others, especially if they were being oppressed and treated unjustly. He didn't do it the right way—he didn't always understand it—but he had a heart desire of compassion. God didn't change the heart desire. He claimed the man. God redeemed Moses' experience and shaped Moses for his service.

How do I respond to injustice and bullying?

As I reflect on my personal "holy history," what are some of the heart desires I see behind my actions?

Even if my actions have been misguided, such as some of Moses' were, what do they reveal about my longings?

What Do You Hold in Your Hand?

Moses was a deliverer. He was a caregiver, a rescuer. The shepherd's staff was a visual representation of this heart desire. With its hook on the end, he could reach down and rescue a sheep that had fallen into a hole. The staff had a knot on the end, making it a weapon he could throw at predators. The staff was used to guide the herd. Moses looked at this staff and saw all of this. His identity was in that staff.

This is how you begin to get in touch with your heart desire: Ask yourself, What am I holding in my hand? Where am I? You may feel that you are on the far side of the desert, a little bit east of nowhere. You may have never expected to be doing what you are doing or to be living where you are living, but there you are. So what are you holding as a result? Look at your staff, be it a computer, a piano, a textbook, a diaper. Or a backhoe, a hammer, a calculator, a stethoscope, a wheelchair. Or a football, a legal brief, a financial projection, a calligraphy pen, a dish towel. What are you holding? And what does it say about your heart desire?

Remember, not everybody understands all the links immediately. It takes some soul-searching. You may be holding something right now that reminds you of a lot of pain. Moses' staff represented a lot of pain, struggle, and difficulty in his own life. What does that thing in your hand say about your life? What does it say about your Lord? Take time to observe who you are and what you've been given, and it will remind you of where you have come from and where God may want to lead you. What are you holding in your hand?

What am I holding in my hand?

What skills and experiences do I have?

What desires burn within me?

God didn't change Moses' heart, but he did change Moses. God redeemed Moses. He redeemed Moses' experience and shaped him for service. How did that happen? It happened when God commanded Moses, "Throw it down."

Throw It Down

When Moses acknowledged what he was holding in his hand, the Lord then said, "Throw it down!" That's hard to do! Release it, let it go, drop it. Put that thing down. The Hebrew word here is urgent. It doesn't mean "Set it down nicely now." It means to throw.

If God asks you to throw down your gift—your heart desire—what happens to you? You hold on more tightly. Why? Because you are afraid you may never get it back. We're afraid to trust our heart desire to God. We're afraid to release it. We don't realize that letting go allows God to reveal its power and its gift. We fear that either we won't get it back at all, or it will come back changed, and we don't want change.

Until we let go of everything else we cannot claim that God is first. And until God is first, we cannot discover our deepest joy and greatest satisfaction. When we release our heart desire, we may find God revealing something awesome. And I mean "awesome" in the richest sense of the word—something wonderful that will truly inspire awe.

What does Moses' staff become when he throws it down? A serpent. Contemporary people living in the Western Hemisphere don't understand this passage very well. We associate serpents with poisonous venom that will kill us. Many of us immediately associate them with the Garden of Eden. To the Western mind, serpents are always wicked and evil.

However, they are not always a symbol of evil, and they are not always to be dreaded. In the ancient Near East, the serpent was a symbol for special wisdom, fertility, and healing. The familiar insignia of medical doctors is a rod with the wings at the top and a serpent entwined around it. That's the symbol of the Greco-Roman god Aesculapius, the god of healing. As a little child, I couldn't understand why a doctor would have a snake on his door! I wasn't too sure I wanted to go in there. But it was a symbol of healing. When Moses saw the serpent, he may well have thought of healing.

What else might have come to mind when Moses saw the serpent? He may have thought of Pharaoh's headdress, which was adorned with the head of a cobra, its cowl fully spread, ready to strike. The serpent was a symbol of sovereignty. So when Moses threw down his staff and it became a serpent, he didn't run for cover from a dreaded symbol of wickedness and evil. Instead, Moses saw that God had revealed in his own staff the symbol of wisdom and of healing, sovereign power:

- sovereign power to liberate the people and overcome Pharaoh;
- healing power to restore the people who had been oppressed and abused; and
- wisdom to know how to serve them.

Until we throw them down, we may never fully appreciate our gifts. But when we throw them down, surrendering them to God, he may reveal their awesome power to work in ways we never imagined. He may reveal a special wisdom we hadn't yet perceived. He may even reveal an aspect of the authority that he's put into our hands as his covenant partners. Until we throw down our gifts, we may never fully understand their potential for others as well as ourself.

Randy and Tina White are members of our congregation. Randy is the national director for urban projects for Inter-Varsity Christian Fellowship. They lived with their two boys in suburbia but were active in ministry in our downtown. In his book *Journey to the Center of the City,* Randy tells how God moved them to "throw down" their home and suburban lifestyle. It took four or five years for them to follow through. Now God has given them—and all of us—a vision of his power and grace to transform lives and neighborhoods. Randy writes:

Are there areas of my life and gifts I have "thrown down"?

What have I learned from them?

Are there areas I'm withholding? Why?

> God called us to leave a suburban neighborhood which we felt was fairly stable and predictable and to live here in Lowell [where 99.4 percent of all children live below the poverty line]. And he has opened the door for college students to live with us, using our home as a base for partnering with the poor in the healing of the city. We have joined a small network of people who are attempting to fly upside down for the sake of the gospel and, in the process, are taking another look at life and God.[1]

Once you have thrown something down, though, you have to move on. A lot of people can get lost in the introspection. Introspection is essential to wise service, but we can't stay there.

Take the Risk

Moses looked at what he was holding in his hand, his staff, and threw it down. He saw the awesome revelation of God in it. Then he was called to take the next step. Following the time of introspection and soul-searching, he was called to action—a new, more powerful, more exciting action. An action that required more courage than Moses ever knew he had.

God said to Moses, "Take hold of [the serpent's] tail." Imagine that! Moses may have thought, *Lord, don't you know how these things work? If you pick a serpent up by the tail, it coils around and strikes, injecting its deadly poison.* God said to Moses, "Pick it up by the tail," and I think there was a holy twinkle in God's eye.

The Hebrew conveys that Moses snatched it. He didn't reach down gingerly and pick it up. He grabbed it. I think I know why: He was going to grab and be ready to fling it away if it threatened to strike. Moses obeyed God, but he didn't know what would happen. We can't blame him for bracing himself and grabbing the tail.

God often asks us to do things that may not only look foolish but may actually be foolish (under ordinary circumstances), full of risk and danger. God may ask us to do things in a way that shows that we value God's direction more than human convention. God may ask us to do things in a way that shows that we trust God's Word more than human wisdom. "Pick it up by the tail." Are you taking any risks in your business? in your home? in your neighborhood?

Several years ago a person Sarah and I knew only as an acquaintance got into serious trouble. We cared, so I wrote him a letter. Then I wrote him another letter but never heard a word back. Then Sarah wrote him a letter, and then she, too, wrote another letter. Still no response. Then, after two years and four letters, this person called on the phone. "I want you guys to know that I have every one of your letters. In fact, I just put them in my new Bible. Last week I committed my life to Jesus Christ. I think your letters helped plant the seeds."

Now, it was a small risk indeed for us to send a letter to this man. But the additional letters we wrote, receiving no response, felt a bit more foolish each time. We asked ourselves what he might be thinking. Would he feel that we were too pushy or preachy? Still, we grabbed it by the tail. It's a pretty small tail for us, but we grabbed it. And then, after two years, Sarah and I each had a forty-five minute conversation separately with this person, and we saw the seeds bear fruit.

Risk is essential. In the movie *Raging Bull,* boxer Jake La Motta's manager-brother explains to him why he should shed some weight and fight an unknown opponent. After an intricate argument that leaves La Motta baffled (probably had too many hits upside the head), he concludes, "So do it. If you win, you win, and if you lose, you win."

Did you get that? "If you win, you win, if you lose, you win." That's what risk is all about. Often a risk is worth taking simply for the sake of taking it. A risk wakes us from our routine and our apathy. A risk tests our sense of who we are and helps us see in new ways who God is. If God says to you, "Grab it by the tail," you better believe that something

How do I respond to risks?

Am I a risk taker, or am I more cautious?

What risks have I taken? How have they affected my spiritual vitality?

What have I learned about myself and about God through risks?

is going to happen! That's what a risk is all about. We select a challenge, and it creates a sense of new power. It also creates a sense of new understanding of God. "If you win, you win, if you lose, you win." God has a plan no matter what happens.

In the process of risk taking, the staff of ordinary experience, the staff of our heart desire, becomes the staff of God.

As Moses' encounter with God concludes, we read, "So Moses took his wife and sons, put them on a donkey, and headed back to the land of Egypt. In his hand he carried the staff of God" (Exodus 4:20). It is no longer Moses' staff; it is the staff of God. God takes what Moses knows best and transforms it into the best means for doing God's work. Moses sees his heart desire now in a whole new way. He knows that God is not limited to Moses' abilities or resources. God will work through them in wonderful ways as Moses yields them to the Lord.

God Uses the Ordinary

God uses the ordinary things he has given us to serve his purposes and to fulfill our heart desire. When I was preaching on the material in this chapter, I invited the congregation to take a moment to go through their pockets, wallets, or purses to find some symbol of their "staff." They could even write something on a piece of paper. I invited them to hold it up and then asked them to drop it (with adequate precautions for breakables!). It was an amazing moment: There was hesitation, as if everyone was holding their breath. Then I heard a coin ping, then someone dropped a book, then a flutter of a few papers, and in a few moments the sanctuary was filled with the sounds of holy surrender. After the services countless people commented that God did something in their hearts in that time.

What about You?

You can do the same thing right now. What is symbolic of your "staff"? Pick it up, and prayerfully reflect on its meaning for you. Then throw it down. As a salesperson, you may throw down an order form, inviting God to open the doors of conversation to spiritual things so that you see your work as touching people, not simply providing a service or product. As a student, you may throw down your student ID, inviting God to enable you to witness to your values and convictions in the midst of your classes or during mealtimes, at sports or other activities. You may have a symbol from a service club. Throw it down.

Perhaps you've come across something that reminds you of something you've always wanted to do. I often talk with people who are aspiring authors who are yet to be published. Their discouragement may go very deep. I don't know what it might be for you, but bring your dream before the Lord. Throw it down, and let God give it back to you as his!

NOTES

1. Randy White, *Journey to the Center of the City* (Downers Grove, Ill.: InterVarsity Press, 1996), 27.

CHAPTER 9

"*Where is your security?*" Taking Unholy Inventory

1 Chronicles 21:1-2

HITTING IT BIG may not bring all the security it seems to promise. Just ask Curtis Sharp. When Sharp, a thirty-thousand-dollar-a-year Bell Labs janitor, showed up to collect his lottery winnings in 1982, he appeared with two women on his arm—his estranged wife and his girlfriend. He married the girlfriend in a hundred-thousand-dollar wedding. Fifteen years after winning $5 million (to be paid out in twenty annual payments) in the New York lottery, Sharp declared bankruptcy. His annual two-hundred-thousand-dollar (after taxes) checks were insufficient to cover his accumulated debts. He lost his $550,000 house in West Orange, New Jersey, which he'd purchased for his new wife, and his fleet of Cadillacs. His five remaining checks were sold to pay off his debts, and he'll live the rest of his life on an $825 monthly pension. "They say a fool and his money are soon parted," Sharp says. "Easy come, easy go."[1]

An Issue of Security

Security is a big issue for all of us. Psychologist Abraham Maslow produced what he called a hierarchy of human need, which put personal security and safety as essential before all other needs. His hierarchy begins with the most basic physiological needs of keeping the body alive and satisfying our basic appetites. On the second level are our safety and security needs. Following these come our need for belonging and love. Fourth are our esteem needs by which we seek affirmation, recognition, and appreciation. At the top of the hierarchy is the need for what Maslow calls self-actualization. He writes, "Even if all these needs are satisfied, we may still often (if not always) expect that a new discontent and restlessness will soon develop, unless the individual is doing what *he,* individually, is fitted for. A musician must make music, an artist must paint, a poet must write, if he is to be ultimately at peace with himself."[2] While Maslow nowhere affirms the need for faith in God, his analysis of the human condition prods us to take a closer look at the elements of our security, our sense of well-being.

Reviewing Maslow's hierarchy, what needs does Maslow ignore?

What needs are of greatest concern to me?

How do these needs affect my spiritual vitality?

One of the fundamental battles of faith is that of security. Where is my trust, my confidence that my welfare is assured? Faith calls to a type of security far different from anything offered by this world. One of the basic tools of the evil one is to get us to bank on the wrong things. When we think there are quick answers to solve our security needs, we are sorely tempted. And he can attack us at a number of levels.

Security—A Prime Target of the Evil One

Security—or lack of it—determines to some extent the quality of our life. The lack of security makes us nervous and afraid. We are unable to rest in the Lord or to take risks in his service. For this reason, our security is a prime target of the evil one. The devil would like us to be shaken and insecure. He would like us to look anywhere but to God for our confidence in life.

Near the end of King David's life, he had done very well. He'd won many battles and established a powerful nation under God. Then something very strange happened.

> **Satan rose up against Israel and caused David to take a census of the Israelites. David gave these orders to Joab and his commanders: "Take a census of all the people in the land—from Beersheba in the south to Dan in the north—and**

> **bring me the totals so I may know how many there are."**
>
> **But Joab replied, "May the Lord increase the number of his people a hundred times over! But why, my lord, do you want to do this? Are they not all your servants? Why must you cause Israel to sin?"**
>
> **But the king insisted that Joab take the census, so Joab traveled throughout Israel to count the people. Then he returned to Jerusalem and reported the number of people to David. There were 1,100,000 men of military age in Israel, and 470,000 in Judah. But Joab did not include the tribes of Levi and Benjamin in the census because he was so distressed at what the king had made him do. (1 Chronicles 21:1-6)**

People reading this passage for the first time are usually puzzled and ask, "What is the big deal here? Why all this upset over a census? Hadn't Israel taken a census before?" As we read further in the story, we see that God's wrath breaks out because of this census. The Lord gives David several options in judgment, none of which are pleasant. The result is that there is destruction in Israel—all because of the census. And we think, *Isn't God overreacting?*

If we look more closely at this passage though, we see that David is trying to measure the human, tangible basis for his security. The unsettling fact is that this had not been an issue in his earlier life.

Starting Well Is Good, But It's Not Good Enough

David demonstrated total trust in God alone from the very beginning. We can go clear back to the story of David and Goliath (1 Samuel 17) and see this. When the Philistine giant had the Israelites paralyzed with fright, David had come forward to fight Goliath single-handedly. Saul gave David his own armor to wear, but the armor didn't fit. Instead, David wore his regular clothes and took a slingshot as his human weapon. But his real confidence was in the Lord.

> **David shouted in reply, "You come to me with sword, spear, and javelin, but I come to you in the name of the Lord Almighty—the God of the armies of Israel, whom you have defied. Today the Lord will conquer you, and I will kill you and cut off your head. And then I will give the dead bodies of your men to the birds and wild animals, and the whole world will know that there is a God in Israel! And everyone will know that the Lord does not need weapons to rescue his people. It is his battle, not ours. The Lord will give you to us!" (1 Samuel 17:45-47)**

David did not rely on the protection nor the weapons of the world. David relied on God's power as he went into battle. He started very well.

David continued to do well as he waited to become king of Israel. Following his anointing, he was hunted by a jealous Saul. David had several chances to assassinate Saul, but he refused to trust his own hand to force God's plan. David trusted not in human force but in God's timing. And when the time came to take the throne, David honored God as he solidified his new kingdom, continually expressing his confidence in God.

When have I been tempted to rely on worldly armor? How did it affect the battle?

But David didn't finish well. His story is a sober reminder to all of us. I think of a girl I'll call Annalisa who prayed to receive Christ at a Young Life camp during her sophomore year of high school. She got off to a great start. But then she got into a music group that did a number of weekend parties. She said she wanted to be a witness to the party scene. But instead of bringing others to Christ, they drew her from Christ. When I bumped into her at the mall after months of not seeing her at church, she said, "I don't really belong there anymore. I have finally found a place where I can be me." In other words, she'd found a place of "security," but it took her far from her once-vibrant faith.

The world offers a number of security traps. What ones attract me the most?

We are in danger of going spiritually backward as we move upward in the world.

My guess is that something in the climb kept David's eyes on the summit. As he was climbing the hill of spiritual progress, step-by-step, he continually looked to God. He fought every battle in the confidence that it was the Lord's. But once he got to the top, all he did was look down. Down at his own successes, down at his own desires, down at his own securities. He looked down instead of looking up to the next summit, up to the next peak that God had for him. And he failed at a terrible, terrible cost.

Have I trusted in any securities that have weakened my faith?

There is a warning here to us. The warning is that we need to know how to go forward in spite of success. We are in danger of going spiritually backward as we move upward in the world. Those who have known the Lord for a long time have to be aware of losing their spiritual vitality.

"Oh, I've been to prayer meetings before," you say. "I don't need to go to this next prayer vigil." You may be drifting.

"I've been in worship all my life. I don't need to go anymore on a regular basis." You may be drifting.

"Oh, I used to sing in the choir, but now let someone else do it."

"I used to teach Sunday school, or I was a youth advisor, but I'm tired and want to rest now." You may be drifting.

"Oh, I don't need to be so diligent about tithing anymore."

What are some areas of my spiritual life that were once stronger and more important than they are now?

Ironically, we may reach a place where God's blessing lulls us into complacency—and we become targets of Satan's scheme.

When did those areas start to fade? Is God asking me to attend to them again?

The Danger of Taking God for Granted

There are times in our life when we take God for granted. We don't pray as we used to—when we *had* to, when we were on our knees because we weren't sure where the finances were going to come from, or we were desperately afraid of what might happen to our children, or our parents were in uncertain times. But when those times are past, we take God for granted. Or we "slack off" from our spiritual self-watch. That's a great old Puritan term—the self-watch, which is a way of maintaining your spiritual integrity and vitality on a daily basis.

When we are most secure in the worldly sense, we are most vulnerable in the spiritual sense. That is precisely when Satan raises his questions and says, "So, now that you have arrived, why don't you count it?" *The evil one urges us to turn from counting on God to counting what we have.* Satan asks us to trust what we can see. Satan asks us to put our trust in things we can count. Ironically, David fell into what I call the security trap. That trap teaches us to say, If I can *see* it, I can count it. If I can *count* it, I can count on it. Satan urges us to take an unholy inventory. And in the process, we lose not only the very "security" we can see, but we lose God himself.

When am I most vulnerable to spiritual complacency?

Worldly Power Can Make You Powerless

David was taking a census to assess his military power. He wanted to know how many soldiers he had. That's what he was counting. He wanted to know how many soldiers he could conscript. (I still remember getting my draft number and realizing that this military stuff is serious business!) But remember that this is near the end of his life. God has helped David win every battle. Why should he count now? It doesn't make any sense. And yet Satan moved David, and David wanted to count. Even his own chief of staff, Joab, said, "Don't do this." David said, "I'm doing it." He ignored the warning.

The security trap of power

David's story demonstrates how people get caught in the power trap. We are vulnerable to this trap if we say to ourself, *If I have more, I can get my way.* This happens in the church, at work, in politics, in business. If I have more power in a relationship, I can get my way.

God warns us against the deceptions of human power. Psalm 20:7 reads: "Some trust in chariots and some in horses, but we trust in the name of the Lord our God" (NIV). Psalm 33:16-19 gives us a similar passage: "No king is saved by the size of his army; no warrior escapes by his great strength. A horse is a vain hope for deliverance; despite all its great strength it cannot save. But the eyes of the Lord are on those who fear him, on those whose hope is in his unfailing love, to deliver them from death and keep them alive" (NIV).

Until the time of Solomon, the Hebrews never used horses or chariots. There were practical reasons for this. Israel is a hilly country in which chariots aren't practical. They are too heavy and awkward for the terrain. Chariots are best used for battles on the plains. But the Israelites also considered the horse to be a pagan luxury. Only people who didn't trust in God used horses.

Many of us are tempted to be like those ancient chariot owners. Unlike the righteous psalmist, we want the symbols of prestige and power. We want to place our confidence in material objects and resources. We think those things give us greater security. But chariots and horses, the most powerful things in the ancient world, reminded the Israelites of the Red Sea. What happened at the Red Sea? All the horses (with their chariots) of Pharaoh were drowned! The Israelites crossed the Red Sea safely on foot, but not the chariots of Pharaoh. The Israelites knew from their own experience that human power is a vain hope. Rather, you and I trust in resources that cannot be seen.

There is a spiritual principle here: Worldly power can make you powerless. And those who buy into worldly power will soon be made powerless.

The security trap of position

We are vulnerable to this trap if we say to ourself, *I have a secure place. I have a place I can count on.* People used to say this in the job market. They don't say it as much anymore. But again, you can transfer that statement to other

Have I put undue trust in any position?

situations. People say, "I'm secure. I have a position of power and respect."

It's been awhile since most ordinary Americans put a lot of security in their positions at the workplace. Many people—people who certainly had what appeared to be strong, secure positions at one time—have fallen victim to corporate "downsizing." One Christian who worked as a producer/director in Hollywood enjoyed an enviable status a number of years ago. But even while he was on the top, he told film students at Wheaton College that he could be totally forgotten within a year or two; he had learned to enjoy the blessing while he had it but not to count on it.

The trap is in basing your worth on your place in a worldly system—whether it's a job, a neighborhood, a service organization, or even your national citizenship. Worldly systems can change. Companies are taken over, and jobs are lost. Neighbors come and go, and real estate values change. If our security is tied to externals, we are subject to volatile forces beyond our control. On closer examination, you see, these positions are not nearly as secure as they appear.

I have a friend who was the CEO of a leading corporation. The board called in a consultant to review the company and prepare it for the next century. Within several months, my friend, who'd been in the company for over twenty years, holding the top position for over a decade, was "outplaced"—and the consultant was hired as CEO! It was a bitter reminder that positions come and go.

Consider a realm with which we are most familiar: friendships. Think about all the jockeying for position that goes on in relationships and how quickly a person can be left out in the cold, forgotten, or betrayed. Position is a flimsy security, but it traps many people nevertheless.

Only God makes us free. And isn't it fun just to be able to walk around valuing yourself for who you are, not for what position you have? There is great joy when you don't feel you have to guard it, protect it, or control it.

The security trap of possessions and money

We are vulnerable to this trap if we say to ourself, *If I have material things, I have a shield against pain and problems.* Don't be seduced by that one. Yes, money has a good place in our life. If you don't have the basics of financial security, you are in a difficult place. It is appropriate that we provide wisely for ourself and our families (see 1 Timothy 5:8). We all appreciate when God gives us some discretionary money so that we can do more than just survive. We can give to others as well as enjoy ourself.

Have I put undue trust in material possessions?

The trouble with money is that it magnifies a person's weaknesses. Someone has said that money simply makes us more of what we already are. As many as four in every ten lottery winners wind up in distress and sell their remaining checks to companies that will provide immediate cash to cover their mounting debts. This shows us that people who were careless with their money when they had only a little are likely to be careless when they have more.

We forget how limited money is. Has your money ever protected you from gossip or an accident? Has your money ever protected you from a quarrel? Has money brought a person back to life or brought a relationship back from disintegration? More often than not, money is a source of worry, not security. Our possessions possess us. They may offer the basic security that keeps us from starving or sleeping out in the street, but they don't offer ultimate security or protection.

The security trap of popularity

"I am secure because people know me and like me." If we say this, we are setting ourself up for a fall. We may feel secure when we get invitations to the important events. It's fine to enjoy it while it lasts, but we can't count on it lasting. Social circles shift. Rumors circulate. People are fickle. And popularity is no protection from the way we feel about ourself. Marilyn Monroe seemed to be at the height of her popularity when she died, causes uncertain. Her friends weren't able to save her.

Have I put undue trust in people?

Think of your own life. Have your friends ever let you down? Have *you* ever let someone down? Even if it's not intentional, your friends may not have the intelligence, the resources, or even the health that you need to get you through. There is a spiritual principle here: People are limited.

The security trap of pleasure

"I am secure because I can do things that make me feel good." Our hedonistic culture seeks security in pleasure. If we simply take the culture of rock music from the sixties and seventies, we can list numerous names of musicians known for their unapologetic pursuit of pleasure: Jimmy Hendricks, Jim Morrison of the Doors, Elvis Presley, Janis Joplin. Those are just a few of the long list of people who literally pleased themselves to death.

But there are even more illustrations of people who have access to every pleasure this world can supply—and still find no security or happiness. They are anxious and dissatisfied. I call this the "Ecclesiastes syndrome." The author, presumably Solomon, the richest king in Israel's history, wrote:

What pleasures tempt me?

> I said to myself, "Come now, let's give pleasure a try. Let's look for the 'good things' in life." But I found that this, too, was meaningless. "It is silly to be laughing all the time," I said. "What good does it do to seek only pleasure?" (Ecclesiastes 2:1-2)

Are there ways in which these pleasures function as sources of security for me? What is their attraction?

Think of the people still alive who, in spite of their many pleasures, have not found security. They can afford to buy boats and trips and recreations of every sort. Or, even if they're not rich, maybe they still "have a way" with the ladies or men—taking pleasure in relationships right and left. But they can't escape the inevitable problems of life.

The downfall of David began with the story of Bathsheba. His desire for pleasure overrode his integrity. And judgment never departed from his house (see 2 Samuel

12:10). When his children were grown, there were serious problems in the household. Amnon, one of David's sons, raped his half sister (David's daughter), Tamar. In revenge, Absalom, Tamar's brother, killed Amnon. Later, Absalom rose up in rebellion and tried to take over David's throne. This "royal" family was incredibly messed up! David the king lost the battle, not when he was young, but later, when he was a successful ruler.

SECURITY IN THE ROCK OF AGES

God wants us to trust in things that are not seen. Hebrews 11:1 gives us the definition of faith: "Now faith is being sure of what we hope for and certain of what we do not see" (NIV). Satan wanted David to count what he could see so that he would count *on* what he could see. And the Bible tells us that the secret to security is counting on things you cannot see. If we simply attach to what we see in this world, we will be deceived. What we see will never be strong enough to save us.

Consider rock climbing. You may have the best ropes and equipment money can buy, but if you try climbing a sandstone surface, you are doomed to failure and possibly death! The pitons (which go in the crevices of the rock so you can attach and move on up the rock wall) may hold at first, but the rock itself is too weak and brittle to sustain much weight for long. You may climb to one hundred feet off the ground, then give it a jerk to pull yourself up to the next level—and find yourself breaking free and falling. Why? Because you were anchored to an unstable, unsecure surface. You don't just climb any rock. You climb a solid, granite rock. You climb a rock that will hold you and that has proven to hold others.

So it is with our security in Christ. We don't anchor ourself to the sandstone of power. Worldly power can make us powerless. We anchor to the Rock of Ages, who has spiritual resources we cannot see.

We don't anchor ourself to the sandstone of position. Positions can hold us captive. Only the Lord can make us free.

We don't anchor ourself to the sandstone of possessions and money. Possessions possess us, but the Lord provides.

We don't anchor ourself to the sandstone of popularity. People are limited, but the Lord will never forsake us.

We don't anchor ourself to the sandstone of pleasure. Only the Lord, not the momentary pleasures of life, can satisfy our deepest hungers.

What about You?

We count on God. So that leaves us with a basic question: How do we anchor our security in the Lord?

I need to be gentle with myself if this is an especially painful subject. I also may be unable to make any sense of a tragedy I have suffered. Still, it may be worth asking myself: Has anything I have trusted in been removed from me? How have I responded?

IT MAY BEGIN WITH A COSTLY WAKE-UP CALL, SUCH AS DAVID'S PUNISHMENT. After David counted the full numbers of Israel's men, God judged him. A prophet announced that the nation would be visited with judgment. They would suffer three years of famine, come under enemy military siege for three months, or experience three days of divine pestilence.

David did not want to fall to the forces of nature through famine and drought. Nor did he want to fall into the hands of his enemies, other human beings. Human beings could perform atrocities that he wouldn't want to endure. So he surrendered to the plague. And in three days seventy thousand fighting men were killed. Why? Because many more would have been put at risk if David had stopped trusting God. We, too, often fail to understand that point. Many more would have died if their king had stopped trusting God. If he had shifted from his full trust in God with which he went against Goliath, then many more than seventy thousand would have died.

I want to say something that is very hard: *What you trust in may be taken away from you so that you will trust in the one who will never forsake you.* That doesn't mean that every time we lose something, God is judging us; we would be foolish to jump to that conclusion. But sometimes God does take away our false securities so that we'll put our trust in him and save ourself many worse troubles.

Ask yourself what it is that you're looking to for security. Be ready to acknowledge false securities and turn from them.

REMEMBER HOW GOD HAS RESCUED YOU AND PROVIDED FOR YOU IN COUNTLESS WAYS. Remember when you were young and you fought Goliath and you won. Remember that. As we move forward, so many of us forget God's goodness in the past—and we end up going backward spiritually.

When has God touched my life in a special way?

Recall your stories of God providing for you, guiding you, answering your prayers, protecting you. What is your holy history?

If I were writing my "holy history," what are some (at least three) stories that I would tell?

TELL YOURSELF THE TRUTH ABOUT WHERE YOU HAVE PUT YOUR TRUST. Are you caught in any of the security traps mentioned in this chapter? Are you caught in a trap of power or possessions or popularity or position or pleasure? If you are, learn to tell yourself the truth. Review these spiritual principles:

- Worldly power can make you powerless.
- Positions can hold you captive and may be quickly lost.
- People are limited.
- Possessions possess you.
- Only the Lord, not momentary pleasure, can satisfy your deepest hunger.

Learn to say to yourself, "If I have God, I have enough." If we trust in anything less than God, we will always have less than we need. If we trust in God, we will always have enough. So you and I do not count our worldly possessions, our securities. We count on God.

NOTES

1. Paul Sharp, "Lottery Raises Issues of Cents and Sensibility," *New York Post*, 1997.
2. Abraham H. Maslow, *Motivation and Personality,* 2d ed. (New York: Harper & Row, 1970), 46.

CHAPTER 10

"Why don't you use what you have to get what you want?" The Temptations of Desire

Matthew 4:1-4

THE GRIM FACT of temptation is that where we are strongest we are weakest. We are the most vulnerable at those very places where we are the most confident. We are given the choice to use our gifts, skills, and abilities however we like. To use them one way leads to life. To use them the other way can lead to death.

In the mystery of God, Satan and the forces of evil are part of the grand scheme of our spiritual growth. Nowhere is this more clear than in the temptations of Jesus described in Matthew 4. This is the first of three chapters in which we will examine the questions inherent in Satan's temptation of Jesus. In order to understand these temptations, we first need to understand the context of Jesus' life. These are the very first days of Jesus' public ministry. He was a carpenter, helping in the trade of his father, and he went out on his own into ministry. I want to look first at the story of John the Baptist with Jesus.

Where do I feel most confident?

Where am I strongest?

In what ways could these areas be avenues for spiritual failure? Have I seen this happen in the past?

Jesus was embarking on his public ministry. Luke tells us he was thirty years old at this time. His father was a carpenter, so we surmise that Jesus followed in his father's footsteps until he received God's call to begin his ministry. In Matthew 3 we read the account of Jesus' baptism, which some have called Jesus' inauguration. It will be followed immediately by one of the greatest tests he'd ever face.

Then Jesus came from Galilee to the Jordan to John, to be baptized by him. John would have prevented him, saying, "I need to be baptized by you, and do you come to me?" But Jesus answered him, "Let it be so now, for thus it is fitting for us to fulfil all righteousness." Then he consented. And when Jesus was baptized, he went up immediately from the water, and behold, the heavens were opened and he saw the Spirit of God descending like a dove, and alighting on him; and lo, a voice from heaven, saying, "This is my beloved Son, with whom I am well pleased."

Then Jesus was led up by the Spirit into the wilderness to be tempted by the devil. And he fasted forty days and forty nights, and afterward he was hungry. And the tempter came and said to him, "If you are the Son of God, command these stones to become loaves of bread."

But he answered, "It is written, 'Man shall not live by bread alone, but by every word that proceeds from the mouth of God.'" (Matthew 3:13–4:4, RSV)

After the High Point

One of life's great truths is that after a really high time, there is usually a very difficult low time. After every great moment there is a letdown. Championship athletes will often go through a postseason depression. This is partly because a person can't maintain a certain level of excitement all the time. Our body needs to recover. Another part of the letdown is wondering, Can we do it again?

New mothers are often ambushed by a dramatic letdown. After the baby is born, they might go into a depression. Logically, it doesn't seem to make sense. She is holding a baby—in most cases a child she really wanted—and she is happy. At the same time, she's also got the postpartum blues.

We may experience letdown when we come back from a

great conference, or when we finally finish a project that's taken our energy for weeks or months. And when we're at that low, we are very vulnerable. Often we fall into situations or behaviors after a high point that we would have more energy to fend off at another time.

Jesus was at a very high point when he was baptized. His baptism from John was, in part, his anointing for ministry. The Holy Spirit came upon him, and his Father spoke from heaven, saying, "This is my beloved Son, and I am fully pleased with him." Isn't that something? Before Jesus had done anything, God said, "I am pleased with you." That's the biblical basis for self-esteem; before you have done anything, God says, "I am so happy with you. I love you so much. There's nothing more you need to do to make me love you more." That's what God says to Jesus. And that's what God says to us.

When have I had "the high point and the letdown"?

How did this affect me spiritually?

How did it affect me in other ways?

But at the height of Jesus' joy, at the brink of his greatly anticipated ministry, we read: "Then Jesus was led out into the wilderness by the Holy Spirit." Is this what you expected to read? I would expect the story to say that Jesus was led to success or to the temple or to a wonderful place for ministry. That's what we might expect, but instead the Bible says: "Then Jesus was led up by the Spirit into the wilderness to be tempted by the devil" (Matthew 4:1, RSV).

What was going on? We would hardly expect the Spirit and the devil to be used in the same sentence in this way. Jesus was at his strongest. He was about to begin the greatest ministry of all time. What was this desert time all about?

The Way We Begin Often Determines the Way We Finish

When I started college, I decided that I wanted to be identified as a Christian from the very first day. So I had my Bible out on my desk. As I met guys on my dorm floor, the conversation would usually turn to summer activities, and I would tell about a Young Life camp I attended. I wasn't pushy (at least, I don't think I was!), but I wanted to make my faith a natural part of my relationships from the beginning. The first few days of school, InterVarsity had gatherings for students to meet and get acquainted with each other and IV's ministry. So I asked my roommate and the other guys (including my Jewish residence advisor) if they wanted to check out IV. "Hey, you going to the InterVarsity thing?"

"What's InterVarsity?"

"Well, come and find out," I'd say with a smile.

It was so much easier for me to be with all those guys in the dorm and in classes later on because they already knew I was one of those Jesus people. I'd made a good beginning. The way you start often determines the way you end. The way you begin sets the tone.

Likewise with Jesus' ministry. What happened at the beginning would set the tone for the rest of his ministry. From the very outset—beginning with this time in the wilderness—it would be clear to Jesus that his ministry would happen in a tough setting. He would face opposition, struggle, and temptation. And the way he chose in the beginning made all the difference.

What new beginnings have I had? How intentional was I?

If I were beginning in a new place, a new school, a new job, a new friendship, what would I do differently to set a healthy "spiritual tone"?

The Holy Spirit was teaching Jesus something here. We read in the book of Hebrews that Jesus learned from the things he suffered:

> So even though Jesus was God's Son, he learned obedience from the things he suffered. In this way, God qualified him as a perfect High Priest, and he became the source of eternal salvation for all those who obey him. (Hebrews 5:8-9)

Why Are We Tested?

Why would a Christian ever be tested or tempted? Because, as Hebrews tells us, testing is essential in our training. It's part of the reality that God's children will face the toughest tests. It's because God loves and values us so much that he tests us.

As our children are heading into college, we are learning all about testing. We are well acquainted with PSATs and

SATs and so on. When they were younger, our children didn't understand then how their class work and tests would affect their future choices and options. But they do now. Tests are part of life; they determine more than simply which college we'll attend. They measure us in many ways. And in many ways, they teach us.

I was with a couple who first noticed that their eight-month-old child wasn't developing like other babies. A series of tests and examinations over several months revealed their worst fear. Their child had permanent brain damage. Of course, they were devastated. Their faith-fiber was exerted to support a burden heavier than they felt they could bear. Yes, the faith-fiber burst in their anguish. But a spiritual blood supply was rushed to them in the form of Christian friends, who agreed to help pattern the child, pray with the parents, and support them financially. "I'd never wish this for anyone," Tim (real names not used) told me. "But I can also say that we never had any idea what our faith meant to us or what the body of Christ was all about until this happened. Jeremy [their son] may not know his multiplication tables, but his favorite song is 'Jesus Loves Me This I Know.' " The very circumstances that might have devastated many others led Tim and Tina to spiritual growth.

God tests us to help us unlearn and learn.

We're also tested in our spiritual life. God tests his people. And you know how the Bible says God tests us? In the wilderness. In the Bible, the wilderness is the school.

The Israelites' journey from Egypt to the Promised Land was less than two hundred miles, or about as far as from Fresno (my home in central California) to San Francisco, or from Boston to New York City. Even if you're on foot, you can make that distance in, at most, a matter of weeks.

Spiritually, however, the Israelites had a much longer trip to make. Because of their disbelief and their unwillingness to obey God, they would wander for forty years. They sent spies out into the Promised Land, and two of these spies said, "God is with us; we can go in there." The other ten said, "No way. There are giants in the land. Those people will kill us." The people believed the unfaithful spies. They didn't trust God to help them in the battle. And so they began a period of wandering. God will let us wander until we learn.

What was the wandering all about for Israel? It was a time of unlearning their old habits. They had to unlearn the ways of Egypt, which had taken deep root in their souls. They needed to unlearn their desires for worldly life. They also needed to learn God's ways. How does God provide? What does God care about? What does God expect of us? Those were things they had to learn. And it was going to take the wilderness to teach them.

In her book *Education That Is Christian,* Lois E. LeBar says, "God has long before determined that a person's character would be a growth, not a gift."[1] We don't become the people God wants us to become by some supernatural zap. Men and women must cooperate voluntarily with God to bear his likeness in thought and in action.

LeBar also talks about the wilderness classroom. "The barrenness of the wilderness, in contrast with the fertile Nile Valley, had its part in shutting the people up to concentrate upon what God's voice was saying."[2] When you leave the distractions of the world and you are faced with the starkness of the wilderness, you start to listen to God. You start to rely on God. You start to realize how many things have prevented this kind of listening and attentiveness in the past.

For God's purposes, separation from other heathen societies was essential at the beginning of Israel's liberation. The world's roots were deep within the people, and their fallen nature responded readily to worldly attractions and habits because of their affinity to evil. In God's school, they had to unlearn their self-confidence. They had to learn their utter inadequacy before God. This knowledge of self is the only prelude to the knowledge of salvation. God will put you and me in places where we will learn that.

When we're in tough situations, our natural inclinations

come out, don't they? Our natural way of dealing with stress or fatigue or injustice shows up. Our prejudices and opinions and weaknesses make their appearances. We find out what we really believe and whom we rely on. Ingrained habits of the soul pop right out into the open.

In *A Mother's Grief Observed,* Rebecca Faber recounts her grieving process following the drowning death of her child. On "Day One Hundred and Sixty" of that first year's grief, Rebecca writes:

> Year after year, as I have gone to church, attended Bible studies, and read the Scriptures, I have never acknowledged the sin of my heart's outlook, my inner voice saying, This life is too hard! God, You are wrong to make life so difficult and sour for us! I seldom admitted my betrayal and was ashamed of this well-entrenched, ugly voice. I knew it wasn't good. Wasn't right. Being a life hater is completely inappropriate for someone who says she believes in God.
>
> I have to face this now. I cannot go on saying such evil things in my heart.[3]

What are some of the wilderness times in my life?

Looking back, can I see some of the "unlearning lessons"?

If I were asked to teach a class, what are some of the lessons I would share that I've learned in the wilderness school?

In the wilderness God doesn't test us in order to see what we'll do; he already knows us. He tests us so that we can see who we really are.

God tests us for our success.

God puts us to the test—for our own success. We are tested so that we can learn more. We're tested so that we will push harder and see what we can achieve in Christ. We are tested so that we can be spiritually fruitful in this life. Satan tempts us to make us fail—to tear us down, show us how little we know, and destroy us. The same event can serve God's purposes as well.

Satan comes to Jesus at what he thinks will be Jesus' greatest time of weakness. After all, Jesus is very hungry. That's when Satan attacks. He waits until he thinks he can get you down, and then he attacks. But he's not as smart as he thinks he is. Was Jesus weak after forty days of fasting? No. He was strong! The devil does make mistakes. You've got to realize that. Don't give him so much credit. Don't arrogantly mock the devil (see Jude 1:9), but don't give him too much credit either. He made a huge mistake when he tangled with Jesus in the wilderness. He got three knockout punches. He failed to recognize the power of the Spirit within Jesus.

He may attack at the time when you have experienced a tremendous tragedy, only to find that God is already there and God is already working. You see, Satan tempts us to make us fall. But God tests us to help us rise. To walk with greater confidence, greater certainty, greater power in our life in Christ.

Why Don't You Use What You Have to Get What You Want?

Jesus was led into the wilderness because God wanted to teach his Son how to minister and what kind of a person he was to be. Following his baptism, Jesus was thinking about his call to ministry. He'd been endowed with miracle-working power. How was he going to do this? How was he supposed to meet people's needs? These are heavy questions, so Jesus withdrew from the distractions of daily life. He was meditating on God's Word. He was setting his holy agenda. Jesus was focusing, not on the food he was missing, but on the feast he was enjoying with God. I don't think Jesus thought about the fact that he hadn't eaten for forty days.

Jesus knew what we all have to learn: Unless we intentionally stop and spend time with God, we will always be reacting to the world, doing what other people want us to do or being controlled by our own desires. The world, other people's agendas, and our own desires can be very dangerous.

Temptation and giftedness

"If you are the Son of God, change these stones into loaves of bread."

This first temptation tests Jesus' intentions. It focuses both on Jesus' self-gratification and also on his method in ministry. Would Jesus do what other people wanted him to do and give them what they wanted him to give them? Would he use what he had to get what he wanted? This is about stewardship. Would Jesus use his own independent authority for his own personal gain, or would he remain obedient to God? Would he be diverted by material gain from the pursuit of spiritual welfare and priorities and preoccupation? What would happen?

What are my gifts? How have they been avenues of blessing?

How have my gifts become areas of testing and temptation?

What can I do to use my gifts so that I consistently honor God and serve others with them?

Jesus was tempted at his point of giftedness. It's obvious that Satan suspects Jesus to be gifted with incredible power. Do you think the evil one would walk up to any of us and say, "Hey, turn these stones into bread. Come on and do it." None of us could do that, but Jesus could. He was tempted at the point of his giftedness.

Although we are not gifted in the same way, we, too, are tempted in the areas of our gifts. Are you a good singer? Satan will tempt you to use that gift for your own advancement. Are you good with numbers and finances? Satan will tempt you to use that for your own advancement. Are you good in relating with people? He'll tempt you to use your charm to be a deceiver. Are you good with words? He will tempt you to use your words in a glib way that excuses and impresses without giving substance.

Name your gift. You do have a gift—probably lots of them. The devil will tempt you to use it in destructive ways. You see, again and again we are tempted through our gifts. The grim fact of temptation is that where you are strongest he will make you weakest. So Jesus was called to use his powers in a wrong way.

Exposing the Illusion of Worldly Satisfaction

This particular temptation could also be called the temptation to secure popularity through prosperity. How would Jesus serve the poor and the oppressed? How would he deal with Rome's oppressive presence? What would he do with people's expectations as they anticipated a messiah who would bring the nation into a golden era such as they had in the times of David and King Solomon? One of the toughest assignments is to minister to people with a great past. They are clinging to their past greatness, but they don't want to pay the price that often accompanied that past greatness.

How would Jesus use his power to deal with bodily needs? Jesus would encounter all kinds of needs—physical healing, material poverty. How would he meet those needs? In his intriguing book *In The Name of Jesus,* Henri Nouwen says that this is the temptation to be relevant—to give people what they want.

Should we give what people want?

This first temptation challenged Jesus to break free from the illusion of worldly satisfaction. It's a matter of seeing the real needs and the genuine source of lasting satisfaction for those needs.

Which types of needs do I most feel and want to meet: inner needs such as peace or release from guilt, or outer needs such as justice and compassion?

There are two primary ways to give people what they want. Some Christians think that the gospel is about giving people personal peace—an inner satisfaction. Others think the gospel is about social justice and righteousness and liberating the oppressed and setting them free—an external blessing. Often we are operating on both fronts. Often we experience tension, trying to figure out which type of giving is most beneficial in which situation.

The question for Jesus was, Should I give people what they want—inside and outside? If getting what we want becomes our drive in life, and if giving others what they want becomes our strategy for ministry, we will miss what we truly need. Jesus resisted this temptation because he knew that the only way to win people for the kingdom was by starting with their external need. Not with bribes but with the blessing that comes from knowing God. If we focus mainly on those outward things, whether it is simply personal peace and prosperity or social justice and righteousness, we will miss the transformation of the heart. We have all we need in Jesus Christ.

What do we really need?

Consider this question: Is there anything you currently lack that could truly fulfill you? I am coming to believe that there is nothing we currently lack that could fulfill us. Of course, every one of us has a number of voids in our life—things we are lacking. But think about where you were a year ago, or five years ago, or ten or twenty years ago. Do you have more now than you did then? Do you have many of the very things now that you thought would make you happy back then? Most people do. Most of us have a lot more of what we always wanted. But those things haven't made our life better.

The vast majority of people are no happier with the things they always wanted than they were without them. In fact, if you talk with many people, you'll find them nostalgic for the good old days when they had only two pennies to rub together. Why? Because they had the things that made life fulfilling—a dream, hope, love, freedom—all the things that progress took from them.

When Jesus was in the wilderness, he was meditating on God's Word. We know this because Jesus answered every temptation with Scripture. Our deep fellowship with God's Word sustains us. Jesus was meditating on Israel's own wilderness experience. We read in Deuteronomy 8:3: "He humbled you, causing you to hunger and then feeding you with manna, which neither you nor your fathers had known, to teach you that man does not live on bread alone but on every word that comes from the mouth of the Lord" (NIV). Nobody had ever thought of manna. They knew about leeks and onions and garlic and the breads of Egypt, but nobody had ever thought of manna. When did they discover manna? When they were starving. When they were starving, they found the bread of heaven.

Jesus had learned this from the very beginning. We have everything we need in Jesus Christ. We can be content today with Jesus Christ. There is nothing more we need. He's the answer to our anxiety. He's the answer to our desire—and to our fear. He is the answer to our distorted value systems, to our freedom from self-centeredness, guilt, and indirection. There is nothing we need that we can't find in Jesus right now. So how do we resist and stand strong when this evil temptation comes, when we are tempted to use what we have to get what we want? Well, we break free and stay free through the nourishment of God's Word. This is what will keep us strong. And this help is in Christ alone, through prayer and the power of the Spirit.

Has there ever been a time when I finally got something I'd always wanted or I "arrived" at a position I'd always wanted?

Sarah and I have been spiritually starving in some times of personal crisis. That's when we found God's manna of love and healing. You won't get manna if you keep chasing stones. You will never find it. It will always allude you. Because God loves you too much to let you break your teeth on stones.

In what ways was it what I'd thought it would be?

God's Word is the only thing that will deeply satisfy us. That Word will strip away false teaching and expose sordid values. That Word will lead us into that obedience to God, which is the most satisfying thing in the world.

In what ways was it different?

How did this affect me spiritually?

What about You?

God's love does not remove us from the area of testing. A sailor who sails first on a small lake and then sails out on the ocean doesn't expect the ocean to be like the lake. The sailor understands that ocean currents are strong and the weather is intense. The sailor goes out into the ocean to test his skills. Likewise, as followers of Jesus Christ, we don't simply sail in a very small lake anymore. We are in the oceans of life. And you and I have to learn how to navigate the storms that will come. They are promised to us. And God often teaches us the most in those wilderness times.

What is your wilderness?

We've all been in the wilderness. No matter how old you are, you've had a dark time. If you're having trouble thinking of your wilderness, consider this partial list:

- conflict with others
- job crisis

- identity crisis
- financial difficulties
- family troubles
- other problems

Have you been disappointed by people not coming through for you? Have you been burdened with guilt to where you can't imagine God still loving you? Have you been forced to face your own limitations? Has someone you trusted hurt you? Have you been bored? That may not sound like much of a wilderness, but think of how easy it is to drift when you're bored.

I suggest that you make a simple list. Write: "What are my wilderness times?" at the top of the paper, and list them. Start another list with this question: "What have I learned from those wilderness times?"

What have I done with what I have?

You may not have been tempted to turn stones into bread, but each of us has been tempted to use our gifts for our own agendas. We may have never even considered what God would like us to do. I'd like to give you some challenging questions as we close this chapter.

- How does the quality of my life suffer because of my preoccupation with material concerns?
- As I am growing older, do I love Jesus more?
- Has success put my soul in danger?

And one that sort of summarizes them:

- Is my greatest desire to please the Lord or myself?

According to Matthew's Gospel, following Jesus' temptations, he would preach the Sermon on the Mount. In the message, Jesus would urge us to ask and to seek, to knock upon the doors of heaven for whatever we needed. In describing the love and generosity of God, Jesus compares it to the relationship between parents and children. And Jesus says, "Which of you, if your child asks for bread, will give him a stone?" God never gives us stones that we have to turn into bread. Never! He is the Lord of the universe who loves us. He invites us to feast at the table of the food that endures to eternal life. He *will give us this day our daily bread.* The question is this: Will we give him this day our daily love?

NOTES

1. Lois E. LeBar, *Education That Is Christian* (Old Tappan, N.J.: Fleming H. Revell, 1963), 88.
2. Ibid., 89.
3. Rebecca Faber, *A Mother's Grief Observed* (Wheaton, Ill.: Tyndale House Publishers, Inc., 1997).

CHAPTER 11

"If your faith is so great, why not put God to the test?" The Temptations of Pride

Matthew 4:5-7

HOW STRONG IS your faith? I think about that question in a variety of situations. For example, when I'm facing a problem and I don't see an immediate solution, I'll often say, "I wonder if my faith is strong enough to handle this?" Because there are a lot of problems that I don't honestly see how God is going to solve, I get pretty worried.

I find myself asking this question when I hear someone tell a marvelous story of what God has done in his life. And I think, *Wow, God answered his prayers. I've never prayed like that; I've never seen God work like that.* And there's a kind of spiritual jealousy that sometimes arises. *I wonder if I could pray those kinds of prayers and see those kinds of answers?*

I also wonder how strong my faith is when doubts crowd in. I'm not in a time of my life when I have a lot of intellectual doubts about the gospel. I've studied it, and I believe it; I'm convinced. But I have a lot of practical doubts in terms of God's will and direction for my life and the way God is going to work in terms of solving problems. And I wonder how strong my faith really is.

Jesus' second temptation in the wilderness was a direct challenge to the strength of his faith.

> **Then the devil took him to the holy city, and set him on the pinnacle of the temple, and said to**

> **him, "If you are the Son of God, throw yourself down; for it is written,**
>
> **'He will give his angels charge of you,' and**
> **'On their hands they will bear you up, lest you strike your foot against a stone.'"**
>
> **Jesus said to him, "Again it is written, 'You shall not tempt the Lord your God.'" (Matthew 4:5-7, RSV)**

Before we explore this second temptation of Jesus, we need to remember the first one. In the first temptation, Jesus was asked to turn stones into bread. He was tempted to focus on self-gratification and material prosperity and blessing and to use that as his method for bringing others to know the gospel. Would he simply put a chicken in every pot, as Hitler promised in Nazi Germany? A lot of Hitler's power came from his promises to meet the people's physical needs. Jesus was tempted to give priority to people's perceived needs rather than God's eternal purposes.

Now in the second temptation, Jesus is going to be forced to look at his trust in God. Does he really trust God? How strong is his faith? And what strategies will he use to inspire faith in others? Would Jesus really know that God loves him and cares for him? How would he show others that love, especially the people who doubted that God was real? That's a tough thing to show other people. If somebody walked up to you and said, "Prove to me that God is real," What would you say? How would you proceed?

Complete This Sentence

Complete these two sentences. They are similar; they are both meant to bring you to the same point.

- I will know I can trust God when ______________ ____.

- If only God would ______________________________; then I would really believe.

How would I complete these sentences?

Is there some situation, circumstance, a blessing, a need you have that must be filled before you'll trust God? How you answer these questions will give you an insight into your faith and the strength of your faith. We will look at that more at the end of the chapter.

If Satan cannot distract you with material things, then he will go after your faith. All of us probably struggle with material things to one degree or another. But many of us understand that more money or a better job or a bigger house may be nice in their place, but they won't really satisfy. So Satan goes after the next level with us. We need to understand his strategy here. He starts with our most basic, fleshly nature. If he can distract us with money or sex, he won't waste time with anything else. But he'll work all the way up to spiritual desires and ambitions if we don't respond to anything else. If you have learned how to deal with material temptations, the enemy will go after your faith. If he can't get you to give up your faith, then he'll try to pervert your faith—he'll skew it in some way.

In what ways am I vulnerable in the the following areas and why?

material things

my fleshly nature

my spiritual desires and ambitions

Satan tries to intimidate.

Satan tries to deceive us concerning his power over us. Now here's what happened. Jesus was in the wilderness; he had been fasting. The evil one attacked him, and Jesus fought off the temptation with Scripture: "Man shall not live by bread alone, but by every word that proceeds from the mouth of God" (Matthew 4:4, RSV). So Satan took Jesus and—we don't know how this happened—took him out of the wilderness and put him on the highest point of the temple in Jerusalem. That's a move of intimidation. That was meant to put Jesus on the spot.

At this point we need to realize that the evil one is both stronger and weaker than we think. He is able to take Jesus into the Holy City. Now wouldn't you expect that Jerusalem, the Holy City, would be impervious to Satan? Think of all those prayers, sacrifices, and worship activities. Yet Satan walks right in.

And then he puts Jesus on the highest point of the temple. We see an analogy here. High places are dangerous places. If you are ever in any position of leadership, no matter what group it is, whether it's a small group or just a couple of friends, a club or a class, a business or a community, you are in a slippery place. Especially in those places of faith where you are seeking to serve the Lord, you are in greater danger of falling.

Who or what am I most likely to blame for my failings?

And so the evil one takes Jesus to the place that would represent being at the pinnacle, and he tempts him. You and I need to realize that the devil is strong. He can take you to dangerous places. But he is also weaker than you may think. Back in the seventies there was a comedian on television named Flip Wilson. And one of his characters had this trademark line, whenever he got into trouble: "The devil made me do it." In that context, it was a very funny line, but it's a tragic line when most people use it. I've heard people say, "It was the devil. I couldn't help myself."

Are we really helpless victims and puppets? On October 1, 1997, Luke Woodham, sixteen, of Pearl, Mississippi, is alleged to have stabbed his mother in her bed before going to school and opening fire on a group of students. Two girls, including his ex-girlfriend, were killed. In five pages of small handwritten scrawl, Woodham described his anger at society and God. He is accused of having acted at the command of Grant Boyette, who is charged with being the mastermind in the shooting spree of October 1 at Pearl High. Boyette talked about following Satan and proclaimed the power of the devil.[1]

Such horrors are almost too much to imagine. Unfortunately, we hear more and more about them these days. But are the perpetrators just puppets? Have they lost control of themselves? Do you think the devil can force them, against their will, to do such things? Jesus' encounter with the devil reveals the answer.

Satan tries to lure us to act.

When Satan takes Jesus to the high place in Matthew 4:6, he says, "If you are the Son of God, throw yourself down" (RSV). What's Satan doing? He's is trying to persuade Jesus to act. What's interesting about that is that Satan couldn't just push Jesus off the pinnacle! All he could do was coax Jesus to do it himself.

The devil's power is real, but his power has limits. You and I need to understand that. He can persuade, but he cannot compel. He can persuade you to do something, but he can't force you to do it. He can hold out the drugs, but he can't put them in your veins or make you swallow them. He can hold out the lustful temptation, but he can't make you get involved. He can hold out the bribe, but he can't make you take it. He may set the stage, but we are the actors.

How do I respond to the thought that Satan can persuade, but he cannot compel?

The devil's only means of success is to get us to say yes—to provoke our willing participation, making us fully responsible. He can take us to the highest places, but he cannot make us leap. Now, if you think about it, that is *good news!* And a lot of us have never heard that. I know that I've been surprised at times by the intensity of the temptations I've faced. I've felt as if I were being overpowered. I need to be reminded that I really can say no. James 4:7 says, "Resist the Devil, and he will flee from you." First Peter 5:9 says, "Resist him, standing firm in the faith" (NIV). He may take us to some very high places, but the Lord can help us stand firm.

How does this affect my spiritual life?

Satan tries to distort the meaning of our faith.

What is faith? How do we demonstrate our faith to other people? That's the question Jesus was being asked here. Satan confronts Jesus with twisted Scriptures. Professor Dale Bruner writes, "If the evil one cannot make us super spiritual by wonder bread, perhaps he can make us super spiritual by suggesting leaps of faith."[2]

The devil presents Jesus with a crass interpretation of Psalm 91. I once visited a woman in a nursing home, and I happened to pick Psalm 91 to read. As I finished reading the sentence "He will give his angels charge of you . . . lest you dash your foot against a stone," she said, "I love that psalm. I've got it memorized." And she recited it to me. I asked, "How did you learn that?" She said, "I used to sew it into the uniforms of soldiers." I'd never heard that before, but that was a practice of many people in wartime. They would sew Scriptures into uniforms as a sign of love and God's care and protection. She was not a superstitious woman. She believed that God's Word could literally provide protection.

Psalm 91 is a very encouraging passage—when you and I take it as it was meant to be given. Psalm 91 says that God will protect us if danger comes upon us:

> He who dwells in the shelter of the Most High will rest in the shadow of the Almighty. I will say of the Lord, "He is my refuge and my fortress, my God in whom I trust." . . .
>
> He will cover you with his feathers, and under his wings you will find refuge; his faithfulness will be your shield and rampart. You will not fear the terror of night, nor the arrow that flies by day, nor the pestilence that stalks in the darkness, nor the plague that destroys at midday. A thousand may fall at your side, ten thousand at your right hand, but it will not come near you. . . . For he will command his angels concerning you to guard you in all your ways. (vv. 1-2, 4-7, 11, NIV)

I can see how this psalm would mean a lot to a soldier under fire. These are very encouraging words for any time we are in danger.

What the evil one was trying to do, however, was to take that very passage and say, "Put yourself in a place of danger, and see if God rescues you." Do you see how different that is? It's kind of subtle in some ways but very blatant in others. Here's God's promise: God will protect you in time of danger. Here's Satan's temptation: So go do something dangerous and see what God does.

God promises no protection for a spiritual Evel Knievel—someone who deliberately places himself in danger in order to show that God is faithful. There's no protection for that. I know people who say, "It won't matter because God will forgive me in the morning." Oh, but you have no idea what that forgiveness may cost you. I don't mean that you can't be forgiven, but there can be terrible consequences even with forgiveness.

Jesus shows us how to interpret the Word of God. People who tear these passages out of their context will turn a promise into a lie. They will turn a promise into a temptation. And it happens all the time. But Jesus interprets this passage the right way.

What Bible promises are meaningful to me?

Are there ways in which I have taken these promises out of context?

What promise comes to mind now, and how does it encourage me with something I am facing right now?

Know How to Use Scripture

In order to interpret God's Word properly, we need to use the proper tools. I want to give you two principles of interpretation that are essential in rightly understanding and applying God's Word to our life.

The analogy of Scripture

The analogy of Scripture means that we use the whole of Scripture as a basis for interpreting any part of Scripture. We look for the analogy across the whole Bible. For example, James 2:20 says: "Faith without deeds is useless" (NIV), but Romans 1:17 says: "The righteous will live by faith" (NIV). At first glance, people looking at those two passages side by side say, "Total contradiction! See, the Bible is full of contradictions. You can't trust it." But by the analogy of Scripture we solve the dilemma. James means *faith without fruit isn't genuine.* Faith in Jesus Christ, whose death on the cross secures our salvation, is all that is necessary for salvation. There is nothing more we have to do to be saved. We simply put our faith in all that he has done. But if our faith is genuine it will bear fruit. If I say, "I love God with all of my heart, mind, soul, and strength, and I love my neighbor as myself," I won't be rude and mean and ungodly toward you. If I am, I will at least bear the fruit of repentance. James is not contradicting Romans. By the analogy of Scripture we understand that justification by faith bears fruit in a changed life. These verses are not contradictory but complementary.

Taking the didactic over the narrative

Didactic refers to the Scriptures whose explicit purpose is to teach or to command. Narrative refers to the biblical stories of people's experiences. This principle teaches us that the Bible's explicit teaching on a subject is to be normative. People's experiences can be informative, but not necessarily prescriptive for us. The stories will illustrate spiritual principles; however, we must be careful not to draw definitive commands from narratives without the full support of didactic teaching.

Let's take the example of speaking in tongues. Many people have said that if a person doesn't speak in tongues, he doesn't have the Holy Spirit. Some even say the person who doesn't speak in tongues isn't redeemed. Why? Because tongues is a sign of the Holy Spirit in the book of Acts. Yet Paul makes it very clear in passages from Ephesians 1 and 2 and Romans 8 that the Holy Spirit is given to all who believe, with no demand that tongues be exercised. Naturally, this is a very complex subject deserving more explanation than I can provide at this point. My concern is that I have seen people literally stop going to church because they didn't understand the analogy of Scripture or the concept of didactic over narrative. They feared for their salvation. We must understand how to interpret God's Word correctly, or we will fall into many snares.

Seeing through the illogical logic of temptation

We need to learn how to use God's Word more effectively. When Satan distorted the biblical promise into an invitation to irresponsibility, Jesus said, in effect, "I can't misuse God's promise when I have the clear command: 'You shall not put the Lord your God to a test.' To leap would test God, and that I cannot do. We don't test God." Jesus saw through Satan's faulty logic and exposed it without hesitation.

Many illogical arguments threaten our faith. If we don't know how to recognize and answer these from the Word of God, Satan will trip us up. For example, you may have heard this one in high school or college: Can God make a rock so big that he cannot move it? This is a philosophical question meant to catch us in a conundrum. The question is supposed to pose a dilemma for us. If you say yes, then you are saying that God isn't all-powerful because he has created something that exceeds his abilities. But God, by definition, is to have no limitations. If you say no, then God is not all-powerful because there is something he cannot do. The problem is that it is a false dilemma. My simple answer to the question is: God doesn't do stupid things.

Here's a more practical illustration. Your neighbor comes over to your house and says, "We'd like you to pray for our son. He is very, very ill. We have heard you are Christians. We have also heard that if you pray for him, he will be healed. In fact, we believe so much in what your Christian faith is teaching that we are not going to take him to a doctor, because if we took him to a doctor, it would show that we don't have full faith in God. So pray for our child will you?" Your neighbor has created a false definition of faith and in so doing created a terrible dilemma. There is no essential antagonism between faith and medicine. In God's plan they can work together in the healing process.

Jesus shows us that we are to expose the illogical logic that is presented in many arguments. He understood didactical over narrative. He understood the analogy of Scripture. He understood that a text without a context becomes a pretext. He understood that if you take a promise out of the Bible without understanding how that promise was given and use it as a rationale for foolhardy actions, you will pay the price. If we take things out of context, we will do damage to our faith.

Foolish Leaps—or Simple Trust?

Satan was trying to lure Jesus to destroy himself. Jesus was tempted to destruction by Satan's distorting the meaning of faith. Great faith is not seen in foolish leaps. It is seen in simple trust. That's all. If you want to see faith, just look at people who are simply trusting God for the next job, for their daily needs, for healing in their homes. Simple trust. That's what God loves. The spectacular can fascinate, but it cannot touch a heart.

I am fascinated by magicians who can make an airplane disappear. That's fascinating. But it doesn't help me as I pray for my children or for hard situations. We may admire a magician, but we cannot adore him. Clever tricks cannot move us to repentance. So Satan tries to discourage us through intimidation. He tries to distort God's Word, and then finally he tries to discourage us by discrediting God's love.

Satan tries to discredit God's love.

There was something else going on at the temple temptation. Satan was saying to Jesus, "You know, if God really loves you, he will save you. You go ahead and jump, and see if he loves you."

It reminds me of a card our three teenage boys got me for Father's Day one year. On the front it said, "Dad, when I need someone to talk to, you're always there. When I need a comforting hug, you're always there. When I need advice, you're always there." Then you open the card and read, "Dad, I need a car!" I am thankful we all saw it as a joke! But we've all heard it said, sometimes humorously and sometimes seriously, "Mom and Dad, if you really love me, you will . . ." Love is measured on the basis of performance. The evil one was tempting Jesus to say, in essence, "Father, if you really love me, you'll back me up here. Make me look good."

Jesus answered, "Do not put the Lord your God to the test" (Matthew 4:7, NIV). He was drawing from Exodus 17, when the Israelites were thirsty in the wilderness. The people were challenging God to show his presence and power. Yet they were forgetting that he was *already there*. God had already done so much for them—major miracles—but they still were saying, "If you really love us, you will . . ."

People today say the same thing: "God, what have you done for me lately?" It isn't enough that he offers them eternal life through Christ or that he's given all his countless gifts of daily protection and provision. It's "What have you done for me lately?"

Do I have this type of attitude toward the Lord?

What If Jesus Had Jumped?

Did you ever think what faith would be like if Jesus had jumped? What would that have taught us about faith and discipleship? What would have happened to the followers of Jesus if he had jumped? I can imagine some very significant problems that would have arisen. Jesus' followers would have been tempted to similar exhibitions of faith. Those who were too timid to throw themselves off would have felt disqualified and dropped out. If Jesus had jumped, our priests would have been the foolhardy followers. Our faith would have turned into a circus. H. L. Mencken, a cynical journalist, once defined faith as "an illogical belief in the irrational." If Jesus had jumped, Mencken would have been right. If it was crazy, then it would be faith.

Am I disappointed or demanding of God's provision?

How does this affect my spiritual vitality?

Jesus refused to leap because he knew that God had a different way to reach our heart. A show of power may fascinate the imagination, but it cannot penetrate the heart and awaken devotion. God would not win us through foolhardy acts. The way to the heart is not through spectacle but through sacrifice. Think about it. What has won your heart? Not the spectacle but the sacrifice. Sacrifice is the surest means to win respect. When you sacrifice, you inspire love.

I was doing some research in the area of missions, and I came across the story of Lough Fook, a Chinese Christian. He was moved with compassion for the coolies who were working in the mines of South Africa. He sold himself for a period of five years to be a slave so that he could go into the mines to share the gospel with the miners. Soon he began to

When have I experienced or observed sacrificial love?

How did it affect me?

lead person after person to know Jesus Christ as Savior and Lord! When he died, nearly two hundred disciples had formed a church because of him. These slaves had come to know Christ. Why? Not because someone stood outside the mine and began to preach to them, but because someone went into the mine with them.[3]

Jesus didn't need to go to the highest place of the temple to leap. He had already come from a higher place! He came down from heaven to be with us. There was another time when Jesus was lifted to a high place, and again he chose not to leap. Do you know where it was? It was when he was on the cross. Jesus said, "When I am lifted up on the cross, I will draw everyone to myself" (John 12:32). He didn't jump down from the cross, either, although he had the power to do that. Aren't we glad Jesus wasn't out to make a spectacle and win awe through his power? If that had been his motivation, he would never have gone to Calvary for us.

What about You?

Has Satan tried to intimidate you lately? Are you assuming he has more power than he has? Remember that God has expressed love to us by limiting the devil's power. Satan can lead you to the pinnacle, but he can't push you off.

Has the enemy tried to skew your faith, putting a "new" spin on Scripture? Remember the principles of interpretation: (1) Use Scripture to interpret Scripture, and (2) give the teaching precedence over the incident.

Has the devil tried to woo you with displays of power? Remember that real power and life come not from spectacular events but from your growing relationship with God, who loves you and will give you all you need.

Ephesians 3:20-21 says: "Now to him who by the power at work within us is able to do far more abundantly than all that we ask or think, to him be glory in the church and in Christ Jesus to all generations, for ever and ever" (RSV). Think of what great things God can do in and through your simple faith. It doesn't take a leap; it merely takes a step.

NOTES

1. Gina Holland, The Associated Press, "Officials: Teens May Have Used Net in Plot," *The Sun Herald,* 1997 (http://www.sunherald.com/news/docs/pearl11016.htm).
2. Frederick Dale Bruner, *The Christbook* (Waco, Tex.: Word Books, 1987), 108.
3. Paul Lee Tan, *Encyclopedia of 7700 Illustrations* (Rockville, Md.: Assurance Publishers, 1979), 5178.

CHAPTER 12

"Why don't you take a shortcut?" The Temptations of Power

Matthew 4:8-11

IN GERMANY DURING the first half of the sixteenth century lived a man named Dr. Johann Faust. He was a student of magic, astrology, and chemistry. He provided the model for the protagonist in *The History of the Damnable Life and Deserved Death of Dr. Johann Faustus,* written by an unknown author. That story circulated throughout Europe and captured the imagination, not only of many readers, but of many authors. These authors (including Christopher Marlow, the English playwright and contemporary of Shakespeare; Johann Goethe, the profound nineteenth-century German author; Thomas Mann of the twentieth century) each wrote his own variation of the Faust legend. For four centuries this has been one of the most intriguing stories of human ambition ever told.

In the legend Faust is a proud, ambitious man who longs for knowledge and power and is willing to do anything to get them. So he strikes a bargain with the devil. He sells his soul to the devil, Mephistopheles (also known as Lucifer and Beelzebub), in exchange for knowledge and especially magical power. Faust obtains his long-sought knowledge and power, but he cannot handle them. As the story progresses, Faust degenerates into hedonism until finally—pathetically, pitifully—his soul is carried off to hell by his diabolic masters. He cannot and will not repent. He learns too late that it isn't what we possess, but what possesses us that determines our destiny.

What temptations have I faced?

What have they taught me about myself?

What have they taught me about my faith?

Temptation itself is not an evil, but our response to it can make temptation a cause for good or evil. In the wilderness God's people use their temptations as times of testing. Martin Luther said, "My temptations have been my masters in divinity." He meant his temptations were an essential aspect in the theological curriculum of life. His temptations taught him much about himself and God. Temptations reveal our vulnerabilities so that we can cultivate intentional protection. They reveal the forces that control us apart from God so that we can break free from them. They hold up a mirror in which we see the truth about our need for God's transforming power. When handled properly, temptations are like a wind tunnel in a laboratory, exposing defects that need attention. If attended to early, this knowledge can prevent far worse disasters later. Without God's help, however, we may learn more about evil than we can handle.

I see the seeds of the Faust legend in this third temptation of Jesus. He was being offered everything this world has to offer but at the cost of selling his soul. This temptation poses the ultimate test of Jesus' purpose and his mission. He has come as the Messiah to secure the kingdom of God. The question now is how will he get it and what will it look like?

> **Again, the devil took him to a very high mountain, and showed him all the kingdoms of the world and the glory of them; and he said to him, "All these I will give you, if you will fall down and worship me." Then Jesus said to him, "Begone, Satan! for it is written,**
>
> **'You shall worship the Lord your God and him only shall you serve.'"**
>
> **Then the devil left him, and behold, angels came and ministered to him. (Matthew 4:8-11, RSV)**

SATAN'S POWER—AND LIMITS

Satan offers shortcuts to worldly success. We read that the devil showed Jesus the kingdoms of this world and all their glory. Some of us may stop right there and say, "Wait a minute, we sing the hymn, 'This Is My Father's World.' How can we say the kingdoms of this world would be shown to Jesus by Satan? How could Satan make the claim that he could give all the kingdoms of this earth?" Well, listen to what Jesus himself says about Satan. In John 12:30-32, Jesus is preparing to conclude his public ministry and go into the upper room, where he will have a private ministry with the disciples and then go to the cross. After Jesus has heard again the voice of God saying, "This is my beloved Son, listen to him," Jesus says to the crowd, "This voice was for your benefit, not mine. Now is the time for judgment on this world; now the prince of this world will be driven out. But I, when I am lifted up from the earth, will draw all men to myself" (NIV). Jesus calls Satan the prince of this world.

In John 14:29-31, Jesus says, "I have told you now before it happens, so that when it does happen you will believe. I will not speak with you much longer, for the prince of this world is coming. He has no hold on me, but the world must learn that I love the Father and that I do exactly what my Father has commanded me" (NIV). Then in John 16:10-11 we read again (he is speaking of the Holy Spirit's role of convicting people of sin): ". . . in regard to righteousness, because I am going to the Father, where you can see me no longer; and in regard to judgment, because the prince of this world now stands condemned" (NIV).

For whatever reason, God has delivered this world to the rulership of Satan. Now that does not mean the entire created order bears no reflection or sign of God. God is still at work in this world. But this world has come under the domination of the evil one. This is mysterious and difficult to understand, but it is true. The devil does have some kind of power and some kind of influence. It is not ultimate, but it is significant. So he offered Jesus all the kingdoms of this earth.

Now, think about it for a moment. Jesus, so Satan thought, came to establish the kingdom of God in Israel—little Israel, a small nation dwarfed by the power of Rome. So what does Satan do? "I've got a better deal for you: You wanted Israel, you can have Syria, too. You can have Egypt, and the regions of Asia Minor (speaking in our modern-day geographical terms!): Iran, Iraq, Turkey. You can have Rome and its entire empire! You can have all the kingdoms of the world!" You see, the devil thought he understood what Jesus wanted. He knew that Jesus was the Messiah. He figured that Jesus had come to establish an earthly kingdom, along the lines of the kingdom of Israel during the time of David and Solomon.

Here we have a major clue about the devil. He has limited knowledge, and he jumps to the wrong conclusions. Many people treat the devil as if he is omniscient and omnipotent. He is not. And here he is dead wrong. He thinks Jesus is like him. Satan acted on the assumption that Jesus had the same desires that he had.

What assumptions have I made about Satan's knowledge and power?

How Could Jesus Have Been Tempted?

As we read about Jesus' temptation, we might wonder, How could Jesus ever be tempted by something like this?

Jesus could be tempted because, although he was God, he was also human. Hebrews 2:14-18 reveals the wisdom of God in the Incarnation. It tells us why Jesus was fully human, subject to all the temptations we face.

How can I test these assumptions against God's Word?

What difference do they make in my spiritual life?

> Because God's children are human beings—made of flesh and blood—Jesus also became flesh and blood by being born in human form. For only as a human being could he die, and only by dying could he break the power of the Devil, who had the power of death. Only in this way could he deliver those who have lived all their lives as slaves to the fear of dying.

> We all know that Jesus came to help the descendants of Abraham, not to help the angels. Therefore, it was necessary for Jesus to be in every respect like us, his brothers and sisters, so that he could be our merciful and faithful High Priest before God. He then could offer a sacrifice that would take away the sins of the people. Since he himself has gone through suffering and temptation, he is able to help us when we are being tempted. (Hebrews 2:14-18)

In his humanity, Jesus, throughout his life, sought his heavenly Father every day. He needed God's presence and wisdom and encouragement and instruction. I think most people see Jesus as someone who knew everything in advance. If that was true, it's hard to believe that Satan could have tempted Jesus with anything. Jesus would have already known what the temptations would be! Passages such as the following in Matthew 24:36 indicate that there were some limitations on Jesus' knowledge: "However, no one knows the day or the hour when these things will happen, not even the angels in heaven or the Son himself. Only the Father knows."

I don't believe Jesus was born knowing exactly everything that was going to happen to him or how and when it would happen. We know he understood at some point that he would be betrayed and turned over to the religious leaders and eventually crucified, but we don't really know when that was clear to him. For all we know, when Jesus was at the end of this wilderness test, he had only a few clues about exactly how his ministry was supposed to take shape. Maybe God gave him only a few instructions at a time—just as we rarely have much of the picture in front of us. Admittedly, this is a very complex subject. Whatever the case, the Bible teaches us that Jesus was truly tempted, as we are. He also resisted temptation and revealed how—in his power—we can, too. Jesus was strong in the Spirit when the devil came to him, but there could have been enough questions in his mind that Satan's propositions sounded like possible answers.

How could this suggestion of Satan's be appealing to Jesus at all? Why would it even be a temptation? I think there were two ways in which this proposition would have looked good to Jesus.

The temptation of impatience

Jesus could—in his humanness—have been in a hurry to possess the kingdom of God. Do you realize that Jesus had not openly practiced his ministry for the first thirty years of his life? That's a long time to wait. I know that I was champing at the bit when I entered seminary at the age of twenty-two. I wanted to get out there and start changing the world for Jesus! I really struggled with the idea of three more years' delay.

Jesus waited until he was thirty, which was more in line with Hebrew custom for rabbis. The common time for a rabbi to begin was actually age thirty-five. We can imagine Jesus' eagerness to begin his public ministry. And when we hurry, we are vulnerable to temptation.

Dale was a pastor who wanted to see his congregation make some important changes that would attract new members. He was tired of the endless committee meetings that went nowhere, so he decided to take control.

"I figured the people would see how these changes weren't really so bad. We've got to take some chances, don't we?"

So after six months with this hundred-year-old congregation, Dale appeared in the front of the church without his customary robe. Instead of preaching from the pulpit, he preached from the platform with just his Bible and a few notes. They sang one hymn, but the rest of the music consisted of contemporary worship choruses.

"Talk about meetings! I had more to clean up after that service than Noah must have had on the ark!"

There's more to Dale's story. He received so many expressions of concern and hurt that he had to convene a special board meeting. They worked through the crisis and set up a task force to study worship and to get feedback from the congregation. They studied both God's Word and the unchurched culture around them. They talked about the meaning of worship and evangelism, about tradition and relevance. They made some significant changes over the course of time.

"I guess I learned that the process is the product. I was in such a hurry that I was missing a great opportunity to bring the people on board. Now, what we've done isn't viewed as 'the pastor's thing.' It's 'our thing.' That's much better."

Have you ever noticed God to be in a hurry? He doesn't seem to be in much of a rush. I think the only time God is pictured in the Bible as hurrying is in the parable of the Prodigal Son—when the father ran to welcome home his runaway son. That's the only time God rushes in the Bible. He welcomes his runaways home.

But Jesus could have been tempted to rush into ministry. The pressure of all the people who needed him could have been enough to tempt him.

The temptation of expediency and convenience

When you've come to establish a kingdom from the ground up and someone offers a quick way to get there, the expedient way can certainly be tempting. Much more convenient to have a territory handed to you than to have to conquer it town by town. Cowardice would be another reason to opt for the easier method. We know the end of the story—the tremendous suffering Jesus went through to bring all of God's will to pass. Jesus was well studied in the writings of the prophets, and he undoubtedly knew that his mission would carry with it much agony. Why not bypass all that? To say yes to Satan would have shortcut Jesus' mission, saving him much time and trouble. Saving him much of the agony.

But Jesus understood that the way to fulfill God's ultimate purpose was as important as simply fulfilling it. In other words, in God's economy, the ends *are* the means. The process *is* the product.

Is impatience an issue for me?

In what areas?

How does impatience affect my spiritual life?

What are some specific shortcuts that tempt you? What are some of the things you'd like to just get out of the way so you can get on with it? Do any of these strike home?

QUICK GAIN INSTEAD OF STEADY WORK. We are tempted and shaped by the lottery mentality. I am astounded to see how the lottery mentality has infected our Christian culture. We rely on "luck" instead of God's provision. We look for the big hit instead of the steady work. And we ignore the advice of the book of Proverbs, which says many times things like "a greedy person tries to get rich quick, but it only leads to poverty" (Proverbs 28:22).

VENDING MACHINE PRAYER. This mentality convinces us that if we put in a prayer, we should expect the blessings to come out. This mechanistic view misses the whole purpose of prayer. God wants a relationship, and we look solely for selfish results. We spend so little time in prayer, yet we get upset when God doesn't answer right away. How sad! We're not willing to invest in a relationship with God; what we want is a service contract!

BIBLE ROULETTE. Many of us have a Cliff Notes approach to the Bible. Instead of investing time to understand it, we simply open it randomly and read a verse or two. Then we are disappointed when it doesn't seem to speak to us right away. That's like randomly opening a phone book, dialing any number, and expecting to get a friend on the line. It just doesn't work that way. The Bible's truth and power shape our life as we cultivate our knowledge of God's Word.

I am grateful for the tools in contemporary Bibles that guide us to specific passages that speak to specific problems. Perhaps you've seen such lists that deal with anger, depression, fear, or comfort. I don't want to discourage the use of these, because they serve a useful purpose. But Jesus' followers need to go deeper. When God's Word lives in your heart, you gain not only the knowledge of his Word but the knowledge of the author. And knowing the author makes all the difference.

WRITE-A-CHECK SYNDROME. I'm all for stewardship. As

a pastor partly responsible for funding a large church budget, I'm very grateful that people write checks to the church! But we often write a check when God is calling us to get involved. True joy comes not from the shortcut of the occasional check but from a lifestyle of stewardship. Sacrificial giving becomes the fountain of life for God's Word and a fountain of joy for our soul. If God doesn't have you, he isn't interested in your money.

FORMULA EVANGELISM. We often become impatient with people who haven't come to know the Lord. Sometimes we have reduced evangelism (and many other areas of ministry) to a formula that we simply walk through and expect to elicit a quick response. But there's no shortcut to love—which is the heart of evangelism and ministry. And God calls us to invest ourself in people. When they are loved, they will love.

You and I are often in a hurry to secure what we want, and we go about it in ways that do not honor God. And this question is meant to drive us to deep examination of our soul. Why don't you take a shortcut? Because a shortcut cuts short the blessing of God. It also cuts short the knowledge of God. And a shortcut cuts short the fruit of God in our life.

As I review these shortcuts, which most often tempt me?

What other shortcuts, not listed here, do I struggle with?

The master of distraction

It's very easy to get sidetracked into focusing on the wrong goals, thereby giving in to the wrong needs. Satan is a master of distraction. I am astounded at what he uses. In the wilderness Satan had set out very appealing bait. The offer was legitimate in a sense, and it could have saved Jesus a lot of hassle in the short run. But there is a hook underneath that bait. Satan's shortcuts always demand spiritual compromise. What's the fine print here? You can have all the kingdoms of the earth—if you will just bow down and worship me. That's the fine print on the contract. Jesus could take the shortcut, but in so doing, he would lose God. Satan would take God's place in his life.

A Culture Blind to the Bargain

In this temptation we have a dark bargain: The ultimate gift—all the kingdoms of the world—for the ultimate betrayal—giving ourself to God's enemy. But what disturbs me these days is that I'm afraid too many people don't understand this temptation. They just don't get it. Our culture is very much caught in the mind-set of Faust. They work on the principle that getting what they want matters most and the means don't really matter. In many ways people in our day cannot even understand this temptation. They've lost sight of nobility, of integrity, of the importance of the means as well as the ends.

You may have heard of the movie *Indecent Proposal.* I've not seen it and don't plan to. My understanding is that the plot centers on a husband who is offered one million dollars by a man who wants to sleep with his wife. My question here is, Where is the debate? I don't understand why this movie wasn't five minutes long! The couple, it is argued, will gain financial freedom. At what price? Their compromise would forever haunt them. Every time they spent money, how could they not be reminded of how they'd come by it? Their marriage sanctity had been violated. What would they say when their children asked them, "How did you come into our inheritance? What's the story of our family wealth?" The real riches in life are found in promises kept, in relationships that stand the test of time.

But we are becoming a no-conscience culture—and therefore all the more vulnerable to the shortcut temptation. We've lost the sense of manners. Crude speech is the norm. I hear it on the soccer field from both elementary school children and from their parents. We've lost the value of character because there is little reward for integrity. How long can our elected officials and other leaders simply brush off and delay facing the inevitable consequences of their immoral behavior? They are our models. What are they modeling? We've lost the sense of honor indicated by caring about a name and a reputation. There are people who do not seem to care about their name anymore so long as it represents power. Personally, I'll give anything for my name to represent integrity.

Many have lost the ability to value the quality of the journey and care only about the quantity of the results. And, my friend, they are buying the kingdoms of this world. And selling their souls to own them.

What's your kingdom? Each of us has one—at least one. What have you sold? You may resent my implying that you've stepped over this line. But it's so easy to step over it these days. I urge you to search your soul today. What kingdom are you seeking—and what are you tempted to sell to get it? The price will always be too high.

How's my conscience?

The Great Compromise

I see the devil's power over our world now. All around us people have sold their souls. They no longer believe in the authority of God. They no longer believe in the authority of an objective truth, and they have been compromised in every turn.

Are there things I've grown used to that at one time offended me?

I was listening to a review by Alan Jacobs comparing Louisa May Alcott's original book, *Little Women,* with the movie version produced in 1995 and the renovelization of the book, written by Laurie Lawler. Jacobs notes that there are two significant alterations in addition to the modernizing of vocabulary and literary style. There are significant changes in the moral universe. The original story began with Mrs. March and her girls gathering together on Christmas morning. Their father is away as an army chaplain in the Civil War. As they are sitting down to their very meager but still delightful Christmas breakfast, Mrs. March thinks of the German immigrants down the street who have nothing. She suggests that they give their meal to the immigrants. And the girls, at first hesitantly but then willingly, agree. In the remake of the movie and in the new novelization, Mrs. March is nowhere to be found on Christmas morning. She is out at the equivalent of a homeless shelter, and the girls themselves come up with this idea on their

Are there behaviors I've come to accept, not because they are biblical, but simply because they are now viewed as normal?

How does all this affect my spiritual life?

own. Jacobs comments on the radical change in the vision of the role of parents. The new version presents a "vision of children and of childhood that sees parents as, at best, indifferent or unnecessary appendages to the children's lives, at worst, encumbrances and problem-causers. In the original, the girls are always under their mother's authority, they listen to her, they respect her wisdom and her counsel. . . . [In the new version] the best thing for parents to do is to stay out of the way."

There is also a complete excision of spiritual and religious framework that is an essential for the original *Little Women.* The primary interest of the original did not lie in its spiritual aspect. But there is an underlying framework of spiritual experience based on recurrent allusions to John Bunyan's *Pilgrim's Progress,* including chapter titles. Jacobs asserts that the Alcotts' message concurs with Bunyan's premise that this life is a difficult pilgrimage that you should expect to be full of trouble and testing, but it will have its ultimate end, not in getting married (as suggested by what Jacobs calls "Little Women Lite,"), but in dying in this world and going to be with God. This would have been familiar to Louisa May Alcott's audience, but it is not understood by audiences in our day.[1]

Forsaking conscience and spiritual values for the sake of culture will lead to being forsaken by God. That is the chilling reality of a shortcut. You may find a shortcut to the kingdoms of this world, but you will lose the kingdom of God.

Recapturing Our Conscience

How do we recapture conscience? How do we resist the temptations of impatience and expediency so that we can get results—not quick results but real results? This comes when we are committed to God's vision and version of success.

What was Jesus' real mission? Satan assumed that Jesus' real mission was to create the kingdom of God. After all, John the Baptist had been preaching it: "Repent, for the kingdom of heaven is near" (Matthew 3:2, NIV). Satan was listening to the preacher. Satan listens very carefully to preachers.

Mission and worship

There is a sense in which your mission grows out of what you worship. Those who teach on mission often miss this central principle. Your mission, your vision in life, grows out of what you worship, out of your ultimate value. Your eternal direction motivates your purpose. Jesus' mission, ultimately, was *not* to establish the kingdom of God. His mission was to honor his Father in everything. That's all he cared about. That's all he wanted to achieve—to honor God, every step of the way. Now one way he could do that was to accomplish his calling to bring redemption. But this would lead him to death on the cross. And there could be no shortcut to that. But honoring God was first and foremost.

We have often missed the fact that God is to be first and always! "And whatever you do, whether in word or deed, do it all in the name of the Lord Jesus, giving thanks to God the Father through him" (Colossians 3:17, NIV). When we miss this fact we fall into expediency, confusion, compromise, and utilitarianism. Satan's goal is to distract us to valuing the world instead of the Creator of the world. *He wants us to covet the kingdom instead of consecrate the King.*

What about You?

I want to raise some soul-searching questions for you. As you are pursuing your daily activities, simply ask yourself:

- Why am I doing this?
- Do the things that I do honor God first and always?
- Do I do them in a way that inspires worship, thanksgiving, gratitude, and praise to God?
- Would God rather have my works or my worship?

Any kingdom without God as King is a kingdom that will fall. There are many shortcuts to power. They will deter us, possibly forever, from our real destination. In order to rule the kingdoms of this world, you must agree to be ruled by them. Those who rule the kingdoms of this world are actually held fast by the very kingdoms they claim to rule.

One of my favorite poems is "Ozymandias" by Percy Bysshe Shelley. It's a poem of great irony.

> I met a traveler from an ancient land
> Who said, "Two vast and trunkless legs of stone
> Stand in the desert . . . Near them on the sand
> Half sunk, a shattered visage lies, whose frown,
> And wrinkled lip, and sneer of cold command,
> Tell that its sculptor well those passions read
> Which yet survived, stamped on these lifeless
>   things,
> The hand that mocked them, and the heart that fed;
> And on the pedestal these words appear:
> "My name is Ozymandias, king of kings:
> Look on my works, ye Mighty and despair!"
> Nothing beside remains. Round the decay
> Of that colossal wreck, boundless and bare
> The lone and level sand stretch far away.

The kingdoms of this world will all crumble to dust. At the end of time, only Jesus' cross will stand, with the entire universe illuminated in its light.

Temptation is only for a season.

This little profound story of temptation concludes with a very simple phrase. After Jesus said, "Satan, be gone," we read, "Then the Devil went away, and angels came and cared for Jesus."

"And the Devil went away." This is one little phrase that can give us as much hope as any other we've shared. Temptation is but for a season. Temptation does not go on forever. Perhaps you can remember a time when you were feeling sorely tempted and something interrupted you. The temptation vanished.

We will get through it if we cling fast to Christ and don't compromise. We are to hold on and shoo the devil away. He will flee, and we will find God's gracious comfort.

NOTES

1. Alan Jacobs, *On Morals and Manners in Films Based on Jane Austen's Novels.* Audiotape interview with Ken Myers, March–April, 1995. Vol. 14. (Charlottesville, VA: Mars Hill Tapes, 1995).

CHAPTER 13

"What are you looking for?" The Longing That Won't Let Go

John 1:38

"None of us ever desired anything more ardently than God desires to bring men to a knowledge of himself." JOHNN TAULER[1]

Augustine said it: "You have made us for yourself, and our hearts are restless until they find their peace in you."[2] Someone has said there is a God-shaped vacuum in each one of us. It remains empty until God fills it.

We are a restless race, always looking for something. When we get what we think we're looking for, it is far less than we had hoped. This question is an "onion" question—that is, one that is meant to take us to deeper and deeper levels of reflection and soul-searching. What exactly are we looking for in life? The answers may be very unsettling.

This is the day after Jesus has been revealed, in a sense, to John the Baptist. He has been baptized. Now we read of what happens the next day after Jesus's baptism.

> **The next day John again was standing with two of his disciples, and as he watched Jesus walk by, he exclaimed, "Look, here is the Lamb of God!" [A reference to the Passover Lamb.] The two disciples heard him say this, and they followed Jesus. When Jesus turned and saw them**

following, he said to them, "What are you looking for?" They said to him, "Rabbi" (which translated means Teacher), "where are you staying?" He said to them, "Come and see." They came and saw where he was staying, and they remained with him that day. It was about four o'clock in the afternoon. One of the two who heard John speak and followed him was Andrew, Simon Peter's brother. He first found his brother Simon and said to him, "We have found the Messiah" (which is translated Anointed). He brought Simon to Jesus, who looked at him and said, "You are Simon son of John. You are to be called Cephas" (which is translated Peter). (John 1:35-42, NRSV)

If Jesus asked me at this very moment what I am looking for, I would have to say . . .

Our Heart Hungers for Something More

You can tell a great deal about what people long for by looking at the company they keep, the activities they pursue, and the interests they invest in. The quality of Jesus' first disciples is evident by the fact that they were with John the Baptist. Now, I'm not sure we would want to be with John the Baptist. We probably wouldn't have found him very inviting. He was an awesome figure. He was tearing down the traditions of Israel and undoing the religious leaders of Israel. He was demanding change.

If Andrew and the other disciple (whom most believe to be John, the Gospel's author) were disciples of John the Baptist, we know that they were looking for salvation in a world that seemed to be crumbling around them. They were looking for God to do something new in their day. These were men of moral conviction. They saw their religious leaders subject to corruption and convenience. They longed to see God honored in the lives of transformed people. They wanted to see people repent of their sins and be baptized. These were men of high ideals, and they were risk takers. They were willing to pay the price of pursuing those high ideals. As the disciples of John, we can imagine that they were looking for a purpose worth dying for, for a hope worth living for, and for a person who would lead them to God.

I'm reminded of a passage in Ecclesiastes 3:11. The New Revised Standard Version reads: "He has made everything suitable for its time; moreover he has put a sense of past and future into their minds, yet they cannot find out what God has done from the beginning to the end." The New Living Translation says: "He has planted eternity in the human heart." There's a hunger in our heart for something more. Not simply for understanding the past, nor for anticipating the future. It's a yearning for the eternal, a yearning for God.

We Often Misunderstand Our Longings

We may feel restless, thinking an outward change is demanded when, in fact, an inner need is clamoring for attention. We may pursue financial wealth when we're longing for a security that money can never buy. We may pursue sexual adventure when we are longing for love that transcends the physical. We may pursue ambitious plans because we want to feel important, not understanding that the only sense of lasting affirmation comes from God.

I was reading recently about an author named Dan Wakefield. He's one who demonstrates for us that success, as many have discovered, isn't the salvation it's cracked up to be. Dan Wakefield wrote for *Atlantic Monthly, Harper's Magazine, Esquire, The Nation.* He also wrote four novels. One of them, *Starting Over,* was made into a movie with Candace Bergen and Burt Reynolds. He wrote screenplays and wrote for TV. His first novel, *Going All the Way,* was published in 1970. It was chosen as the duo main selection of the Literary Guild. It hit *Time* magazine's best-seller list for three weeks and sold more than eight hundred thousand copies in paperback. Now, that is like hitting a grand-slam in the seventh game of the World Series to clinch the title. No writer could dream of more for a first novel.

Here's what Dan Wakefield writes about his success:

> The dream of a lifetime had been realized and I was delighted. I was also nervous and anxious. I learned what people had testified from the beginning of time but that no one really believes until he or she has the experience. That is, success and achievements and awards are all fine, but they do not transform you. They do not bring about a state of built-in contentment or inner peace or security, much less salvation. The novel was not the answer to all life's problems. So I had another drink.[3]

In his book *Returning: A Spiritual Journey,* Wakefield tells about crashing into alcoholism and nearly losing everything until God entered his life.

What are some of my "I'll-finally-be-happy-when . . ." longings?

Which ones have been fulfilled?

How have I felt as a result?

How has my experience been similar to and different from those of Wakefield and Phillips?

Now another writer, far more widely known than Wakefield, had a similar experience. J. B. Phillips, the British New Testament scholar and author, slipped into a horrible depression following his widespread acclaim. He went into a spiraling depression upon the completion of his beloved paraphrase of the New Testament. And he wrote about that later in an autobiography entitled *The Price of Success.*[4] In the first instance we have Dan Wakefield, a man who did not yet claim to know Jesus Christ, and J. B. Phillips, a man who absolutely knew and loved Jesus Christ. And both of them experienced a hunger for something more.

When we begin to listen to our longings, we begin to look for signs of hope. The disciples who were there with John the Baptist knew from John that they were in the penultimate place. They were not at the ultimate destination yet. So when John said, "There is the Lamb of God who takes away the sin of the world," they left John and began to follow Jesus. But they followed cautiously.

We often follow at a distance, doubting anything good could ever happen to us. I get that clue if you read carefully here in John's Gospel. It says in chapter 1, verse 36: "As Jesus walked by, John declared, 'Look! There is the Lamb of God!' " The two disciples heard him say this, and they followed Jesus. Now, you may think they went right up alongside him. No, because listen to what happens next.

WE DON'T EXPECT GOD TO WANT OR WELCOME US

When Jesus turned and saw them following him, he said to them, "What are you looking for?" They cautiously followed at a distance. Why? They were following from a distance because they didn't have a relationship with him yet, and they didn't want to presume upon him. They wanted to be near him—but they weren't sure that he wanted to be with them.

I remember, as a young pastor, longing to be published. I had some thoughts that I really wanted to share through writing. My first endeavor was an article I submitted to *Christianity Today* on how seminarians can get the most from their seminary preparation. About a month later, a letter finally came from Dr. Kenneth Kantzer, the editor. It was a form letter of rejection. I was crushed. But at the bottom of the form letter was a hand-written note from Dr. Kantzer. He wrote, "Doug, this article needs to be written, but most of our readers are pastors who've already completed seminary or lay leaders who don't plan to go. You've written for seminarians. Please try it again from a different angle."

At the time I didn't appreciate how special it was to have an editor take the time to make such comments. All I knew was: I was a failure. I wasn't wanted. I gave up my hopes of writing for a year and a half. Then one day the idea for rewriting the article flashed in my head. I wrote it, and it was published within three months in *Christianity Today.* That was February 1981. That was a thrill, but there's more to the story.

That summer I was at the American Festival of Evangelism in Kansas City. I tried as hard as I could to meet Dr. Kantzer. I hung around the Christianity Today display booth. Everywhere I went I just missed him. Finally, I screwed up the courage and called his hotel room. I still can't believe I did it.

"Dr. Kantzer?"

"Yes, this is Kenneth, call me Kenneth."

"This is Doug Rumford; I don't know if you'll remember me."

"Oh, yes, the seminary article." He remembered!

"Well . . . er . . . yes, yes. That's right!"

"That was a very good article. I was really glad you took another chance on that."

"Well, thank you. I really appreciate your saying that. I don't want to be presumptuous, but I was wondering . . . could I meet you?"

"Well, Doug, I'm pressing an editorial deadline this afternoon." And I thought, *What a fool I was. I called him and interrupted him—he's writing important things for the nation to read. How could I be so presumptuous!*

"But," he continued, "what are you doing tomorrow for breakfast?"

"I'm available!"

"Are you here with anyone?"

"My wife is here with me," I said.

"Well, bring her along. You and your wife can have breakfast with my wife and me, and then maybe I can introduce you to some other people with Christianity Today and our new journal, *Leadership.*"

I couldn't believe it! It was like a dream come true. But did you see how much I was captive to negative anticipation? I expected rejection. Don't you? When I reach out to people, time and again I find a welcome. But while I long for a welcome, I expect rejection.

"What are you looking for?" Jesus asked the disciples. When we finally can turn to God and hear his question to us, when we begin to consider that question, we begin to search our soul and get down to business with God. Until you ask that question, your religion will merely be a hobby. Until you ask that question, your life will merely be marking time. What are you looking for?

We Need to Be Reminded Again and Again That God Is Ready to Welcome Us

Am I more likely to expect immediate acceptance or rejection from God? from others? Why?

It's tempting to doubt that God really cares about us or that he would bend down from heaven and reveal himself to us. Even those who have known God's power have hit hard times that cause them to doubt God's openness to us.

I was reading about the singer Amy Grant. In the 1980s she was on her way to the top. But her life was not as charmed as it appeared. There were troubles in her marriage. Her husband, Gary, was on cocaine. Other difficulties led to frequent talk of divorce. Amy said about that time, "For a few days I just stayed in bed and mourned my life." Remember as you read that this is a Christian musical superstar talking:

> The only hope I could seem to see was just junking it all and moving to Europe and starting everything all over again. It was then that my sister, in a last ditch visit, marched up right beside my bed and said, "Fine, go to Europe, leave it all behind and start your life over, but before you go I just want you to tell [my little girl] how you can sing that Jesus can help her through anything in life but he couldn't help you."
>
> The words hit home. Gary and I began to seek marriage and personal counseling, and we have rebuilt our relationship with each other and with God.[5]

The superstar Christian singer had stopped believing that her God was a welcoming God. We lose sight so easily of what God has done for us and how, in our past, he has come to us time and time again.

When Jesus asked, "What are you looking for?" the disciples said to him, "Rabbi, where are you staying?"

"Where are you staying?" Initially we might think the disciples were simply making small talk, that they were caught off guard.

Was it simply a surface interchange? Perhaps John and Andrew were conversing among themselves: "Jesus spoke to us! What do we say now? Oh, I have an idea!" They turn to Jesus: "Nice day isn't it? By the way, where are you staying? We're staying at the Locust Inn down here by the Jordan River. Where are you staying?"

I think there was more to it than that! They were saying, straightforwardly, "Can we be with you?" They longed to be in his presence. They may have hung back, fearing rejection, but now they expressed their simple desire.

And Jesus said, "Come and see." He welcomed them readily.

We hunger for something more, but we often follow at a distance, wondering if it could ever be ours. Then he turns and says, "What are you looking for?" And we say, "Could we just be with you?"

That is a powerful request. And it receives a gracious affirmation. Our Lord invites us to find what we need with him and in him. And notice how the Lord makes the first move.

Another interesting detail is the time indication. John's Gospel says that it was about four o'clock in the afternoon. I think that's an incredible detail. The fact that it was later in the day didn't deter Jesus. Some of us procrastinate—or at least we know people who do! They hem and haw until it's too late to do anything. The fact is, it's never too late—it's never inconvenient—for Jesus.

Jesus Gives More Than an Answer— He Gives Himself

And what does Jesus say to them? Jesus doesn't give an answer. He gives himself. Jesus doesn't give a program. He gives himself. Jesus doesn't give a quick-fix solution. He gives a long-term relationship. First he says, "Come." It's as if he were saying, "Come—join me, be with me. I could *tell you* many things, but then you'll think of God as a philosophy. I could *zap you* with a blessing, but then you'll think of God as simply a wonder-worker. I could *give you a formula for success,* but then you'd think of God as a sterile plan for self-achievement. Instead, I give myself, and with me, the way, the truth, and the life. . . ."

What limitations do I impose on God?

What does God's Word show me and teach me about such limitations?

Then Jesus said to them, "See." Again, I hear him saying, "See not only where I live but how I live." You can come alongside, join him, but while you do you must observe and learn.

This is an amazing little passage. It seems so small, so ordinary, so unimpressive. Yet it's the headwaters of the holy river of discipleship. If you go to the upper regions of Minnesota, there are many places where you can step across the Mississippi River. These are the tributaries that will feed into the mighty river. Jesus' encounter with these disciples is one such place.

Discipleship is a matter of small beginnings. Many of us have expectations for dramatic events and profound experiences. But it all begins with simple friendship, as we answer his question: "What are you looking for?"

"Where are you staying, Lord?"

"Come and see." It's the gospel in a nutshell. Jesus invited them to take the next step. They stayed with him, and then they shared what they learned. And those were the headwaters of the holy river that changed the landscape of history. They found what they were looking for. They were scared. And so they found peace through faith in God's care. They were lost. They found hope in God's direction. They were lonely. They found comfort in God's love. Everything you're looking for can be found when you look first to Christ. Everything.

What about You? What Are You Looking For?

It often takes a soul-shaking event to push us to examine our priorities in life. Bob Buford is a very successful Texas businessman in the cable television industry. He's also the founder of Leadership Network, which is a support ministry to leaders of large churches. In his book *Halftime,* Buford tells about an experience with his only

What are some of the small beginnings that Jesus has made in my life through friends?

Christian workers?

Bible study?

Books?

What is Jesus doing in my life now?

son, Ross, that changed what he was looking for. "Ross," he said, "was one of my heroes." Ross graduated from Texas Christian University. The plan was for Ross to assume leadership of his father's company in a few years. But first Ross wanted to get some broader business experience. He worked as an investment banker in Denver. At the age of twenty-four he made $150,000. And he was on his way to making $500,000. But on January 3, 1987, Bob got a call from his brother Jeff. Ross and two other boys had tried to swim the Rio Grande. They wanted to experience what it was like for illegal aliens to cross the watery border into a land of promise. Bob flew down from his home in Dallas. The Texas Rangers were coordinating the search, but Bob also hired trackers, helicopters, and scuba divers—everything money could buy—to search the river. When he looked into the eyes of one of the trackers at the end of the day, he knew that they weren't going to find his son alive.

Bob writes:

> I remember walking along a limestone bluff perhaps 200 feet above the muddy, treacherous river as frightened as I've ever felt. Here's something you can't dream your way out of, I told myself. Here's something you can't think your way out of, buy your way out of, or work your way out of. It was all too clear in this maddening solitude on the river bluff. "This is," I thought to myself, "something you can only trust your way out of." The incomprehensible was breaking out all around me, and there was no way I could understand it apart from an eternal perspective. Albert Einstein once said, "What is incomprehensible is beyond the realm of science, it is in the realm of God." Well, this was in the realm of God. I remember sending up a prayer that in retrospect seems to be the most intelligent prayer I've ever asked. "Dear God," I pleaded, "somehow give me the ability to accept and absorb

> whatever grace people might bring me in this terrible time. Amen."[6]

The search for Ross continued, but his body wasn't recovered for four months. But as Bob was wrapping up Ross's business affairs in Denver, he went through his desk and found a handwritten copy of his will, dated eleven months earlier. When Ross wrote this, he was probably twenty-three years old.

> "Well if you're reading my will, then obviously I'm dead," Ross began. "I wonder how I died. Probably suddenly because otherwise I would have taken the time to rewrite this. Even if I am dead, I think one thing should be remembered and that is I had a really great time along the way. More important, it should be noted that I am in a much better place now." The will directed how he wanted his earthly goods distributed, and then Ross concluded the document with this benediction. "In closing, I love you all and thank you. You have made it a great life. Make sure you all go up instead of down, and I'll be waiting for you at heaven's gate. Just look for the guy in the old khaki Stetson and a faded shirt, wearing a pair of Ray Bans and a Jack Nicholson smile. I also thank God for giving me the chance to write this before I departed. Thanks. Adios, Ross."[7]

Buford says clearly what he is now looking for:

> One of the most common characteristics of a person who is nearing the end of the first half of life is the unquenchable desire to move from success to significance. After a first half of doing what we are supposed to do, we'd like to do something in the second half that is more meaningful. Something that rises above purpose and paycheck into the stratosphere of significance.[8]

Am I more caught up in success or significance?

How do I define each of these?

What has influenced my pursuing one or the other?

What about You?

What are you looking for? When Jesus asked John's disciples, he didn't give them a destination. He gave them an invitation. He made no apologies for what he was about to ask. He didn't conceal any of the problems that would come their way.

The disciples were asked to walk by faith. If God calls me, how much must I know before I say yes? Do I have to be convinced that all of my efforts will always be successful? Do I have to be convinced that I'll always be safe, comfortable, and secure? that I'll never be put on the spot to speak for my faith? that I won't be pushed too far, too fast? that I'll agree right away with anything the Lord asks me to do or to be? Do I have to be convinced that everyone else will go along with me so that I'll never be alone? And that I will gain far more than I will ever lose?

Everything you are looking for can be found when you look first to the Lord. As I consider Jesus' invitation, I can almost see him looking into my eyes and saying, "It should be enough for you to know that you only go where I have already gone and that I'm with you all the way."

Notes

1. Tony Castle, *The New Book of Christian Quotations* (New York: Crossroad, 1984), 61.
2. Rex Warner, trans., *The Confessions of St. Augustine* (New York: New American Library, 1963), 17.
3. Donald W. McCullough, *The Trivialization of God* (Colorado Springs: NavPress Publishing Group, 1995), 45–46.
4. Ibid.
5. Roberta Croteau in *Aspire,* quoted in *Leadership* 16 (fall 1995): 4, 40.
6. Bob Buford, *Halftime* (Grand Rapids, Mich.: Zondervan Publishing House, 1994), 54–57.
7. Ibid., 84.
8. Ibid.

CHAPTER 14

"What would you have me do for you?" Getting beyond Requests

Matthew 20:21, 32

IN 1994 IN Modesto, California, Pastor Glen Berteau of Calvary Temple church called his congregation to pray and fast for revival. Then the pastors in Modesto gathered in a prayer summit to pray for revival. Then they brought in *Heaven's Gates, Hell's Flames,* a dramatic gospel presentation. Everyone was utterly amazed by what occurred. The first night, over eight hundred people came forward to say, "I want my name written in the Book of Life" and committed their lives to Christ. The following two evenings, crowds grew to more than three thousand. The drama was eventually continued nightly for eight weeks, with more than eighty thousand people attending. At least thirty-three thousand decision packets were given out, and more than twenty-five thousand decision cards were signed and returned. That's revival![1]

But let me tell you the rest of the story. The pastors and church leaders were faced with an unusual crisis: What do you do with more than twenty-five thousand new believers? To put it in perspective, remember that there are entire denominations that don't have as many as twenty thousand members! These new believers had to be fed and connected with a body of believers. How was this community going to care for the harvest? The pastors gathered together as the end of eight weeks approached to decide what to do. After intense prayer and discussion, they decided to end the drama presentation. From a practical point, I would concur. How do you handle follow-up in that kind of situation? How do you prevent your leaders from burning out while trying to take care of all the new converts? How do you deal with the logistics of so many new people being enfolded into churches? So I don't criticize the leaders. Their faith and faithfulness have blessed thousands directly. And their example has been a model for countless communities. Most of us may never see such an outpouring of the Holy Spirit. Still, a haunting thought arises: It appears that a revival was stopped.

Do we understand what we're praying for? Do we have any idea what we are asking for? It has become clear to me that the pastors and churches of today (beginning with me and the congregation I serve) are not prepared to receive what we pray for. If every member of most congregations showed up on a Sunday morning, I'm not sure we would have any seating available for visitors or new believers. It is estimated that if all of the people on the rolls of the churches of America went to church on a given Sunday, there would be less than 4 percent capacity for the unchurched. If an unchurched person came, she wouldn't find a place in the parking lot or a seat to sit in. But, of course, it's more than a matter of buildings. What about leaders who are equipped to disciple? What about small groups that will provide care and support? In other words, if the revival we pray for came our way, most of us would not be prepared.

The Law of Unintended Consequences tells us that many things have side effects we never anticipated. How have I seen this in my life, especially in terms of my prayer life?

Have my answered prayers brought with them new, even more difficult challenges than I anticipated?

Prayer is more than a heavenly business transaction. Whether it's the issue of unintended consequences resulting from requests that are closest to God's heart, or a matter of reexamining our motivations, prayer is a window into the soul. If we consider it carefully, our prayer reveals much about us. It also gives us clues for our spiritual vitality.

To better understand these dynamics of prayer, I want to explore Jesus' response to two different requests. I'd like us to see these as a model for our coming to God with prayer requests. In both of these situations Jesus receives a specific request, and he says, "What do you want me to do for you?" In both of these situations Jesus greets with respect the people who ask him for help, even though he gives very different answers to their requests. And in both of these situations we will see that Jesus' question—"What do you want me to do for you?"—is not a request for information; it's an invitation to a relationship in which all of our other needs will be met.

Imagine this scene: Jesus has just told his disciples he's going to be flogged, crucified, buried, and resurrected. Those are the immediate words preceding this incident. Then we read this in Matthew 20:20-34:

> **Then the mother of Zebedee's sons came to Jesus with her sons and, kneeling down, asked a favor of him.**
>
> **"What is it you want?" he asked.**
>
> **She said, "Grant that one of these two sons of mine may sit at your right and the other at your left in your kingdom."**
>
> **"You don't know what you are asking," Jesus said to them. "Can you drink the cup I am going to drink?" [alluding to the Crucifixion and torture he was about to go through].**
>
> **"We can," they answered.**
>
> **Jesus said to them, "You will indeed drink from my cup, but to sit at my right or left is not for me to grant. These places belong to those for whom they have been prepared by my Father."**
>
> **When the ten heard about this, they were indignant with the two brothers. Jesus called them together and said, "You know that the rulers of the Gentiles lord it over them, and their high officials exercise authority over them. Not so with you. Instead, whoever wants to become great among you must be your servant, and whoever wants to be first must be your slave—just as the Son of Man did not come to be served,**

but to serve, and to give his life as a ransom for many."

As Jesus and his disciples were leaving Jericho, a large crowd followed him. Two blind men were sitting by the roadside, and when they heard that Jesus was going by, they shouted, "Lord, Son of David, have mercy on us!"

The crowd rebuked them and told them to be quiet, but they shouted all the louder, "Lord, Son of David, have mercy on us!"

Jesus stopped and called them. "What do you want me to do for you?" he asked.

"Lord," they answered, "we want our sight."

Jesus had compassion on them and touched their eyes. Immediately they received their sight and followed him. (NIV)

God Uses Prayer to Search Our Heart

There's much more to the prayer encounter than many of us often assume. In the first section of Matthew 20:20 we see that God searches our heart in prayer. When you and I come to God in prayer, there is much going on. It's not just that God is some sort of cosmic vending machine—you put in a prayer and out comes an answer. Instead, God wants an encounter with us, and during that encounter he searches our heart.

Missing the point

In this situation recorded in Matthew 20, a mother makes a request concerning her sons. We can understand that, can't we? My wife wants the best for our children. My mother wanted the best for me. That's how mothers (and fathers!) are. But when the mother of James and John comes to Jesus, her request is totally inappropriate. Jesus has just said, "I'm going to die for you. I'm going to give up my life for you. It's going to be a torturous experience, and I will be killed." Immediately following this, she comes to Jesus, falls down on her knees before him, and says, "I have a favor to ask.

When all that ugly stuff is over and you're up there in glory, can my boys be at your right hand and your left hand?"

As a side note, it occurs to me that we may have some insight here as to how James and John got their nicknames—"the sons of thunder." To be candid, I always assumed that their dad was the firecracker in the family. Now I'm beginning to think it was their mother. This is one very powerful woman. Her sons grew up saying, "If Mama wants something, she gets it. And we're going to be just like that!"

How does Jesus respond? How would you respond? Would you be tempted to lecture her about selfishness and pride? Would you be tempted to dismiss her for her presumption? Jesus, however, responds with warmth and respect. He simply says to her, "You don't know what you're asking! You really don't know." Then he uses that opportunity to teach her about her request. He uses her own desires to take her to a new level of understanding.

Romans 8:26 tells us, "We do not know what we ought to pray for, but the Spirit himself intercedes for us with groans that words cannot express" (NIV). We don't know how to pray as we ought. But that should not keep us from asking! The fascinating aspect of this mother's request is that *she isn't rejected.* When you don't know how to pray, God doesn't slap your wrists or ridicule you. He doesn't reject you. Instead, he searches you, and he asks you to go with him on the search. In this sense, the mother's request is not all bad. It would lead to a greater revelation of God's purpose and model for leadership. Our prayer requests can lead to true soul-searching.

Godly ambition and just plain ambition

There is a sense in which God is grateful for godly ambition—for ambition to do great things for God, to see God do wonderful things in the world. God is grateful for a person who says, "I'll do it. I'll take the responsibility." There's a place for the request to be in on the action—right up there with Jesus.

But many times our requests are what I call "striped." By that I mean they are checkered with desires that are light and dark. We have a holy desire to be about God's business, but we have the dark desire to make a name for ourself, too. Pride enters in. Greediness enters in. Sometimes we want that place of honor because we really think, *I know how to do this and nobody else may do it as well, so of course I should have the position.* We don't know how to pray as we ought. So Jesus asks us to search the complexity of the request.

The implications of answered prayer

There are times when we really don't know what we're asking. We may not understand the implications of our prayer. What Jesus is saying to this mother and her two sons is, "You know what? You're going to have to drink of the same cup that I drink of if you want that place in glory."

GETTING A CROSS. When we follow Jesus into glory, we acquire a cross to bear. To James and John, it could have meant a literal cross—execution. What does that cross mean to us now? I think it could mean surrendering control. If I'm to be right there with Jesus doing the kingdom's work, I'm sharing the glory, but I'm giving up control of my own life. A cross to me is letting down the boundaries, giving up the right to say, "I'll go this far, but no farther." When Jesus surrendered to the cross, when he was spread out on that beam, he had given up control.

As I review my prayer requests, what are some of the crosses that may be inherent in my requests?

How do I respond to these?

BEING VULNERABLE. The Bible also says that Jesus was naked. He was stripped of everything and put on display. Just think of the physical realities: When you're in pain, do you really want people to see you—to witness your cries and tears and groans? Jesus was naked and in excruciating pain, and all of it was on display. Even his spiritual agony was on display, or we wouldn't have the record of his words, "My God, my God, why have you forsaken me?" Here he was the spiritual leader, and in his hour of darkness his enemies heard him say that. Jesus had no protection at all. He was a living picture of vulnerability on several levels. When we pray for great things, is that what we have in mind?

When I pray, I take a risk with God and with others with whom I pray. I risk showing my deep desires. I risk being disappointed. I risk being judged. How have these risks and others affected my prayer life?

The unforseen consequences of answered prayer

There's a rather fascinating story in 2 Kings 20. A man prayed to be healed, and his prayer was answered. The story is about King Hezekiah. Now, we often call King Hezekiah a good king because he was a king of Judah, the southern nation, a direct heir of King David, and he did good things in Israel. All their leaders were not good kings, but Hezekiah was. When he was around the age of thirty-eight or thirty-nine, he became seriously ill, and God told him he was going to die. Well, Hezekiah wasn't ready to die. So he prayed for healing.

God gave Isaiah the prophet instructions for Hezekiah to prepare a poultice, and God healed Hezekiah through that. It's interesting that God used a poultice when he could have healed Hezekiah outright. I think there's a lesson there for us—that any healing, medical or not, is ultimately from God's hand. Hezekiah was healed. His prayer was answered.

After he was healed, he and his wife had a baby boy, whom they named Manasseh. Manasseh's history begins in 2 Kings 21. He was twelve years old when he became king. Now, Manasseh was one of the worst kings to ever serve Judah. He took God's people backward. He undid all the good his father had done. We have an unsettling fact here: The consequence of Hezekiah's prayer was that he was healed, but he wasn't prepared to care for a child that came his way. He was busy pursuing the establishment of his kingdom, but he wasn't taking care of the heir of the kingdom. So as we pray for things, we must also watch the priorities God has already given us for our marriage, family, friendships, and community.

The mystery of unanswered prayer

In Matthew 20:23, Jesus says, "You will indeed drink from my cup, but to sit at my right or left is not for me to grant. These places belong to those for whom they have been prepared by my Father (NIV)." Do you hear that? Jesus didn't have a right to answer that particular prayer. Within his humanity there were certain limitations. He recognized and accepted those. He did not know the mind of the heavenly Father on everything. (This is partly why he would meet with God regularly in prayer. Jesus didn't automatically have knowledge of God's plans.) He could not speak the mind of the heavenly Father on all issues until he had heard from the Father (see John 5:19-20). He said to his disciples in essence, "I don't know when I'm coming back, the seasons are not for you to know."

What are some of the currently unanswered prayers in my life?

What do I believe God wants me to do concerning them?

There are limitations to what we can or cannot know. There are limitations as to how prayers will or will not be answered. So when Jesus responds to us, "You don't know what you are asking," it may not only be that we don't understand the implications and consequences; it may be that there are spiritual dynamics and eternal realities involved that we are incapable of knowing and understanding.

I know that some of us have a very hard time living with unanswered prayer. I do. I have several prayers that have not been answered for years. They are heartbreaking, and sometimes I wonder if I should keep asking them. I do take courage in the fact that I'm still relatively young and there's still time for God to answer. But you know, praying for twenty-five years is a long time no matter what age you are. You humble yourself before God. You say, "God, teach me then what I'm asking. If I need to prepare, let me prepare. If I need to be responsible for what will happen as a result, then enable me to be responsible. If I need to just stand before you in faith and trust, knowing that you'll give when you give in the right time, I surrender."

I was greatly encouraged to learn about George Müller's experience. This prince of intercessors began to pray for a group of five personal friends in 1846. After five years one of them came to Christ. In ten years, two more of them found peace in the same Savior. He continued to pray for twenty-five years, and the fourth man came to faith in Christ. A few months after Müller's death in 1898, the fifth friend came to Christ. Although Müller didn't see that prayer answered, he had continued to pray for fifty-two years!

You Have Not Because You Ask Not

Two central principles of prayer are presented in James 4:2-3. The first is the simple principle of asking. "You do not have, because you do not ask God" (NIV). Some people simply don't ask God for help. They feel unworthy, afraid of rejection, or don't believe their requests will be heard. I visited a woman in the hospital who was a friend of members of our congregation. She had just been informed that her cancer was unable to be treated and that there was nothing more medicine could do. I asked her if we could pray, and she said, "I would like that very much, but I'm not sure God would hear me. I've never been a churchgoer, but I do believe God loves me." I took some time to share the good news of Jesus' love with her, and we prayed. The next day, when I walked into her room, she was smiling very sweetly.

"The Lord visited me last night," she said, with a touch of awe. "I didn't see anything, but I know he was here. He told me I was going to die, but that it was all right. I feel *so* peaceful. It is all right now."

Some people don't ask because they have no idea how God could possibly solve the problem. So because they see no way out, they figure God can't do any better. We need to heed the example of Jehoshaphat. In 2 Chronicles 20 the Moabites, Ammonites, and some of the Meunites declared war against Judah. These three armies were amassed against the smaller, inadequate forces of Judah. Jehoshaphat prayed, "O our God, won't you stop them? . . . We do not know what to do, but we are looking to you for help" (v. 12). And God answered. While the choirs of Israel sang, the armies started fighting among themselves and destroyed each other without harming Judah. God is infinitely creative in answering prayer. As Paul reminds us, "By his mighty power at work within us, he is able to accomplish infinitely more than we would ever dare to ask or hope"

Have I neglected to pray for certain people and situations because I can't see an immediate possibility or a feasible solution?

How has this affected my prayer life?

(Ephesians 3:20). God's message to us is, "You have not because you ask not. Go ahead and ask."

But there's a second principle right alongside the principle of asking: "When you ask, you do not receive, because you ask with wrong motives, that you may spend what you get on your pleasures" (James 4:3, NIV). This is the principle of self-evaluation. God often schools us when our prayers arise from a selfish agenda, as we saw in the case of the request by the mother of James and John.

Contrast her request with that of King Solomon. In 1 Kings 3, God comes to Solomon, the new king, one night in a dream and asks, "What would you have me do for you?" This is the same question Jesus asked James and John's mother! The same question Jesus asked the blind men.

Solomon said to God, "I am like a little child who doesn't know his way around" (1 Kings 3:7). He says, in effect, "Lord, I don't know enough. I don't understand how to govern these people, *your* people. Lord God, I need wisdom." Then we read,

> The Lord was pleased with Solomon's reply and was glad that he had asked for wisdom. So God replied, "Because you have asked for wisdom in governing my people and have not asked for a long life or riches for yourself or the death of your enemies—I will give you what you asked for! I will give you a wise and understanding mind such as no one else has ever had or ever will have! And I will also give you what you did not ask for—riches and honor! No other king in all the world will be compared to you for the rest of your life! And if you follow me and obey my commands as your father, David, did, I will give you a long life." (1 Kings 3:10-14)

It reminds me of Matthew 6:33: "Seek first his kingdom and his righteousness, and all these things will be given to you as well" (NIV). Solomon asked for wisdom so he could be the servant of others—he could help others and provide the resource that could bring others into the presence of God. And with it God blessed him with everything else.

Here's a way of summarizing these principles: *Ask whatever you want in love and receive whatever he gives in love.* Let him search your heart as you make your request. Let him say, "Do you understand what you're really asking?" Maybe you're asking for a new job. Do you really understand the implications for your family? Could it be that where you are at the present time is best for your family? Maybe you're asking for God to put together a particular relationship. Do you really understand what that could mean? Years ago Ruth Bell was in a relationship with a man and was praying desperately that it would work out. But it fell apart. And then Ruth met Billy Graham, who became her husband. Ruth says, "I thank God for unanswered prayer."

Jesus' words are an invitation to "uncensored prayer," that is, prayer that flows freely from our heart to God, leaving the results to him. What prayers are stirring in my heart right now?

If I could ask anything of God, it would be . . .

God Reveals His Love and Power

Let's look at the story of the blind men, which immediately follows the story of James and John's mother. I believe that these passages in Matthew's Gospel—the mother's request and the blind men's request—are set side by side, not by some coincidence of literature, but by divine appointment of theology. God wants us to understand this material in this sequence so that we may be encouraged when we come to prayer. How do we pray? First, we let God search our heart to understand and shape our requests. Now we see just how God reveals his love and power in response to our requests.

Jesus is leaving Jericho. As he walks along with his disciples, suddenly someone calls out, "Lord, Son of David, have mercy on us" (Matthew 20:30). I want to focus on those two words: *have mercy.* When Jesus hears these words, he stops. Above the noise of the crowd, above the clamoring and shuffling all around, he hears two words, "Have mercy," and he stops cold.

This incident with the blind men is what we might call a summary miracle. This little miracle is the last miracle Jesus performs before he goes to the cross. And in this miracle we see how he works with people and the dynamics of a healing encounter. We see here the mercy of Jesus. If you cry out to God, "Have mercy," he hears. We see the graciousness of his welcome, and we see that he can be interrupted. He stops the whole entourage and says, "I want to see those who are calling out to me." We see the grace and mercy of Jesus' respect for individuals.

It has always fascinated me that Jesus says to the blind men, "What do you want me to do for you?" (v. 32). He could easily have said, "It's obvious what you need," or "I'll fix that for you." But that wouldn't show respect for the person. Jesus doesn't presume to impose what he thinks they need. He wants to know what *they* think they need.

In addition to Jesus' respect, we see the mercy of his touch. He reaches out and touches the blind men. In those days blindness was revolting. There was often seepage from the eyes or disfigurement. They didn't care for themselves; they were beggars. Very few people ever cared for them. We see how the crowd rejects them. So these people are rather unsightly, unwelcoming people, and Jesus touches them. He touches them, and their sight is restored.

There's a boldness to prayer.

The blind men refuse to be silenced. As they are crying out, "Lord, Son of David, have mercy on us!" the crowd is shushing them. "Shut up!" some say with irritation, "Jesus is a busy man. Would you leave him alone? You're interrupting. Shhh!" But the blind men call out all the more.

A little child was playing outside with her kitten when it scampered up a tree. It became stuck on a branch just out of the child's reach and was meowing at the top of its little lungs. The girl ran in to get her mom to help, but her mom was on the phone. When Mom saw her daughter's distress, she interrupted the phone conversation, "Honey, what's wrong?" Then she looked out the window and saw the kitten on the branch, which was only about four feet off the ground.

"Oh, I see. Kitty will be fine. I'll be out to help after this phone call. Kitty's not far off the ground."

"But Mom," insisted the little girl, "it looks a long way down to Kitty!"

When we're in trouble, it looks a long way down. Problems don't wait for convenient times. We need help when we need help.

Hebrews 4:16 says, "Let us come boldly to the throne of our gracious God. There we will receive his mercy, and we will find grace to help us when we need it." There's a boldness to prayer.

There's also a desperation to prayer.

When we are desperate for help, people trying to shush us don't matter anymore. Some of us have been that desperate; we're not intimidated by obstacles to Jesus.

When have I seen or practiced bold prayer?

How can my own prayers become more confident?

But some people are fragile in their desperation. We have to be careful not to squash the hopes of someone in that situation. Don't be too pragmatic when someone is praying for a miracle. Jesus hears that prayer. Above our practicality and our shushing, Jesus hears the cry. He loves when people call out.

It's interesting that the blind men use words for Jesus that recognize him as the Messiah. They call him the Son of David. Jesus is on his way to Jerusalem and to his death, and these blind beggars are the only people in that crowd who see him for what he is. The blind men see what others refuse to see! In the same way, we often see Jesus most clearly when we are in desperate need. We often don't see him in our success or in our sufficiency.

God Wants to Open Our Eyes through Prayer

When Jesus hears our requests, he doesn't see us as a case number. He sees us as people with whom he wants a relationship. When he asks, "What do you want me to do?" he is searching not just for an answer but for a conversation. In the middle of that hustling, bustling crowd, Jesus stops and asks, "So, how's it going? What do you need? What do you really want?"

"Lord, we want to see," say the men. "We haven't seen our wives for years. We haven't seen our children. We haven't seen a sunrise or a sunset. We haven't even seen you, Lord. Let the first thing we see be your face. We want to see you."

Jesus is not a busy executive, wanting a quick one-word answer. God longs to engage us. He wants to open our eyes until we truly see him.

What do you want to see? God wants to open our eyes. And he really wants to make his presence known to you and me in very specific ways. We don't have to tell God how to give us sight. That's God's business. We give God the prescription for fulfilling our requests when all he really needs is a description of what we want. "God, I want to see." And God delights in answering in marvelous ways. Some of us ask for a tiny bit—the next meal—when he's waiting to give us much more—the entire vineyard. He wants to open our eyes to blessings we haven't yet imagined. He wants to answer in marvelous ways.

In the passage about the blind men, we read, "Jesus had compassion on them" (Matthew 20:34, NIV). The Greek word that's used is *splagchnistheis.* It describes emotional compassion at "the gut level" when you are so deeply moved that your insides tremble, your stomach churns, your heart aches with compassion. You may have felt this kind of compassion when you saw a sweet little child in the grocery who whines for a moment, and the parent suddenly grabs him and gives him a hard whack and calls him a foul name. You *splaunch.* You feel compassion deep in your gut for that little guy. Or maybe you're at work, and a client starts yelling at a coworker, insulting and bawling her out in front of everyone. You're dying inside for her. That's what Jesus feels for you and for me. He is not an unmoved God, far out of reach, merely keeping the world going with as little effort as possible as if he were on some retirement plan. He's God of the earth, deeply involved in our life. He always responds to faith. Jesus' question, "What do you want me to do for you?" is not a request for information. It's an invitation to a relationship in which all needs can be met. Where do you long for God to give you sight?

What about You?

In our need we come to know the Lord more deeply than at any other time. His question comes, not simply like a clerk in a store, but like a friend who is ready to listen. W. E. Biederwolf says, "Hannah wanted only a son, but God wanted more."[2] God wanted even more than Hannah for the child to be born who would be Samuel, the prophet and judge of the people. But he also wanted more for Hannah, as we see in her song of praise. Her spiritual life reached a depth of faith and confidence in God for which all of us long.

If God came directly to you, as he did to Solomon, and asked, "What would you have me do for you?" How would you respond? Search your heart, make your prayer, and expect God's best. Remember: *Ask whatever you want in love and receive whatever he gives in love.*

Notes

1. David R. Mains, "Revival Watch," *The Partners Report* (Wheaton, Ill.: The Chapel of the Air Ministries, July 1995), 3.
2. Quoted in E. M. Bounds, *The Essentials of Prayer* (Grand Rapids, Mich.: Baker Book House, 1925), 121.

CHAPTER 15

"Where are your accusers?" Breaking the Power of Accusation

John 8:10

Oscar Wilde said, "No person is rich enough to buy back his past." But many of us have gone poor trying.

IT'S NOT A story I'm proud of. I remember a time in elementary school when I went with several of my friends to a store. One of them thought it would be a great idea to get some things without paying. He said that it was no big deal and that he'd done it before. I was reluctant at first but didn't want to appear uncool. So I went along with the idea. I honestly don't remember taking anything, but I definitely knew what was going on. As we were about to walk out, the store manager stopped us and asked us to come with him. Caught! I was scared. The manager took us into his office and said we'd been seen taking stuff. He pointed at the two-way mirrors through which he could look down the aisles. Then he told us to empty our pockets. He explained that even if only one of us had taken something and the others knew it, we were all guilty. He said he was debating whether he should call the police or our parents. Neither choice seemed good to us, but in the end it seemed better to face our parents and get it over with.

I'll never forget that feeling of getting caught. The flushing of my face, feeling like my heart would pound right out of my chest, the dry mouth, the burning in my stomach, and the regret. "How stupid could you be?" I kept saying to myself. I did a real number on myself for months to come. I was angry at my "friend" for tempting us to do something I knew was wrong. I was angry with myself for going along with it. I was angry at the store manager. And I was deeply shamed. I didn't want to talk about it with anybody. Each day I went to school with dread, fearing that someone would bring it up and make fun of me. I don't think I ever went into that store again. I couldn't bear the memory.

I think many of us think that God is like that store manager: concerned with catching us doing the wrong things. Many of us believe that God loves nothing more than catching us with our hands in the cookie jar, that God is like a highway patrol speed trap. Aha! Gotcha!

When have I been caught?

How did I respond?

How did it affect my future behavior, decisions, and relationships?

Accusation comes in a variety of forms. Our bosses or employees may point their fingers at us. Our family members may ridicule and criticize us for our mistakes. Our friends may jeer and tease us. Even strangers may accuse us, especially if our failure is public. But nothing is quite like the number we do on ourself. If we are honest, many of us have done a variety of inappropriate things and have *not* been caught, but we have felt the guilt just the same. We know we have done wrong, and we have felt that inner accusation.

How would the Lord have us handle the sense of accusation, the guilt, the shame of knowing we've done something wrong? The answer may surprise you.

What Did Jesus Do with the Guilty?

> **Jesus returned to the Mount of Olives, but early the next morning he was back again at the Temple. A crowd soon gathered, and he sat down and taught them. As he was speaking, the teachers of religious law and Pharisees brought a woman they had caught in the act of adultery.**

> **They put her in front of the crowd. "Teacher," they said to Jesus, "this woman was caught in the very act of adultery. The law of Moses says to stone her. What do you say?" They were trying to trap him into saying something they could use against him, but Jesus stooped down and wrote in the dust with his finger. They kept demanding an answer, so he stood up again and said, "All right, stone her. But let those who have never sinned throw the first stones!" Then he stooped down again and wrote in the dust. When the accusers heard this, they slipped away one by one, beginning with the oldest, until only Jesus was left in the middle of the crowd with the woman. Then Jesus stood up again and said to her, "Where are your accusers? Didn't even one of them condemn you?" "No, Lord," she said. And Jesus said, "Neither do I. Go and sin no more." (John 8:1-11)**

"Where are your accusers?" Often, we answer this question too quickly. We know what it feels like to be accused by classmates and playmates, brothers and sisters, parents and teachers, employees or employers. We especially expect that God is ready to accuse us.

In this account, the religious leaders were acting in accordance with their understanding of the law of Moses. Jesus' response, however, helps us move beyond the "letter of the law" to the spirit in which it was given. His purpose, like that of a loving parent with a dearly loved child, was not punishment but restoration. Not damnation but redemption.

Accusers aim to destroy our credibility and worth as individuals.

Now we need to set the scene here. This Gospel tells us that around dawn, Jesus gathered with his followers in the temple and began teaching. Suddenly, in this early morning hour, a woman is brought into the midst of the gathering.

All eyes are on her. Her head is hung in shame. The humiliation and shame of her oh-so-public spectacle burn on her cheeks. The rage of injustice smolders within her. Again, men are using her, she thinks. This time they seized her in her vulnerability and allowed her partner in crime to slip on his robe and escape. Again, she is being abused. Again, she is being used. Only this time in a public setting. We might imagine a hatred for men festering deep within her heart.

So there she is in front of Jesus. And then comes the taunting challenge we read in John 8:4: "Teacher," they said to Jesus, "this woman was caught in the very act of adultery. The law of Moses says to stone her. What do you say?" The real question is this: Whom were the religious leaders trying to accuse? A careful reading shows us that their target was Jesus. The woman is just a pawn. They wanted to put Jesus in a no-win situation. No matter what he answered, he would lose. We have questions like that nowadays. The old (and offensive!) line is, "So when did you stop beating your wife?" The very phrasing assumes you have been practicing that abhorrent behavior. If you say, "Never," then you are interpreted as having never stopped!

So the trap was set for Jesus. If he said, "Stone her," the Roman authorities (who alone had the power of capital punishment) would intervene, and Jesus would be in trouble for ordering capital punishment. If he said, "Don't stone her," the religious leaders would say, "See, Jesus doesn't pay attention to the law of Moses. You should not listen to him." So the taunting challenge is issued. And the goal is not information but condemnation.

Accusers aim to destroy our hope.

But what of the woman? The accusation is aimed at her judgment, her execution. I have deliberately cast this woman with a misanthropic attitude. (A misanthrope is a person who hates men, even as a misogynist is a person who hates women.) I am assuming that men have mistreated and abused her before and that she has behaved like this before. But her treatment by the religious leaders at this time is the worst of all. They are out to destroy her. I think she probably has a justified resentment of men. That doesn't necessarily excuse it, and she needs to be healed and learn the power of forgiveness. But this woman might well hate men. And as she hears the threats of judgment, she could well be losing all hope.

Accusation, whether self-inflicted or inflicted by others, puts us before the court of condemnation. We may lose all sight of hope. Arthur Dimsdale, the unconfessing adulterous minister in Nathaniel Hawthorne's *The Scarlet Letter,* portrayed the devastating effects of guilt and self-accusation. As he reflected on his own death and grave,

> [H]e questioned with himself whether the grass would ever grow on it, because an accursed thing must there be buried! . . .
>
> He longed to speak out from his own pulpit at the full height of his voice, and tell the people what he was. "I, whom you behold in these black garments of the priesthood—I, who ascend the sacred desk, and turn my pale face heavenward, taking upon myself to hold communion, in your behalf, with the Most High Omniscience—I, in whose daily life you discern the sanctity of Enoch—I, whose footsteps, as you suppose, leave a gleam along my earthly track, whereby the pilgrims that shall come after me may be guided to the regions of the blest—I, who have laid the hand of baptism upon your children—I, who have breathed the parting prayer over your dying friends, to whom the Amen sounded faintly from a world which they had quitted—I, your pastor, whom you so reverence and trust, am utterly a pollution and a lie!" . . .
>
> . . . He loved the truth and loathed the lie, as few men ever did. Therefore above all things else, he loathed his miserable self![1]

When have I felt the shame and despair of guilt?

Have I ever felt as bad as Dimsdale? Why or why not?

What did I do with those feelings?

Our guilt leaves us powerless to silence our accusers. Dimsdale, whose very name reflects the encroaching darkness in the deep valley of guilt, was powerless to break free from his crippling self-accusation. The woman crouching before Jesus and the crowd was likewise in no position to help herself. She had been caught. She was guilty. She knew that she was being used, and others knew that, too, but that didn't change her own guilt. She could do nothing but wait for judgment and speak only if spoken to.

This is an accurate picture of each of us. We are guilty. Other people use that guilt against us. Our guilt often puts us in a position of getting used and abused. But the abuse doesn't change the fact that we are sinners. And until our guilt is taken away, we're often stuck with all the abuse that gets attached to it. It's not fair—it's like kicking a person when he's down—but it's how the devil takes advantage of us in a fallen world. The evil one kicks us in our bruises. Where is our redemption?

What is the purpose of guilt?

Does God want me to feel guilty?

What if I've done something wrong and don't feel guilty?

"Where Are Your Accusers?"

When we truly understand our sin, our guilt, our humiliating stance before God, we may be cast into abject despair. Such was the case with Arthur Dimsdale. But the amazing grace of the gospel is that when we finally understand our guilt, only then can we truly understand God's nature and God's grace. As C. S. Lewis has said, "Despair is a greater sin than any that cause it." Why? Because despair says, "God, I know the sacrifice of Jesus Christ was good, but it wasn't enough to cover this." That's like saying, "God, I know you created the heavens and the earth, but you may have a hard time with the crops this year!" If God can create everything from nothing, he can certainly handle one year's crops! And if he gave his own Son for the sins of the world, he certainly didn't exclude a particular sin—when one repents and turns to him in faith.

Jesus shows us God's amazing grace in the way he deals with this woman.

Jesus understands our—and our accusers'—motivations.

Look again at the Gospel account. After the accusation is hurled, Jesus bends down and writes in the dust with his finger. I have actually enacted Jesus' methods when speaking to a youth camp or even when preaching. In the middle of a talk, I will suddenly bend down and touch the floor. What happens? Everybody starts shifting to see what I'm doing. It's instinctive. What is Jesus doing in this situation with the woman? He's doing something unexpected in order to take the attention of the crowd off of the woman. He draws them away from her and toward himself by bending down.

Are there sins I regret and for which I feel unforgiven?

Am I truly unforgiven?

What else might lie behind my feelings?

Then he writes on the ground. What is he writing? I don't believe he's doodling. Jesus doesn't doodle. Jesus doesn't waste time.

I believe Jesus is writing the Ten Commandments on the ground:

> Do not worship any other gods besides me.
> Do not make idols of any kind.
> Do not misuse the name of the LORD your God.
> Remember to observe the Sabbath day by keeping it holy.

And so on. Jesus may also be writing some allusion to the great commandments in Deuteronomy 6 and Leviticus 19:

> "You must love the Lord your God with all your heart, all your soul, and all your mind." This is the first and greatest commandment. A second is equally important: "Love your neighbor as yourself." All the other commandments and all the demands of the prophets are based on these two commandments. (Matthew 22:37-40)

Then Jesus straightens up and looks around the crowd, searching each person's heart. "All right, stone her. But let those who have never sinned throw the first stones." Then he stoops down again and continues writing. Instead of casting stones, the crowd evaporates. Their hearts of stone have been strangely moved. Some withdraw quickly, glad to be gone. Others linger in confusion. Others smolder with rage but leave when their supporters leave.

People who are wounded wound other people. Those who accuse most often are struggling with their own accusers. People who rise up indignantly against others are often dealing with those very problems in their own hearts. Whole people don't knowingly hurt people. Wounded people wound people.

When have I come under the attack of a wounded person?

How did I handle it?

What do I learn from the way Jesus handled wounded people?

But Jesus touches accusers and breaks the power of accusation. If I were Jesus, I would have said, "Let him who is without sin cast the first stone—I dare you!" Then I'd give my best righteous-glaring, sin-exposing, soul-piercing look. But what would that do? It would be antagonistic. In fact, it would be my own form of accusation! My look and words would be contaminated with humiliating anger and condemnation toward the accusers. That would be daring people. And what do people do when you dare them? Many of them may have been provoked to throw their stones.

But Jesus broke the power of accusation by turning people's attention toward their own relationship with the Lord. When he bent down the second time, he gave people the opportunity to be honest with God. He gave them time to consider their own sin without the shame that they had laid on this abused woman. He gave them space to back away without any more humiliation.

And so, without the shame of antagonism or escalating the conflict, the Bible tells us, "beginning with the oldest" the accusers begin to walk away. The elders walk away first. Until finally, no one else is there.

What a fascinating detail: "beginning with the oldest." Every word in the Bible is rich with meaning. John makes a point of saying the older people walked away first. Have you noticed that often it's the middle-aged or younger people who are so driven? "We've got to meet this goal, and you have to hold people accountable." It's usually the older Christian who has the grace to say, "Wait a minute. Give this some time. Let's figure out a different way."

The grace of Jesus gives people the opportunity to consider their own struggles and their own difficulties, without the threat of condemnation, without the threat of accusation, without the threat of punishment. *Jesus doesn't even accuse accusers!* He loves them and seeks to lead them into a redemptive process. He is gracious, even toward those who are condemning and judgmental.

Who are some of the gracious, nonjudgmental people in my life?

How do I feel when they are around?

What is it like to share my heart with them?

Do I need to share with one of them soon?

Jesus sets us free from condemnation.

Let's look again at Jesus' interaction with the crowd, but this time consider what is going on from the woman's perspective.

Jesus says, "All right, stone her. But let those who have never sinned throw the first stones." Can you imagine what she's thinking? *This is worse than I ever imagined. It's happening! This is it!* But then Jesus does something amazing. He stoops down again and begins writing. What is that all about?

There have been a few times in my life when I went to a prayer meeting when I was sure that when I walked in the door they were going to say, "Stop! Stop! Stop! We have a sinner in our midst, ladies and gentlemen! Doug Rumford's here. Doug Rumford, you must come forward, we have to deal with some issues. Here are the charges against you." Then the catalog of my horrific sins is read for all to hear. "How do you plead? Guilty? Of course, GUILTY! Aha! Throw him to the wolves!"

Have you ever felt that sort of guilt? What's wrong with my nightmare? It goes against the consistent witness of Jesus. In John 8 we see how Jesus separates us from the crowd. He doesn't humiliate a broken person in public. Broken people need tender care. Restoration is a private thing.

Jesus sets us free from condemnation by dealing with our brokenness in a way that honors our humanness. He deals with our sin, our failure, our falling short of the mark, our problems in a way that doesn't tear us down or tear us apart. He separates us from the accusing crowd so that we can experience his restoring touch.

And so Jesus isolates the woman in a holy way. When they are alone, he ministers to her. Notice that Jesus doesn't even ask the woman's side of the story. He doesn't give her the responsibility for setting herself free. He deals with the crowd before he even speaks to her. Then he asks, "Where are your accusers?" not "So was it a setup, or did you really do it?" Now she is standing in the presence of a man who has basically begun to set her free. What is she thinking? She has been liberated from the harsh judgment and condemnation of others. For the first time she catches a glimpse of a different way.

Jesus says to the woman, "Neither do I condemn you." The corrosive power of judgmentalism is neutralized by the grace of Jesus Christ. He is not a condemning God. He convicts us of sin without insulting our worth. He convicts us of sin in a way that inspires us to change and be transformed.

Now, we need to remember that this woman has been forced to be in Jesus' presence. She hasn't volunteered to go and see Jesus. We do not know whether she repented of her sin. We do not read anywhere in this passage where she says, "I believe that you are Jesus Christ, the Son of God Almighty." We know nothing about her heart. Nothing. What do we learn? We learn about Jesus' heart. We learn how he accepts people. What's required? Just to be in his presence. That's it. Simply be in his presence. He begins with acceptance, not accusation. Then, it's up to the person to respond.

Jesus sets us free from punishment.

I'm going to say something that may sound like heresy. If you trust in Jesus Christ, you will not be punished for your sins. I want you to think that through. You will not be punished for your sins. Why do I say that? Because *all the punishment was laid on Christ on the cross.*

To say that we won't be punished does not mean there won't be consequences—and some very hard consequences—that stem from our sins. These, however, are natural consequences that come as a result of what we've done. They are not punishment added by God. Punishment has to do with satisfying God's justice—and Jesus Christ's death on the cross has fully satisfied God's justice. He will chasten us to help us grow, but that must not be confused with punishment.

People who don't understand this truth can make themselves miserable. They may sabotage themselves. I know people who deny God's grace and forgiveness. As a result, they sabotage their careers and their families because that is the only way they know to punish themselves for what they have done. That is not the way God works with us. God is like a father disciplining his children.

I've been a father for more than twenty years, and I know what it's like to err on the side of punishing my children when I should discipline them. But I also know what it is like to discipline them. Punishment exacts a price, a fine, for past misbehavior. It keeps a ledger of accounts and assesses the damages. Discipline, however, enables good behavior. It is more like a coach than an accountant, more like a teacher than a judge. There's nothing more joyful than cultivating a mature child who knows right from wrong and who values the right. *In discipline, the focus is not on making up for bad behavior, but on shaping up for good behavior.* That's what Hebrews 12:7-8 tells us:

> As you endure this divine discipline, remember that God is treating you as his own children. Whoever heard of a child who was never disciplined? If God doesn't discipline you as he does all of his children, it means that you are illegitimate and are not really his children after all.

Our God is not a shaming God. Those who trust in Christ have this confidence: "So now there is no condemnation for those who belong to Christ Jesus" (Romans 8:1). We see here a beautiful picture of God's unconditional love. Jesus doesn't wait for the woman to meet the conditions of expressing repentance or faith. He loves her unconditionally. The key is, how will she respond? Will she accept that love and bear the fruit of a changed life?

Whom do I know who needs this unconditional love?

How can I share it with that person?

How should I pray for that person and for an opportunity to share?

Jesus' discipline is geared toward our restoration. Jesus uses accusations as soul-searching questions. He wants people to take their own heart condition far more seriously.

After Jesus silences the accusers and sets this woman free, he says to her, "Didn't even one of them condemn you? . . . Neither do I. Go and sin no more" (John 8:10-11). Jesus doesn't simply conclude with excusing her. He exhorts her toward a new way of living.

If we could expand the paragraph here, I think he says to her, "Now go, and stop leading your life of sin. You're better than that. You are such a valuable person. I don't want you to allow yourself to be abused in these ways. Come on now. I want to teach you a different way to live."

Does he take her hand and help her stand? Jesus calls her to a life of honor. We can imagine her changing from behaving like a prostitute to living like a princess. She walks with an entirely different bearing, as if she wears the royal robes of faith and the crown of salvation on her head.

How have I responded to Jesus' simple command "Go and sin no more"?

Are there particular areas where this applies right now? What am I going to do?

WHAT ABOUT YOU?

An encounter with God's grace is an invitation to change. When you meet love, you want to love. We are not liberated for license but for liberty. Freedom is not found in doing whatever we want to do whenever we want. Freedom is being able to live life with wisdom, not by impulse. Freedom, real freedom, is being able to choose on the basis of godly desires, not because of some necessity that drives us. This woman found freedom and she changed.

I read recently of a girl who said about her father, "You know, when he yells at me, I just want to be worse. But when he is nice to me, I want to do what he asks." Somehow, it's God's kindness, not the threat of punishment, that leads us to transformation.

When we deal with our own guilt, we often battle accusation, a sense of punishment, self-condemnation, or discouragement. Those are not from God but from the self. God's voice says, "I don't condemn you. Go and sin no more."

He loves us as we are but calls us to break with sin and lead a life of honor.

Oscar Wilde said, "No person is rich enough to buy back his past." But many of us have gone poor trying. We've impoverished our relationships because we've felt so rotten within ourself that we couldn't be there for others. We haven't lived boldly for the cause of Christ because we're held back by our self-condemnation and shame. We've impoverished those relationships that are closest to us, and we've cheated God.

Jesus breaks the power of accusation. When you hear those accusers, within or without, show them Jesus, stooped down and writing in the dust. Then hear his words of life to you: "Neither do I condemn you. Go, and lead a new life in me."

NOTES

1. Nathaniel Hawthorne, "The Interior of a Heart" in *The Scarlet Letter* (New York: New American Library, 1959), 139–141.

CHAPTER 16

"Will you also leave me?" Testing the Limits of Commitment

John 6:67

In some, religion exists as a dull habit, in others as an acute fever. Religion as a dull habit is not that for which Christ lived and died. WILLIAM JAMES[1]

WE HAVE DEAR friends (John and Suzi), who have been married for over fifteen years and have two children. Several years ago Suzi was diagnosed with multiple sclerosis. She did quite well for a while but has found her mobility gradually limited by the disease. John and Suzi have sought prayer, medical treatment, and still more prayer, but for the present they are faced with adjusting to this chronic condition.

When I was talking and praying with John one day, I asked him how he was doing with all this. I will never forget his answer: "Well, Doug, God is teaching me to walk more slowly." To walk more slowly—not to push his wife to keep up with him nor to leave her behind, but to adjust his pace to that of his life partner. John is teaching me the cost of commitment.

Our life is shaped by commitments. When a child is born, many parents make a commitment to God through baptism or dedication that shapes the spiritual priorities of their home. In the marriage ceremony, a man and woman make a commitment that they will stand by each other "in plenty and in want, in joy and in sorrow, in sickness and in health." In school, sports, careers, and relationships, we make commitments that determine either the narrow boundaries or the broad expanse of our life.

These commitments have power to make or break our life. There comes a time when we learn that commitment is costly. When the going gets tough, the tough may get going, as they say, but many just go away. Some dig in, but some bale out. It happens when the first-aid training is over and we are faced with using lifesaving methods to save a real life, when the honeymoon is over and we learn what marriage is all about, when the childbirth classes are over and we are leaving the hospital with our child. It happens when we receive our diplomas and learn how little we really know about the real world or when the business is on the line and one decision could make or break us.

Commitment to Jesus is costly. Of course, there are countless benefits, but the time comes when his teachings make us uncomfortable. He challenges us in ways that make us examine our fundamental commitment. He asks us to walk at his pace, not our own. Such a situation is recorded in John 6. After the strong, and in many ways offensive, teaching that "unless you eat the flesh of the Son of Man and drink his blood, you cannot have eternal life within you," the crowds began to leave him. We continue to read,

> **Even his disciples said, "This is very hard to understand. How can anyone accept it?"**
>
> **Jesus knew within himself that his disciples were complaining, so he said to them, "Does this offend you? Then what will you think if you see me, the Son of Man, return to heaven again? It is the Spirit who gives eternal life. Human effort accomplishes nothing. And the very words I have spoken to you are spirit and life. But some of you**

don't believe me." (For Jesus knew from the beginning who didn't believe, and he knew who would betray him.) Then he said, "That is what I meant when I said that people can't come to me unless the Father brings them to me."

At this point many of his disciples turned away and deserted him. Then Jesus turned to the Twelve and asked, "Are you going to leave, too?"

Simon Peter replied, "Lord, to whom would we go? You alone have the words that give eternal life. We believe them, and we know you are the Holy One of God."

Then Jesus said, "I chose the twelve of you, but one is a devil." He was speaking of Judas, son of Simon Iscariot, one of the Twelve, who would betray him. (John 6:60-71)

"Are You Going to Leave, Too?"

Are we religious consumers or committed followers?

There's a difference between being religious consumers and committed followers of Christ. Religious consumers view faith as a means of self-enrichment and self-satisfaction. Their commitment is based on what the faith adds to their lives. Committed followers, on the other hand, have an entirely different mind-set. Their commitment is a response to God's love and to God's valid claim on their lives. Their goal is not self-enrichment, but personal transformation that seeks to honor God. Their goal is not self-satisfaction, but making their lives a "living and holy sacrifice—the kind he will accept" (Romans 12:1).

Do I see any tendencies in myself to be a religious consumer?

Such single-hearted commitment to God was seen clearly in the life of Jim Elliot. As a student at Wheaton College, Jim wrote in his diary: "God, I pray Thee, light these idle sticks of my life, that I may burn for Thee. Consume my life, my God, for it is Thine. I seek not a long life, but a full one, like you, Lord Jesus." As his passion for missions grew, he wrote of his unwavering focus on Christ, "One treasure, a single eye, and a sole Master."

Such consecration led him to establish a mission work among the unreached Quichuas Indians of Ecuador. Then he worked diligently to reach the savage tribe known as the Aucas. He prayed and planned for six years. At the age of twenty-nine, his dream was realized: He took an Auca by the hand. Two days later, on Sunday, January 8, 1956, the men for whom Jim Elliott had prayed for six years killed him and his four companions. That sacrifice, however, eventually opened the way for that tribe and countless others to come to Christ.[2]

Perhaps no epitaph better fits the commitment of Jim Elliot than that of his own words: "He is no fool who gives what he cannot keep to gain what he cannot lose."[3]

But many of us never arrive at the point where Jim Elliot began. We may say we want to know what God wants for our life, but when he shows us, we're not too sure! To be candid, most of us really want what *we* want, not what God wants. We focus on all that there is to lose. We are like religious consumers who make conditional commitments. We measure the return we receive on our investment of faith. If the return is less than we expect or demands even more investment, we give in or give up. The question for us, then, is this: To what extent does the religious consumer mentality control our life?

What conditions have I put on my commitment to the Lord?

Religious consumers are driven by their needs rather than by God's purposes.

In John 6 we read that Jesus had been teaching a crowd of over five thousand men plus women and children. As mealtime arrived, there were no supplies nearby, so Jesus fed them. After Jesus fed them, they wanted to make him king because they saw him meet their needs. Their agenda was simple: They were hungry. He supplied the food, and that was all they needed to be willing to put a crown on Jesus' head. But Jesus slipped away instead, retreating to a quiet place where he could get reoriented with his Father.

Do I expect him to meet specific criteria that I have established concerning areas such as my lifestyle and location?

Maybe he was asking, "Father what's this king stuff all about?" Jesus was faced with this several times during his ministry. Each time he turned to the Father's agenda rather than his own.

The disciples took a boat over to the other side of the lake, and, following his prayer time, Jesus walked across the water to the disciples. But the next morning that whole crowd of people came to Jesus on the other side of the lake. Their devotion would have pleased him *if* it had arisen from selfless commitment. But they came, not to *know more* of Christ, but to *get more* from him. They came, not for the expression of commitment, but simply for more bread to consume. They had missed the meaning of the sign.

Some who initially profess faith in Christ seem to fall back when he doesn't meet their expectations. In the mid-to-late 1970s, many celebrities were professing to be saved. Jimmy Carter was the evangelical president of the United States. One magazine even dubbed one year "The Year of the Evangelical." In 1977 the first Christian record from B. J. Thomas was released. Then Bob Dylan released *Slow Train Comin',* and people began to learn of his new commitment to Christ. Christians, especially of the younger generation, were ecstatic. Dylan was one of "the biggies." He seemed to give a new credibility to faith. But his commitment was short lived.

Many years later, speaking of his Christian commitment "which blindsided his liberal, secular fan base," Dylan said:

> I don't think I'm tangible to myself. I mean, I think one thing today, and I think another thing tomorrow. I change during the course of a day. I wake and I'm one person, and when I go to sleep I know for certain I'm somebody else. I don't know *who* I am most of the time. It doesn't even matter to me. . . .
>
> I find religiosity and philosophy in the music. I don't find it anywhere else. Songs like "Let Me Rest on a Peaceful Mountain" or "I Saw the Light"—that's my religion. I don't adhere to rabbis,

> preachers, evangelists, all of that. I've learned more from the songs than I've learned from any of this kind of entity. The songs are my lexicon. I believe the songs.[4]

There are many stories of people who began and never finished. The whys are as varied as the people, but the fundamental reason often orbits around this principle: We will ultimately leave Christ if we follow him solely for our own needs. Why? Because there will come a time when Christ will disappoint us. If our focus is on our satisfaction rather than the truth, we will not be able to endure, because following Jesus means dying to self.

Have I gone through times of lessening commitment because of my disappointment in God?

Have I seen this in others?

Religious consumers want Jesus on their own terms. The crowds were fair-weather followers. They wanted Jesus on their own terms. They wanted to make Jesus king. But they were not thinking so much of surrendering to his will as of feasting on his generosity. When they found out that kingship had to do with faith, not food, they dropped the crown and left.

Are we ready to have a Lord only when we can crown him?

Are we ready to have a Lord only when we can announce the coronation?

Are we ready to have a Lord only when we are fulfilled in the process?

Are we ready to have a Lord only when we can set the agenda?

Faith is not a menu from which we can pick and choose. It is not a buffet of optional beliefs and practices. In our age of endless options and "the-customer's-always-right," we find it difficult to accept that we do not set the criteria for salvation or for discipleship. We must face the fact that Jesus' comfort comes with his call to the cross. His provision comes with his call to contentment. His power comes with his call to service. *His yoke is easy in the sense that it fits us; it is not easy in the sense that it conforms to us. We are conformed to it.*

When you and I come not for the sake of truth but with our own agendas, we will be disappointed. When we come not to honor God but to fulfill our own desires, we will be disappointed. When we come for the purpose of self-gain instead of self-yielding, we will be disappointed.

Religious consumers simply go through the motions. We can go through the outward motions but keep our heart from God. Judas stayed with Jesus as a pretender. We don't know precisely what his motivation was. In John's Gospel we're told that Judas was the treasurer for the disciples. He would skim a little "fee" off the top for himself. Maybe Jesus' ministry was doing pretty well, and Judas was making a good living off it. We don't know. But for whatever reason, Judas continued to stay with Jesus, and he was not honest with himself, with Jesus, or with the other disciples. At least the deserters were honest enough to desert.

Judas ended up being a follower of Jesus in name only. In the end, Judas did what Judas wanted to do. There is danger in that many of us tolerate a Judas factor in our life. We keep one section of our heart absolutely closed to God.

Commitment Unlocks the Power of Discipleship

The question at the heart of this message is, What does it mean to follow Jesus?

David Livingstone was the missionary who opened the jungles of Africa to the gospel—literally chopping and hacking his way through the thick, uncharted underbrush. He was supported by an English missionary society. One day he received a message from them: "Dr. Livingstone, we wish to send other men to come to your aid. Is there a good road for them to follow?" Livingstone wrote back: "If they are men who need a road, I don't want them."

At the beginning of this chapter I asserted the principle that our life is shaped by commitments. These commitments have power to make or break our life. I recall a quote

Is there a part (or parts) of my life I have kept back from the Lord?

How do these "held-back" areas affect my spiritual vitality?

from an architect: "First we build our buildings, then our buildings build us." The same can be said of our commitments. We make our commitments; then our commitments make us. What kind of commitments have you made in building your life?

If we are dissatisfied with life, an inventory of our experience will most likely reveal two things. Either we are investing ourself too much in things that are unworthy, or we are not truly investing in worthy commitments.

Commitment-powered living teaches us that people rise highest when the commitment is greatest. One of Napoleon's artillery officers, at the siege of Toulon, built a battery in such an exposed position that he was told he would never find men to man it. But Napoleon had a sure instinct for what was required. He put up a placard: "The battery of men without fear," and it was always manned. As James Stewart has said, "This is no time to be offering a reduced, milk-and-water religion. Far too often the world has been presented with a mild and undemanding half-Christianity. The gospel has been emasculated long enough. Preach Christ to-day in the total challenge of His high, imperious claim. Some will be scared, and some offended: but some, and they the most worth winning, will kneel in homage at His feet."[5]

Commitment unlocks the energy of life. I have found time and again that circumstances adapt and resources develop to support my commitments. (Note: For more information on the power of commitment, see my book *SoulShaping: Taking Care of Your Spiritual Life* [Wheaton, Ill.: Tyndale House Publishers, 1996], 91–92.) The following statements are my own "theses" about commitment. They are not fully developed, nor are they arranged in any particular order.

- Commitment is a decision to invest yourself in a course of action. This decision satisfies your mind, energizes your will, and engages your emotions because it is based on your vision and on your values.

- Commitment can never be a "mental thing" alone. That only leads to a double standard for life, to hypocrisy.
- Commitment is the heart's answer to life's important questions. Why am I here? Who do I love? How can I help? What is my gift to life?
- Commitment is the decision that keeps you "tacking into the wind" even when the surf gets rough.
- Commitment is a decision that makes many other decisions unnecessary.
- A commitment is based on logic and emotion, both functioning as a team.
- A commitment is a promise to yourself.
- A commitment must be worthy of the name. It is an investment of your life energy and personal resources in proportion to the value of the object.
- Commitment is the decision to direct your life toward a goal that demands your best. This decision awakens your passion, builds up your self-value, and expresses that you value yourself and others. When we commit ourself, we find that God releases unbelievable power into our life.

When the disciples submitted to waiting upon the Lord between Jesus' ascension and Pentecost, they demonstrated their commitment. They put their lives on the line for God. And God poured out the Holy Spirit. God gave what they needed to fulfill the commitment they made. This is a principle of life. In his book, *The Scottish Himalayan Expedition,* W. H. Murray tells his explorer's experience:

> Until one is committed, there is hesitancy, the chance to draw back, always ineffectiveness. Concerning all acts of initiative there is one elementary truth, the ignorance which kills

> countless ideas and splendid plans: that the moment one definitely commits oneself, then Providence moves too.
>
> All sorts of things occur to help one that would otherwise never have occurred. A whole stream of events issues from the decision, raising in one's favor all manner of incidents and meetings and material assistance no [one] would have believed would have come his way.[6]

Hesitancy and halfhearted commitment rob us. Whatever we hold back from God is paltry compared with what we lose. We hold back our favorite trinkets and lose God's greatest treasures.

Unconditional commitment is the price God asks for the gift he has given us. It does not become the basis for our salvation—that is ours as a free gift through Christ. But unconditional commitment is the basis for a vital life of faith.

After hearing a returned missionary from China, a young lady walked up to her and said, "I'd give the world to have your experience."

"That," said the missionary, "is exactly what it cost me."[7]

How do I define commitment?

When has commitment alone carried me through a difficult situation?

When has my commitment failed?

What made the difference?

What about You?

Committed followers see the futility of all other options. When the crowds left Jesus, his disciples stayed. He wanted them to say why they were staying. They could have been staying out of grudging obligation or fear of looking even more foolish after having followed him for so long. Why were they staying?

> **Simon Peter replied, "Lord, to whom would we go? You alone have the words that give eternal life. We believe them, and we know you are the Holy One of God." (John 6:69)**

Even when Jesus' words are hard, they are "good hard." We know they are true. We know they strip away the illusions that deceive us. They are honest feedback, accurate portraits of reality. Only the truth sets us free.

As tempting as it may be at times to walk away from our faith, we know all too well that nothing else in this world satisfies like Jesus. One of the most powerful testimonies to enduring discipleship comes from the pen of the fourth-century church historian Eusebius. He tells the story of the martyrdom of Polycarp in Smyrna, Asia Minor, who may have been the last survivor of those who had talked with the eyewitnesses of Jesus. Eusebius writes about the appearance of Polycarp before the Roman proconsul:

When have I been tempted to walk away from my faith?

How did I respond?

What kept me or brought me back?

> He stepped forward and was asked by the proconsul if he really was Polycarp. When he said yes, the proconsul urged him to deny the charge.
>
> "Respect your years!" he exclaimed, adding similar appeals regularly made on such occasions. "Swear by Caesar's fortune: Change your attitude; say: Away with the godless!"
>
> But Polycarp, with his face set, looked at all the crowd in the stadium and waved his hand towards them, sighed, looked up to heaven, and cried: "Away with the godless!"
>
> The governor pressed him further: "Swear, and I will set you free: Execrate Christ."
>
> "For eighty-six years," replied Polycarp, "I have been his servant, and he has never done me wrong. How can I blaspheme my king who saved me?"
>
> "I have wild beasts," said the proconsul. "I shall throw you to them, if you don't change your attitude."
>
> "Call them," replied the old man. "We cannot change our attitude if it means a change from better to worse. But it is a splendid thing to change from cruelty to justice."
>
> "If you make light of the beasts," retorted the governor, "I'll have you destroyed by fire, unless you change your attitude."

> Polycarp answered, "The fire you threaten burns for a time and is soon extinguished. There is a fire you know nothing about—the fire of the judgement to come and of eternal punishment, the fire reserved for the ungodly. But why do you hesitate? Do what you want.". . .
>
> The proconsul was amazed, and sent the crier to stand in the middle of the arena and announce three times:
>
> "Polycarp has confessed that he is a Christian.". . . Then a shout went up from every throat that Polycarp must be burnt alive. . . .
>
> The rest followed in less time than it takes to describe: The crowds rushed to collect logs and faggots from workshop and public baths. . . . When the pyre was ready . . . Polycarp prayed:
>
> "O Father of thy beloved and blessed Son, Jesus Christ, through whom we have come to know thee, the God of angels and powers and all creation, and of the whole family of the righteous who live in thy presence; I bless thee for counting me worthy of this day and hour, that in the number of the martyrs I may partake of Christ's cup, to the resurrection of eternal life of both soul and body in the imperishability that is the gift of the Holy Spirit."
>
> When he had offered up the Amen and completed his prayer, the men in charge lit the fire, and a great flame shot up.[8]

Commitment is the fire that fuels the life of faith and our witness in the world. When tested, we find a faith more precious than gold, refined by the fire. When tested, even the world is forced to stand in awe.

Notes

1. Quoted in Thomas R. Kelly, *A Testament of Devotion* (New York: Harper & Row, 1941), 53.
2. Elisabeth Elliot, *The Shadow of the Almighty* (Grand

Rapids, Mich.: Zondervan Publishing House, 1958), 247.

3. Ibid.
4. David Gates, "Dylan Revisited," *Newsweek,* 6 October 1997.
5. James S. Stewart, *Heralds of God* (Grand Rapids, Mich.: Baker Book House, 1946), 26–27.
6. Julia Cameron, *The Artist's Way* (New York: G. P. Putnam's Sons, 1992), 66–67.
7. John Haggai, *Winning over Pain, Fear and Worry* (New York: Inspirational Press, 1991), 447–448.
8. Eusebius, *History of the Church* 4.15, quoted in *Eerdmans' Handbook to the History of Christianity* (England: Lion Publishing, 1977), 81.

CHAPTER 17

"Why do you worry?" Seeing the Lies That Lead to Worry

Matthew 6:28

Worry does not empty tomorrow of its sorrow.
It empties today of its strength.
CORRIE TEN BOOM

IN FIFTY YEARS of ministry, John Wesley, founder of Methodism, faced countless challenges that could have consumed him many times over if he had been given to worry. He and his brother Charles were chased from pulpits and towns for their "unorthodox" ways. They were tested financially, physically, and spiritually. It is even reported that John Wesley had a very unhappy marriage. In spite of these struggles, he maintained his confidence in God. He said, "Ten thousand cares trouble me no more than ten thousand hairs upon my head. Yes, I feel certain things, and at times I may even grieve over them, but I fret at nothing." Perhaps an incident early in his ministry helped cultivate his holy optimism. He wrote in his *Journal,* "Today I visited one who was ill in bed. She had buried seven of her family in six months, and had just heard that her beloved husband was cast away at sea. I asked, 'Don't you fret at any of these things?' She answered with a loving smile, 'Oh, no! How can I fret at anything which is in the will of God? Let him take all besides: he has given himself. I have learned to love and praise him every moment.'"[1]

For most of us, worry is a way of life. It's a part of every day. When asked to imagine a day without care, one friend said, "I think I'd either be an infant or a demented old man. I don't think conscious people can ever be free from worry." Not only is worry a way of life, worry is a *weight* of life. It is a burden on our life, making everything heavier and making us weaker.

Worry is no small problem. Surveys have found that worry is an epidemic, especially in Western society. In his book *Every Other Bed,* Mike Gorman, former executive director of the National Mental Health Committee, states that half of all hospital beds in the United States are occupied by people suffering from mental disturbance. Many of those people are suffering from complications of stress, tension, and worry.[2] We are horrified that approximately fifty-five thousand American soldiers died in the Vietnam War. But what do we make of the fact that over 350,000 people die every year from heart disease—much of which is the result of hypertension, anxiety, and worry?

Where does worry come from? Is there any way we can break free from it? In the Greek, *worry* is based on two words that have been brought together, meaning "to divide the mind." A person who is worried is carrying on a constant debate in her mind: "I really want to do this, but what about that? Will God take care of me? Is this—or that—the right decision?" We go back and forth, playing a soul-draining game of mental Ping-Pong.

Our word *worry* comes from the Old English word *wyrgan.* To me that sounds like *werewolf*—and that's an image of what it means. It means "to grab by the throat and strangle." The word conveys being choked, strangled by cares, as when an animal attacks, going right for the throat. When you and I allow worry to put a stranglehold on our life, we suffocate. Our enthusiasm is stifled; our energy is drained; and our spirit is choked because we are caught in the jaws of anxiety.

In the Sermon on the Mount, Jesus helps us to recognize

and overcome the dangers of a divided, worry-strangled life.

> **So I tell you, don't worry about everyday life—whether you have enough food, drink, and clothes. Doesn't life consist of more than food and clothing? Look at the birds. They don't need to plant or harvest or put food in barns because your heavenly Father feeds them. And you are far more valuable to him than they are. Can all your worries add a single moment to your life? Of course not.**
>
> **And why worry about your clothes? Look at the lilies and how they grow. They don't work or make their clothing, yet Solomon in all his glory was not dressed as beautifully as they are. And if God cares so wonderfully for flowers that are here today and gone tomorrow, won't he more surely care for you? You have so little faith!**
>
> **So don't worry about having enough food or drink or clothing. Why be like the pagans who are so deeply concerned about these things? Your heavenly Father already knows all your needs, and he will give you all you need from day to day if you live for him and make the Kingdom of God your primary concern.**
>
> **So don't worry about tomorrow, for tomorrow will bring its own worries. Today's trouble is enough for today. (Matthew 6:25-34)**

Looking at Worry the Wrong Way

Jesus understands the practical needs of life. In this passage he calls us to face the realities in order to break free from worry's stranglehold. He exposes the failure of worry and invites us to trust God for our daily survival.

Worry is a weed that grows in the garden of careless thoughts. Worry grows from the seeds of misplaced concerns, misdirected efforts, and misunderstood priorities.

The point Jesus makes is that worry itself is not realistic. Some people say to me, "I am realistic, that's why I worry." The fact is, however, that worry distorts reality.

Have you ever looked through a pair of binoculars from the wrong end? Instead of looking through the eyepieces, you look through the other end. What happens? Everything looks much farther away. Have things really moved farther away? No. You're just looking through the wrong end of the binoculars.

That's how many people treat God when they worry. They look at God through the wrong end of their worry binoculars, and God seems so very, very far away. Then they turn those binoculars around and look at their problems. And the problems look closer and bigger than ever. Has reality changed? No. You're just looking through the wrong lens. What if we look at God through the eyepiece of promises and see how much bigger he really is? What if we look at our problems through that eyepiece also and see how much smaller they are in comparison with the Lord?

Which lenses do I use to look at God and my problems?

Many people claim that worry is pragmatic. On closer examination, we see that worry, according to the Bible, is foolishness. Worry is like a mirror in a fun house. It distorts reality. I don't look in a fun house mirror to figure what I really look like. When you and I worry, we are living as if there is no God. We surrender to lies that have no theological truth.

On a scale of one to ten, with one being "big-time worrier" and ten being "total trust in God," how would I rate myself?

Three Lies That Lead to Worry

In Matthew 6 Jesus teaches us that there are three lies that lead to worry.

The here and now is more important than eternal priorities.

Are there areas of life where I'm especially vulnerable to worry?

That's the first lie of worry. Worry distorts life and its values. For example, there are people who say, "I couldn't go to church this past week. I'm really sorry. It's just that I work hard all week slugging through six days, morning till night. Sunday is my only day to sleep in, relax, read the paper, and do my lawn. I may get to church someday—but not until life slows down a bit." Such a person is leading his life in terms of earthly pressures and pleasures. When it comes to eternal priorities, such as attending church, where a person can reset his life compass, he can't find the time.

Worry says, "Earthly things are most important." So when you get in trouble financially or in some other area of life, you begin to worry about how you will solve the problem. You seek earthly solutions and churn and churn instead of looking to God. When you look to the Lord, you say things like, "God, I've made some mistakes. I repent of those mistakes I've made. Now lead me out of this." Or, "Lord, you know there's very little I can control about this situation. I trust you to guide and provide." Developing a God-ward focus can help us over difficulties large and small.

One Sunday morning I woke up and looked out our front window. The trees and bushes in our front yard were covered with snow. That's a very unusual sight when you live in the central valley of California! I rubbed my eyes and looked again. What did I really see? What I took for snow was really toilet paper! We were the victims of a teenage prank.

As a preacher, I like to ease into Sunday morning. I need to pray, to focus on the service and the message. I don't want distractions. I would have let the toilet paper remain in the yard, but there was one major problem: They had also papered my neighbor's bushes. That was not a good thing. So I began to worry, thinking I needed to go out and clean that up. But I needed to go over my sermon and didn't have much time. I thought about waking up our boys, whose friends were no doubt to blame! I fussed that "of course, this just had to happen today, Sunday, of all days." I thought about installing security lights and sirens that would go off if such intruders ever entered our yard at night again. I think you get the idea—I was *not* responding in a godly way! I was worrying about how to get it cleaned up and how to protect against future problems. Then it was as if the Lord

In this example, a small inconvenience spurred a significant "worry" reaction. How do I respond to the little hassles of life?

How could the phrase "Is life not more than . . . ?" help me deal with a current worry?

simply said, "Stop worrying and start doing!" It sounded like something my own father would say. So I dressed and went out to the yard.

You know what I did? I cleaned the whole thing up in about ten minutes. And I prayed for the kids who did it. And after that I felt free. I didn't believe the lie that these earthly things are more important than heavenly things. I thought to myself, *I'm not going to be mad at these kids.* Of course, it was inconvenient and disruptive, but in a few minutes the whole thing was clean, and I felt great because I had connected with God instead of being controlled by my normal reaction.

We could paraphrase Jesus' words with a number of applications. "Is life not more than . . .

- cleaning up after your yard has been toilet papered?
- continuing a grudge match that's been going between you and someone else?
- making it to the top by stepping on other people to get there?

"Is life not more than . . . ?" Say those words whenever you're facing a situation where the earthly things seem to be closing in on you. Is not life more than this? When I go to meet God, my yard won't even be a memory. When I get to heaven, every message I've preached won't even be a memory. When I stand before the Lord, the only thing that will matter is my heart. And my heart is shaped by each choice I make. Instead of a worry-based choice, I want to develop the habit of faith, seeing things in light of the eternal perspective.

The first lie that leads to worry is that earthly things are more important than eternal priorities. Tim Hansel, founder of Ignite! Ministries, says, "Worry often gives a small thing a big shadow." By faith, we shine the light of God on the small thing and drive that shadow away.

You are not going to be taken care of.

The second big lie that leads to worry is the assertion that God won't take care of us. This belief is articulated both directly and indirectly.

It may surprise you, but church ministry provides ample fodder to feed the worry beast within. There are so many needs and so many challenges that it's tough not to worry. Every year around church budget time, my worries used to go up three or four levels. On the whole, I didn't think much about the budget during the rest of the year. Things usually went along with various ups and downs, but we managed. But every fall, when we were putting together the next year's budget, my financial concerns escalated. I would be intimidated by the numbers and wonder how God could possibly pull this budget off. I'd pray, "Lord, I know you've been good in the past, but I just don't know about next year. . . ."

As you read this, you think, *Absurd! Pastor Doug, you of all people should know that God provides!* Right! But have you ever felt that way about *your* budget? "God, I know you've provided in the past, but this time . . . it may be just a little too much."

There are other areas that stir worry in the church. Who will be our church leaders? Who will advise our youth and teach our children's classes? How will we meet the requests of our missionaries? How can we reach out to the unchurched? How can we visit all the sick and inactive members of the congregation? If we thought long enough, we could create a list of worries that would fill pages and pages. The result is that we are overwhelmed by the needs. Worry sets in like a thick fog. We can't see clearly, so we often sit and stew, going nowhere.

Jesus tells us to turn from the situation that causes worry and look instead at the abundant evidence that God cares. Jesus says, "Consider the birds." At the heart of our faith in God's provision is the theological fact that we are of supreme value to God. If God provides for his other creatures, we can trust that he will provide for us. When we worry, we not only see ourself as somehow unworthy of God's care, but we are viewing God as care-less. That is, very bluntly, a lie. God has created this marvelous world and created us in love. If he keeps the planet spinning in its orbit (have you ever worried about that?) and makes the sun rise every morning (do you worry about that?), how much more will he provide for us as we continue in the discipleship orbit of the Son!

During my first two years of seminary I served in a Baptist church in Bedford, Massachusetts. Of the many special people there, Paul and Elsa became dear friends. They were a couple in their early sixties, who knew and shared the joy of the Lord. Paul was a schoolteacher, and Elsa was a nurse, who worked in order to provide the financial means necessary to care for their developmentally disabled grown daughter.

On my last day there, in May 1977, Paul and Elsa arrived early, before the evening service. They asked to speak to Sarah and me privately. They shared how much they had enjoyed our two years with their congregation. He handed me a card but said, "Now before you open it, we need to tell a story.

"Elsa and I have been praying for you two daily for the past few weeks. One morning the Lord impressed on my heart that we were to give you something special. I was a bit surprised by what he seemed to want, but I prayed about it and decided to talk it over with Elsa."

"What Paul didn't know," chimed in Elsa, with a sparkle in her eye, "was that the Lord was saying the same thing to me."

When they discussed it together, they were pleasantly surprised to find that God had put the same idea on their hearts at the same time!

"God wants you to have this! So go ahead and open the card!"

I opened it, and out fell a check.

"We had each written down the amount the Lord told us on a piece of paper, traded papers, and opened them at the same time—and it was the same amount."

It was a check for five hundred dollars! From this dear couple who had little extra to share.

"We felt that the Lord wanted you to have this as you start your family."

I was speechless. Sarah and I both began to cry. How could they have known that we had been praying about starting a family? The gift of money itself was amazing, but the last comment showed the hand of God in a way I had never seen it before. He moved through others to supply a need we hadn't shared with another soul.

I have never been able to share that story without tears welling up in my eyes. Even as I type it now, tears are running down my cheeks. God is so good. And his love is so sweet. God provides. Worry denies or distracts us from the evidence that God takes care of us every single day. The Lord used Paul and Elsa to convince me, as we stood poised on the brink of ministry, that he literally knows our needs before we even ask him. Bless the Lord—and bless his people who listen and are part of his provision!

God values us and will take care of us. Worry wants us to deny that and be eaten up with concern over our daily—and long-term—needs.

It's all up to you.

This may be the biggest lie of all. A worry mind-set is rooted in stubborn self-sufficiency. We think we need to have all the answers, think up all the ideas, and do all the work. Therefore, if we don't have the answer, can't think of an idea, or can't work, we're in big trouble.

At the basis of much of our worry is pride and individualism. We don't want to appear to need help. We don't want to depend on others. We think we have to do it all ourself. This is not something most people admit. In fact, few people see these factors at the heart of worry. But consider the fact that the ordinary church, even the smallest, usually has significant human and material resources to deal with most problems. There are plumbers and bookkeepers, teachers and tradespeople, grandparents, parents, and children. Some have financial resources,

Am I likely to doubt God's provision?

When has he provided for me recently and in the past?

How can I use God's past provision to cultivate my hope?

and some have talent and experience, and all have the love of Christ. If you had a problem and you searched your fellowship, do you think the resources would be there to help you? Your answer, most likely, is yes. Now comes the tough part: Are you willing to make your need known? If not, why not?

One of the most powerful antidotes to worry is community. When we develop vital relationships, we develop spiritual, mental, emotional, and material lines of support. We can both admit our needs and also freely give of ourself to help our brothers and sisters in Christ. "It's *not all up to me!"* Say it aloud right now.

Jesus bluntly addresses our misguided self-sufficiency when he says, "Can all your worries add a single moment to your life?" (Matthew 6:27). Will worrying lengthen your life? According to scientific studies, you'll be what they call a "flat-liner" (referring to the cessation of the heart beating as viewed on a heart monitor) a whole lot sooner if you worry.

In what ways have I been snared by this lie that it's all up to me?

How has that affected my tendency to worry?

Are there areas of concern I have right now that could be addressed by calling upon others to support me?

Are there people I could help?

An alternate reading of this verse is, "Who of you by worrying can add a single cubit to his span of height?" I remember going to see my new physician for the first time. He measured me and said, "Doug, you're really 5 feet 11½ inches." I had always thought I was 6 feet! I was kind of proud of my height. People would ask how tall I was, and I would answer 6 feet. Then my doctor told me, "No, you are about 5 feet 11½ inches." (He also told me things about my weight that I'm sure are lies!) Still, no matter how much I worry, I haven't grown even a half inch taller. Not a bit taller. Worry does nothing. Our life changes, not through doubt, anxiety, and worry, but through faith, hope, and love.

How Do We Break Free?

I may be meddling with what is possibly a lifetime habit of yours. In fact, you may have cultivated this habit of worry with great care. Some of us have certain areas we really know how to worry about. When we are trying to go to sleep at night, we turn to our favorite worry. I don't know why, but it's what we do. You won't break a lifetime of habit through reading one book chapter. But I want to give you four principles that correct the lies we have already talked about. Try to apply these. Our heavenly Father wants you to break free of worry's stranglehold.

Cultivate a deepening assurance of God's love.

God loves you. That's where we start. Nothing else can put worries to rest more quickly than knowing that God loves you and learning to say to yourself, "God loves me. I am not going to be destroyed."

I remember a man associated with our congregation who was going through a financial crisis. A business he had invested in was on the verge of collapse. He faced the loss of his life savings. His retirement plans would have to be severely altered. He even faced the possibility of having to sell his home. But he said to me, "It's not my wife or my life. I'll get through it." He knew that God loved him. And God did get him through it. It did cost him dearly, though the crisis didn't touch those two things that he said were closest to him—his wife and his life. He trusted God and began again.

Jesus says this very clearly just by a simple reference in Matthew 6:26: "Your heavenly Father feeds [the birds]." Your heavenly Father. Up to that point in time, a Jew would never have called God "Father." When Jesus taught them to pray, "Our Father in heaven," it stunned them. We don't appreciate the impact of this in our day because we are so casual and informal. But for the Hebrew, God was God Almighty and you couldn't even pronounce his name: Yahweh. Yet Jesus invites us to draw close to God, building our relationship not only on the awe and respect that are due the Creator of the universe but also on the love that our heavenly Father has for us.

How do you do that? Read Psalm 103:13: "As a father pities his children, so the Lord pities those who fear him" (RSV).God is not like so many parents in the morning, behind the newspaper, while the children get ready on their own for school. God is not a detached observer, preoccupied with "more important things." He is paying attention and moved with compassion for his children.

Cultivate a growing awareness of your worth.
Jesus says, "Are you not of more value than the birds?" The heavenly Father takes care of the birds because he values them. How much more, Jesus reminds us, does God value us! As a parent, I value my children. There's nothing I won't do to make sure they are provided for. Both my wife and I are blessed with parents who feel the same way. We can ask things of them we'd hesitate asking of others because we know how much they care.

God has compassion for me. Is that easy or difficult for me to believe?

If the Lord spoke to me in a compassionate way about a situation I am currently facing, what might he say?

A rich vision of our worth to God is found in Psalm 139:13-16:

> **You made all the delicate, inner parts of my body**
> **and knit me together in my mother's womb.**
> **Thank you for making me so wonderfully complex!**
> **Your workmanship is marvelous—and how well I know it.**
> **You watched me as I was being formed in utter seclusion,**
> **as I was woven together in the dark of the womb.**
> **You saw me before I was born.**
> **Every day of my life was recorded in your book.**
> **Every moment was laid out**
> **before a single day had passed.**

God has shaped our body and written the story of our life. I don't think that means there is a literal script that we perform, as though we were actors. It is an image of the author who loves his characters and creates a story with mystery, adventure, romance, depth, and spiritual power that brings out the best in those characters. God is the author of life and of your life. I know that, as an author, I care about every word in the story. And that's what God is like. He cares about every word in your life story.

God gives daily signs of his attention to details. How many times do you think our heart beats every day? The normal person has a resting heart rate of 60 beats per minute. Now if your heart beats 60 beats per minutes, 60 minutes per hour, 24 hours a day, the total is 86,400 beats per day! Every day! When was the last time you worried about your heart beating like that? (You will now!) Unless you've had heart problems, you probably haven't even thought about it. What about your breathing? I'd better stop or you'll be hyperventilating! The point is, the body takes care of itself, just as God designed it to do. It's a miracle that this flesh and blood can perform so many complex functions constantly for years and years. If God took such care to create us in this way, why would he not care for all the rest of it?

God's value is the foundation for self-value. How does my sense of my own worth to God affect my spiritual life?

Cultivate a conscious appreciation of God's provision.
Be confident in God. Nothing is impossible. Look what he has provided for you already today. Our confidence in God's provision is impoverished because we take so much for granted. We forget about God's care in the past. We forget about his daily provision not only for our most basic needs but for many of our desires as well.

How has God provided for me in the past?

How has he provided for me recently?

Most, if not all, people reading this book have more than 90 percent of the other people in the world! It is not an issue of quantity—it's a matter of trust. Sarah and I often think of Paul and Elsa and countless others who have been God's hands to provide for us. And by God's grace, we have listened to God and found him putting people on our hearts who have needs. In many situations now, instead of worry, I'm responding with curiosity: Lord, what are you going to do this time?

How can I keep these things in mind to encourage my confidence in his ongoing care?

Cultivate a single focus on God's kingdom.
Many of us create our own worries because we are too eagerly pursuing our own agenda. Jesus says, "Seek first his kingdom and his righteousness, and all these things will be given to you" (Matthew 6:33, NIV). We've heard that verse

many times, but do you realize that this statement was made in the context of Jesus talking about anxiety? He gave us this truth in order to free us from anxiety.

If you seek God first and his righteousness, many of the things you worry about won't even be concerns anymore. Things like having the best and the newest lose their meaning. Things like public acclaim and popularity fade as we live for the one who matters most. At the same time, many of the things you legitimately have concern for are provided naturally.

What about You?

Why do you worry? Jesus is asking you that question now: Why *do* you worry? Have you believed some of the lies of the evil one? "These earthly things are more important than your eternal priorities. You've got to focus on them." Well, that's a lie. Don't believe it. "You won't be taken care of." Don't believe that either.

Have I set my heart on seeking God's kingdom first?

What would that look like for me?

What is the next step I can take to give God first place?

Have you cultivated the growing awareness of God's love? A deepening appreciation of his provision? Have you cultivated a sense of focusing on his provision through the kingdom? Have you cultivated a growing awareness of your own worth?

Jesus said, "Look at the lilies and how they grow" (v. 28). One time when I was preaching on this passage, I compared worry to a weed cultivated in the garden of neglected thoughts. At the conclusion of the service, I had ushers and members of our prayer team come to the front of the sanctuary. The ushers held bouquets of beautiful flowers. I then invited the people to write a "worry weed" on a peace of paper and come forward to exchange it for a flower. After a few moments, as we began to sing quietly, first one member then another came forward. Some simply gave the paper and received a flower. Others knelt and prayed by themselves. Others got their flower and then asked a prayer team for special prayer. I could feel a wonderful lightness entering as the weights of worry were lifted.

What are your worries? Can you discard them like weeds

and take up a flower—of God's love and provision, and of peace?

Notes

1. Excerpted in part from *Our Daily Bread* (Grand Rapids, Mich.: The Radio Bible Class, March 19, 1985).
2. John Haggai, *Winning over Pain, Fear and Worry* (New York: Inspirational Press, 1991), 317–318.

CHAPTER 18

"Who do people say that I am?" Breaking the Power of Indecision

Mark 8:27

BRYAN WAS BORN and raised in a Jewish home. He enjoyed the rich cultural heritage of being Jewish, but he often felt that many of the religious practices were done out of tradition, not faith. Even being a Bar Mitzvah ("son of the covenant") at age thirteen was expected because it was the traditional thing to do. "It didn't reflect my personal faith," he told me. As he grew older, Bryan never felt "attached" to the Jewish heritage that was supposed to have so much meaning. The traditions felt like routine. He was simply going through the motions, doing what people expected him to do.

Things began to change when he met Gail. They were soon married. From the beginning he knew that Gail was a gift from the Lord. Gail was already a Christian, and she wanted to help Bryan find the right road. They wanted to have some kind of religious foundation for themselves and their children. But they never could make a decision. They just drifted along.

During their time of searching, Bryan had decided to coach a baseball team of nine-year-olds. One of the players on his team was my own son Peter. Bryan told me later that he enjoyed meeting me but had no idea of my occupation. Near the end of the baseball season, a friend of Bryan's named Gordon invited him to our church's men's conference. Bryan wasn't too sure he wanted to go but went anyway. When the announcements and singing started, Bryan saw me up front. He asked Gordon why I was up there, explaining he had my son on his team. Was he surprised to find out I was the pastor! God began to stir Bryan's heart that weekend. Decision time was approaching. Here's the rest of the story in Bryan's own words:

> The men's conference woke me up. I began to understand that missing link in my life. The presence of the Lord took a hold of me. It frightened me at first because I didn't understand the tears rolling down my cheeks and the warmth that was surrounding me. But I wanted more.
>
> When we got home, I called Doug and shared what the weekend meant to me. I asked for his direction and assistance in learning more. He invited me to go through the Operation Timothy series of Bible studies. For the next three months, our study and Doug's incredible patience with my never-ending questions showed me the road home. Then in September of 1995, I went with the men from First Presbyterian Church to Promise Keepers in Oakland with over fifty thousand brothers. That Friday night, September 30, it all came together. I found that missing link from my life. I committed my life to Jesus Christ and have not looked back since. What peace I have found in my life and in the Lord! I have found my Shepherd and I am one of his sheep. "My sheep listen to my voice; I know them, and they follow me" (John 10:27).
>
> Finally, I am now a "completed" Jew. It's wonderful to be home.

It's easy to drift through life, carried along by the strong current of routine. Like Bryan, we think we'll get around to making the important decisions sometime. In the meantime, life rolls on, opportunities are lost, and, tragically, eternity hangs in the balance.

One of the secrets to spiritual vitality is making a decision—*our own decision*—about what the Lord means to us. I'm not speaking solely of a first-time decision to trust Jesus Christ as Lord and Savior (though that is included!). I'm speaking about deciding to take the next step in following him.

A pair of incidents in Mark's Gospel show us the power of decision. The two stories in this Scripture passage are intentionally paired. They are linked in tandem on purpose. See if you can see the linkage.

> **When they arrived at Bethsaida, some people brought a blind man to Jesus, and they begged him to touch and heal the man. Jesus took the blind man by the hand and led him out of the village. Then, spitting on the man's eyes, he laid his hands on him and asked, "Can you see anything now?"**
>
> **The man looked around. "Yes," he said, "I see people, but I can't see them very clearly. They look like trees walking around."**
>
> **Then Jesus placed his hands over the man's eyes again. As the man stared intently, his sight was completely restored, and he could see everything clearly. Jesus sent him home, saying, "Don't go back into the village on your way home."**
>
> **Jesus and his disciples left Galilee and went up to the villages of Caesarea Philippi. As they were walking along, he asked them, "Who do people say I am?"**
>
> **"Well," they replied, "some say John the Baptist, some say Elijah, and others say you are one of the other prophets."**
>
> **Then Jesus asked, "Who do you say I am?"**
>
> **Peter replied, "You are the Messiah." But**

Jesus warned them not to tell anyone about him. (Mark 8:22-30)

The Crisis of Decision

One of the most common human tendencies is for us to rely on the opinions of other people. What do others think? What are other people saying? What do the experts think? You cannot look at a paper, read a magazine, listen to a radio, or watch television without being informed about some poll that has been taken. The questions can span the range from what people prefer for breakfast to what they believe about euthanasia.

Polls have value in that they help us understand the pulse of public opinion. But polls also have a drawback. They tend to make us equate majority opinion with what is true and right. *Majority does not equal normality. And normality does not equal morality.* What everybody is doing may not be the right thing to do.

Each one of us has faced times when we had to make a decision that would either allow us to go along with the crowd or force us to stand apart and make our own statement.

I was talking with an executive who serves on the board of a corporation that was debating providing benefits for same-sex partners. "I couldn't blend in with the crowd on that one," he said. "I told them of my personal moral reasons against it as well as my practical business concerns. No one else spoke against it. Only one other person voted with me, but never said why. I'm a marked man now," he concluded, "but that's fine by me."

Each one of us has faced a crisis of decision. It may have been in deciding whether to end a relationship, make a career move, decide on a risky form of medical treatment, or show tough love to a family member. If you have relied only on other people's opinions, you will be unprepared for what it means to own the decision yourself. When we rely solely on other people's opinions, we not only forfeit our responsibility but also the joy and the power that come from saying, "This is what I believe."

INDECISION CRIPPLES: DECISION EMPOWERS

In Mark 8:27 Jesus asked the disciples, "Who do people say I am?" What he learned was that people couldn't decide. The Pharisees continued to test Jesus, most of them clearly set against him. The crowds looked back in their recent history, thinking Jesus was somehow John the Baptist, returned from the dead, or Elijah, the forerunner of the Messiah. Some said he was one of the other prophets. The variety of opinions indicated that many could not decide just what to make of Jesus.

Have there been times when I was faced with going along with the crowd or standing apart?

What did I do? Why?

With this understanding of the situation, Jesus' two-stage healing of the blind man begins to make sense. This is the only miracle in the Gospels where Jesus didn't heal a person on the first try. I don't think this was because Jesus was having a "bad miracle day." Nor was it because there was some peculiar problem with the blind man. This healing was a living parable. The partial restoration of sight followed by the full restoration of sight is paired with the partial understanding people have about Jesus and the subsequent full revelation of who he really is. Jesus' first touch helped the man see the vague shape of things around him, but Jesus' second touch was needed to restore his vision fully. Likewise, the twofold touch of God in faith leads to our full recognition of Christ the Messiah as the way to salvation. He was more than a prophet; he was more than a political messiah who would rescue the people from Roman rule. He was also the suffering Messiah. Immediately after Peter's confession we read:

> **Then Jesus began to tell them that he, the Son of Man, would suffer many terrible things and be rejected by the leaders, the leading priests, and the teachers of religious law. He would be killed, and three days later he would rise again. (Mark 8:31)**

This was hard for the disciples to understand and accept, but it was something they had to see.

The blind man's sight was restored in stages. How has my faith moved through stages?

What names would I give these stages?

The key to lasting change

In our spiritual life we move through a series of stages, understanding more and more about the nature of Christ and the exercise of faith. The key to moving from one stage to another is reaching that point when we make a decision to go forward. Likewise, we stagnate or regress if we decide not to move.

Consider the decision points in Bryan's story. First, he decided there must be something more to faith than tradition and going through the motions. This was the moment of awakening. But then he drifted. He put off a decision to explore his faith or other faiths. This continued in spite of occasional spiritual stirrings or nudges until he decided to accept Gordon's invitation to the men's conference. Then came the decision to study the Bible with me, then to attend Promise Keepers, then to go forward at the speaker's invitation. No lasting change happens without decision.

What decisions am I facing right now?

Am I taking steps to make the decision or drifting? Why?

Decision Detours

A number of factors keep us from traveling directly to a decision. I call these decision detours. Some of these take us the long way to a decision, but some of these may take us totally offtrack. Looking back at the Mark 8 passage, we see several common detours.

We are detoured by thinking we already know what God is all about.

The Pharisees were blinded by prejudice and preconception. They continually demanded signs from Jesus. I guess the miracles of feeding the five thousand and feeding the four thousand just weren't enough for them. These events weren't on their list of Messiah credentials. What does this tell us? It means that they were asking Jesus to live according to their criteria. They wanted to define Jesus according to their terms as their political messiah, or as one who imitated Moses. They had their own preconceptions.

We all come to the issues of faith with preconceptions. For example, I was talking with a college student who said,

"God isn't God if he allows suffering and evil." Two preconceptions detoured her from commitment. First, she was asserting the premise that the suffering and evil in the world are directly God's fault. Second, she assumed that God's methods for dealing with suffering and evil must match her methods. When I challenged her to think that God had *already* taken definitive action to defeat evil through the sacrifice of Christ on the cross, she wasn't impressed. She'd heard that before. But then I said that God holds every person responsible to join God through faith in Jesus Christ in confronting suffering and evil. God calls us to take practical action through things such as prayer for others, loving others, being wise stewards of creation, and leading ethical lives. Much suffering results from our own irresponsible behavior and cannot be blamed on God. "What about the suffering *we* contribute to? What about the evil *we* do?" I asked. These thoughts began to take our conversation into a more fruitful direction.

When you meet people for the first time, you realize that you cannot determine who they are or what they will be like. You don't define the person. That person will reveal himself or herself to you as he or she chooses. How, then, can we come to almighty God and expect to define him? Our own definitions can actually blind us, preventing us from seeing God as God truly is.

What preconceptions or assumptions shape my vision of God?

What ones need to be corrected?

How do I complete the sentence "God is . . . or is not . . ." or "God does . . . or does not . . . ?"

We are detoured by our inattention to the spiritual life. Sometimes God is doing things in our midst, and we just miss it. We simply aren't paying attention. Sometimes we live in a state of unawareness. This was the disciples' experience. They had just seen Jesus multiply food for five thousand and then for four thousand, but when they forgot their lunch, they panicked. They were inattentive to the deeper levels of God's activity. They didn't realize that having Jesus meant they had God's provision for all their needs.

One of the great tragedies of life is that we get too busy to think about God. We fall prey to distractions and lose perspective. Tom Landry, former coach of the Dallas Cowboys football team, came to faith in Christ later in life. He wished he had paid more attention to spiritual things. He said, "Well, I discovered that truth at the age of thirty-three. The most disappointing fact in my life, I believe, is that I waited so long before I discovered the fellowship of Jesus Christ. How much more wonderful my life would have been if I had taken this step many years earlier."[1]

Landry's regret applies not only to a first-time commitment but to daily discipleship. Each day we neglect our spiritual life is a day we've lost in honoring God and growing into the full likeness of Christ.

When am I most likely to be inattentive to my spiritual life?

When has my spiritual life been most vital?

How can I cultivate increasing spiritual awareness today?

We are detoured by forgetting all that God has already done for us.

Another problem with the disciples was their short memory. I think I know what those disciples were going through. Years ago Sarah and I were struggling with requests from several congregations that we consider coming to serve them. I began to get anxious, tossing and turning before going to sleep, wondering which, if any, of the places was God's call for us. Sarah was much more calm. She reminded me that God had clearly guided each of our moves. Still I fretted. As we walked through the process, it became very clear that one of the four situations was just what God had in mind for us. We watched God either close the doors or cool our hearts toward the other three situations. Within several months, it was clear as could be. God came through again, and he impressed on my heart the words, "Remember, remember, remember, remember!"

Do you see a pattern here? We all know what the phrase "clueless" means. That's the way most people are toward God. God is moving in our midst, but we are clueless. He is doing awesome things in our life each and every day, but we don't see it.

I love it when fellow believers come up to me and say, "Doug, I saw the Lord work today." Just recently someone told about a discussion her family was having. She told me, "I went out to the car, and one of your sermon tapes was on the seat. I popped it into the tape player, and it was on the subject we were discussing as a family!" She ended up playing a portion of the tape for her family. "It's just amazing to see how much God cares about us!" she concluded. I hear story after story like that. But if we are inattentive, we will miss these God-touches in our life.

You might be thinking, *If I saw Jesus Christ perform a miracle, I'd believe. Just let me see one miracle, and I'd believe.* Others might say, "But if I could just be with Jesus, if he would come back in the flesh, if he would come today and I could walk alongside him, I think I could believe then." Really? The Pharisees saw Jesus perform a miracle. What did it do? They didn't like that one; they wanted a different one. The disciples were with Jesus. What did that do? They turned to one another in the boat, exclaiming, "Oh my gosh, you forgot lunch? Oh no, we don't even have enough money for french fries!" They were with Jesus, they saw him work, and still they panicked over a forgotten lunch.

On the Road to Decision

"Who do people say I am?" The point of this question is to encourage the honest searching of our heart and faith. Do you see Jesus clearly yet? It is no shame to admit our partial understanding. The blind man wasn't shamed to silence. He wasn't beligerent, chiding Jesus for not healing his sight completely. He wasn't resigned: *Well, I guess Jesus doesn't care enough about me to do the whole job.* He couldn't see completely yet, and he told Jesus that. And Jesus gave the man that second touch. When we admit our confusion, our inability to understand clearly, Jesus has the opportunity to touch us again.

What are some of my great memories of God's touch in my life?

Where can I keep this list so I can add to and reflect on it regularly?

Ask the Lord for his touch that brings understanding.
Our eyes are opened as we request God's touch for whatever need we have. One of the most powerful testimonies in the gospel is that Jesus continually welcomed honest requests. A Roman centurion came to Jesus and Jesus welcomed his request, healing the centurion's servant. He

never refused someone who asked. Do you think he'd refuse you? I don't. Not if you ask for a touch that opens your eyes to see him clearly.

You may ask for something that would be inappropriate, something that might not be good for you at this time. The Lord will make that clear. But we can begin with this prayer: "Lord, touch me. I'm tired of looking at you as if you're just a tree walking. Let me see you clearly."

Our eyes are opened only as we welcome the touch of God in Jesus Christ. After Jesus healed the blind man in two stages, he tested people's spiritual vision. Obviously, Jesus had the power to heal the man in one touch. But the fact that he did it in two stages provided a living parable for the disciples. "Who do other people say I am?" "Well, they say you are Elijah, one of the prophets, whatever." Jesus says, "They see me like trees walking. They've got the shape, but they're not seeing me clearly."

Jesus asked, "Who do you say I am?" And Peter answered, "You are the Messiah, the Son of the living God." In Matthew's narrative, Jesus said, "You are blessed, Simon son of John, because my Father in heaven has revealed this to you. You did not learn this from any human being" (Matthew 16:17). The second touch gave Peter sight. *The crisis of decision, successfully managed, leads to the power of conviction.*

In what area of my life do I long for God's touch?

Study God's Word to learn what he truly is like.

Our eyes are opened first as we receive God's Word. Both Jesus' disciples and the crowds knew God's Word. But they failed to grasp the manifold ways in which Jesus fulfilled the promises stated specifically and implicitly in the Scriptures. One of the more common studies of Christ centers on his fulfillment of the Old Testament roles (or offices) of prophet, priest, and king. I have found these to be a rich source of meditation for expanding not only my intellectual understanding of Christ, but also for nurturing my confidence in prayer, my comfort in trials, my courage in the face of challenges, and my consistency in obedience.

Jesus Christ fulfilled the role of *prophet.* In Israel, the prophet was both a foreteller of the future and a forthteller of God's truth. He spoke to the people for God. We usually emphasize the prophet's gift of prediction but miss the fact that the purpose of prediction was simply to enforce the prophet's message calling for repentance and obedience. Jesus foretold his future trial, crucifixion, and resurrection, but his primary message was what those events meant for people who trusted him in faith. Through the Scriptures, Jesus continues to reveal the way of God and the truth about our shortcomings.

Jesus Christ fulfilled the role of *priest.* In Israel, the priest interceded with God on behalf of the people. He made sacrifices for them and interceded for them. Jesus is both our High Priest and the once-for-all sacrifice. His intercession makes it possible for us to come boldly before God's throne of grace (see Hebrews 4:16).

Jesus Christ fulfilled the role of *king-lord.* The king led the battles and held the people accountable to keep God's commands. He maintained order in the name of the Lord. Jesus is our Lord. He rules over all and is everything we need for our every need. He not only commands our obedience, but he empowers our obedience through the Holy Spirit.

Which of these three roles speaks most to my needs and concerns at this time?

Pay attention to God's presence.

God is here. Learn to pay attention to his daily gifts.

In my book *SoulShaping: Taking Care of Your Spiritual Life,* I talk about a practical way to cultivate a moment-by-moment awareness of God. I call it the discipline of preview. This practice arose as a practical response to some men in a Bible study I was leading. We were meeting for breakfast for a number of weeks, but one of the men suggested we switch to lunch. "Why?" I asked.

"Because by the time it's 9:00 A.M., I have pretty much forgotten about our study. But if we were to meet at lunch, at least I'd see it on my calendar as an appointment and look forward to it all morning."

That triggered an idea. "Let's get out our calendars and planners." I then led the men through a prayer time based on the specific appointments, commitments, and priorities they had for that day. As they prayed over their schedules, I encouraged them to *mark* directly on their calendar a cross or a dove (for the Holy Spirit), or write down any Scripture or thought that came to mind about each item.

Preview today or tomorrow, prayerfully going through your schedule, including your routine activities. "Lord, as I walk through this day with you, I commit each of these matters to your hands."

"We've just previewed your day with the Lord. Now, when you look at that calendar all day, you'll be reminded of this prayer time." Frankly, I was surprised at just how helpful that idea was for me as well as for the other men. I have since found this exercise to be a significant tool for helping us to "practice the presence of God." (Note: For additional material on numerous other spiritual exercises, see my book *SoulShaping: Taking Care of Your Spiritual Life* [Wheaton, Ill.: Tyndale House Publishers, 1996]. Guidelines for the discipline of preview are presented on pages 149–161.)

What about You?

Who do you say Jesus is?

The Son of God is our starting place. The fullness of Christ and who he is for us cannot be captured in a few names, but he is all things to us. Jesus has a threefold office. He is our prophet; he brings the Word of God to our life. He is our Priest; he intercedes on our behalf to God. And he is our King; he sits and reigns and governs all things. As you think of a particular need, who do you need Christ to be for you?

Indecision cripples. Decision empowers. I urge you to search your heart honestly to find those areas in which you have only partial sight and need a second touch.

Maybe you've never put your trust in Jesus Christ—because you haven't had a clear view of him and thus stayed hung up in indecision. Or you may be a Christian, but there are other dimensions of your life that need to be touched by God's power. Each of us needs God's touch for our blindness. We need his presence to strengthen us and to reveal himself to us.

Who do you say he is? It's time to make a decision.

NOTES

1. Josh McDowell, *Evidence That Demands a Verdict* (Campus Crusade for Christ, 1972), 345.

CHAPTER 19

"Could you not keep watch with me one hour?" The Warning and the Wonder of Prayer

Matthew 26:40

But the cost of nondiscipleship is far greater—even when this life alone is considered—than the price paid to walk with Jesus. Nondiscipleship costs abiding peace, a life penetrated throughout by love, faith that sees everything in the light of God's overriding governance for good, hopefulness that stands firm in the most discouraging of circumstances, power to do what is right and withstand the forces of evil. . . . The correct perspective is to see following Christ not only as the necessity it is, but as the fulfillment of the highest human possibilities and as life on the highest plane. DALLAS WILLARD[1]

ONE OF MY boyhood heroes was Pete Rose of the Cincinnati Reds baseball team. As a Little League baseball player growing up in Cincinnati, I wanted to be like Pete. He was the player's player. We called him "Charlie Hustle." He could do it all. In fact, two of my most cherished mementoes are an autographed baseball and poster from the night Pete broke Ty Cobb's all-time hitting record of 4,191, getting his

4,192nd hit on September 11, 1985. No player has ever hustled more or been more committed to the game of baseball. After breaking Ty Cobb's record, Rose went on to a total of 4,256 hits in an unequaled 3,562 games and 14,053 times at bat, for a lifetime batting average of .303. He also held thirty-one other major and National League records. Pete was certain for baseball immortality in the Hall of Fame.

Then came news that Rose gambled on sporting events, along with allegations that he bet on baseball. Although admitting to the charges of gambling and tax evasion, Rose has vigorously denied this last allegation. He was convicted and served his prison sentence for the federal crime. He is still banned from baseball's eligible list and therefore cannot be elected to the Hall of Fame. Although the debate rages about Pete's induction into the Hall of Fame, this one thing we know: He has lost something he valued most because he let down his guard.

This story can be repeated for people in all walks of life, in all ages of history. Many start out well but fall through failing to watch, through failing to be diligent to guard the integrity of their character, moral behavior, and spiritual life. No one is immune to the danger, not even those who were closest to Jesus during his last days.

Jesus has shared the Last Supper with his disciples. He has predicted Peter's betrayal (verse 34), and now Peter declares,

"Even if I have to die with you, I will never disown you." And all the other disciples said the same.

Then Jesus went with his disciples to a place called Gethsemane, and he said to them, "Sit here, while I go over there and pray." He took Peter and the two sons of Zebedee along with him, and he began to be sorrowful and troubled. Then he said to them, "My soul is overwhelmed

> **with sorrow to the point of death. Stay here and keep watch with me."**
>
> **Going a little farther, he fell with his face to the ground and prayed, "My Father, if it is possible, may this cup be taken from me. Yet not as I will, but as you will."**
>
> **Then he returned to his disciples and found them sleeping. "Could you men not keep watch with me for one hour?" he asked Peter. "Watch and pray so that you will not fall into temptation. The spirit is willing, but the body is weak."**
>
> **He went away a second time and prayed, "My Father, if it is not possible for this cup to be taken away unless I drink it, may your will be done."**
>
> **When he came back, he again found them sleeping, because their eyes were heavy. So he left them and went away once more and prayed the third time, saying the same thing.**
>
> **Then he returned to the disciples and said to them, "Are you still sleeping and resting? Look, the hour is near, and the Son of Man is betrayed into the hands of sinners. Rise, let us go! Here comes my betrayer!" (Matthew 26:35-46,** NIV**)**

To me, this is one of the most poignant and heartbreaking moments in the entire drama of Jesus' final days, which we call the passion (or suffering) of Christ. A passion describes a time in which you are acted upon by forces you do not control. And in that final passion of Christ, the most poignant moment is when he turns to his disciples and says, "Could you not keep watch with me for one hour?"

What Does It Mean to Watch?

Before we consider the deeply emotional and theological aspects of Jesus' question, we need to examine the idea of watching. What does it mean to keep watch? It means more than simply staying awake. Our modern translations read,

"Couldn't you stay awake and watch with me even one hour?" That doesn't capture it. It means to be alert. You can be awake and not alert. But you can't be keeping watch and not be alert. It means to be attentive. It means to be spiritually aware of the dynamics of life around you. The watchman who keeps watch over the city isn't simply staying awake. The watchman is on the lookout for signs of the appearance of the enemy or for news from the allies—for signs of danger or news of good. To watch means to be ready, on guard.

How do we keep watch in our daily life? We watch events in the Middle East, staying alert to the dynamics of that volatile region. We watch and are "on guard" as we drive through unfamiliar or rough sections of town. Parents watch as their children go and come from school. Even walking through the mall, parents are watching to be sure nothing happens to their children. A nurse in the Intensive Care Unit of a hospital guards a patient through constant attention to the monitors that track vital signs. A business person watches the stock market, analyzing the economic opportunities and risks. I know of one man who is a leading international investor who literally sleeps with monitors that will awaken him if the markets anywhere in the world rise above or fall below certain levels. This person is leading a very watchful life. Watching, guarding, being alert for danger and opportunity is a part of our daily life. But so often it's missing in our spiritual life.

In what areas of life do I do the most watching?

How does this idea of watchfulness apply to my spiritual life?

Watchfulness is an essential quality for spiritual vitality. Watchful disciples are aware of the snares within themselves and the dangers in the world that can harm them. They are like defensive drivers on the roads, alert and prepared for what others may do that endangers them. Those who fail to watch fail to see danger coming.

In his hour of agony, Jesus continues to instruct his disciples in principles of spiritual growth—in what will make them ready to lead life to the fullest. And this lesson, this time, is literally given in blood, sweat, and tears. He calls his disciples to keep watch. Why?

We Keep Watch to Stay in Fellowship with Christ

I challenge you to find any other time in the life of Jesus Christ when he said that he *needed* someone. We find plenty of examples of Jesus valuing people, but no others which so clearly portray his own longing to be supported by others. In Gethsemane he is crying out literally for support. He says to his disciples, "My soul is overwhelmed with sorrow to the point of death. Stay here and keep watch with me" (Matthew 26:39, NIV).

I've been at the bedside of people who say, "Stay with me, don't leave me now." You have too. You've been with your children when they are terrified in the night and they say, "Don't leave me now." You may have been with someone who has gotten devastating news and says, "Please, stay with me. Don't leave me alone with this." Jesus, the Son of God, was saying that to his own disciples. I don't think there is another time in his life when he expressed such need. This was the disciples' unique opportunity to serve the one who served them always. To be alongside him in a way that they would never be again. That makes it all the more poignant. In his hour of greatest need, Jesus Christ was deserted emotionally by his disciples before he was betrayed by Judas.

Although Jesus is no longer in Gethsemane, he still has the same longing for fellowship with us. Fellowship with the living God is the primary goal of prayer. Most of us have been taught to think of prayer in terms of requests, when in fact it is primarily a matter of relationship. The primary purpose of prayer is not that we get something from God or even give something to God; it's for us to be in communion with God. The psalmist captures this point when he says, "My heart has heard you say, 'Come and talk with me.' And my heart responds, 'Lord, I am coming'" (Psalm 27:8).

The starting point of watchfulness is realizing the simple fact that God's love is not simply utilitarian. God does not merely want to do things for us—he wants *us!* Writing about parents and children, Tim Hansel tells the story about a teenager who had a very obvious birthmark over much of his face. And yet it didn't seem to bother him. His self-esteem seemed secure. He related well with the other students and was well liked. He seemed to be in no way self-conscious about his very large birthmark, which was obvious to everyone else.

Finally, someone asked how this could be.

> "Are you aware of the fact that you have this large birthmark on your face?"
>
> He replied, "Of course I am."
>
> "Can you tell me, then, why it does not seem to bother you in the slightest?"
>
> The young man smiled and said, "When I was very young, my father started telling me that the birthmark was there for two reasons: One, it was where the angel kissed me; two, the angel had done that so my father could always find me easily in a crowd."
>
> He then continued, "My dad told me this so many times with so much love that as I grew up, I actually began to feel sorry for the other kids who weren't kissed by the angel like I was."[2]

The same principles apply to our heavenly Father. Time simply spent with him lets us hear his voice and know of the angel's kiss—indeed, the Lord's kiss—in our life. Such a vital relationship carries us through the toughest times and the greatest disappointments. These very experiences become avenues of God's grace.

At the beginning of his ministry, Jesus called twelve to be with him. We often emphasize the fact that "withness" was itself valuable for the disciples. They got to learn in the informal conversations and events of daily, humdrum life. They saw Jesus on his "off-hours." But did it ever occur to you to that Jesus not only wanted his disciples to be with him, but *he* wanted to be with them? He valued their companionship, their conversations, the richness of experiencing life with them. Make no mistake, fellowship with us is God's delight.

Do I know how to simply enjoy fellowship with the Lord?

WE KEEP WATCH TO PREPARE OURSELF FOR SUFFERING

Read Psalm 27. What are David's insights into the comfort and the benefits of simply being in fellowship with God.

Jesus' concern reached beyond the need for support and fellowship. He was deeply concerned for the welfare of the disciples themselves. Jesus knew what lay ahead. He had already warned the disciples that they were going to be severely tested by the events that were about to transpire. Although Jesus warned them of their impending failure through betrayal and desertion, their protests rang out loud and strong. That's why Matthew's account of Gethsemane is especially vivid. Not once but three times Jesus prays and comes back to find his disciples sleeping. Do you see any correlation here? A threefold denial is preceded by a threefold failure to pray. Those who identified with Christ as he went to trial would face their own trial. They would be tempted to deny him, to disown him, to flee from him. They could have been strengthened if they had prayed. But they would not.

In Gethsemane Jesus prayed three times. Each prayer was a step in letting go of things that would hold him back so that he could take hold of God's will and endure the suffering that lay ahead.

The first prayer was an outburst of grief. It was the step of realization when he felt the full impact of his mission. Jesus shuddered in the chill of death's dark shadow. Prayer was his only refuge. He longed for his companions to comfort and support him. They slept.

The second prayer was one of release. He let go of his agenda and accepted God's will. This was the moment of transformation. Jesus came face-to-face with his choices. Either he would die for us or live without us. If he saved his life, he would lose us. If he lost his life, he would save us. When he saw the matter clearly, having released his grief to the Father, he could clearly see God's will. And God's will became his desire.

The third prayer strengthened his resolution. It was like the tempering of steel in which the refined metal is reheated a second time to increase its strength. As a soldier readies himself going into battle, or a witness calls upon all her courage for going onto the witness stand, or a patient prepares himself for going into a difficult surgery, so Jesus gathered from God all his strength. He left all his cares with God.

What we keep from God keeps us from God. What we give to God becomes a channel to give ourself to God. Prayer enables us to travel the journey from realization to release and from release to resolve. We see this same process at work in the apostle Paul. He also prayed three times for relief from his thorn in the flesh. Each time God told him, "My gracious favor is all you need. My power works best in your weakness" (2 Corinthians 12:9). This word enables Paul to move to acceptance, and even to boasting in his weakness, so that the power of Christ was clear to all.

Is there something God is asking of me that is heavy on my heart?

How can I move through the stages of realization, release, and resolve?

We keep watch in order to prepare ourself for the suffering, the trials, the temptations that are about to befall us. The disciples' threefold failure is something all of us understand. I don't know about you, but I know what it's like to fall asleep in many situations. As a husband, I know that I am to pray with my wife, yet I too often sleep instead. As a parent, I know that I am encouraged to read God's Word with my children, but too often I prefer sleep. As a friend, I know that I have opportunities to share my faith with another, but I am too often asleep at the switch.

Do you know what it's like to feel that the need is there, but you can't bring yourself to act? When an opportunity calls for you to say something, do you find yourself overwhelmed with waves of weariness and resistance? Why are we so vulnerable to sleep? Jesus mentions several reasons.

Our flesh is weak.

First, Jesus says to his disciples, "The spirit is willing, but the body is weak" (Matthew 26:41, NIV). We are limited people.

Psalm 103:14 says: "For he knows how we are formed, he remembers that we are dust" (NIV). In 2 Corinthians 4:7, it says: "We have this treasure in earthen vessels" (RSV). We are weak, we are limited, we are dusty people.

Being subject to hunger, thirst, fatigue, emotions, and spiritual warfare, Christ understood human frailty. And he knew that without the backbone, the steel reinforcement of prayer, and the Spirit, this all-too-human flesh would fail.

"Blessed are the drowsy ones for they shall soon drop off to sleep!" wrote Nietzsche. His cynical beatitude sounds a warning to all of us to beware of "the Gethsemane sleep," to use Pascal's term.

Simone Weil died in 1943 at the age of thirty-three. She was serving with French Resistance forces in England at the time and trying to live on the food ration of a French workman in occupied France. Through her posthumous writings, she became a kind of apostle of the spiritual life of France during the first decade after World War II. At the heart of her insights is her definition of prayer as attention. Sin, then, is distraction. Douglas Steere describes the danger of spiritual sleepiness and the promise of prayer this way.

> Pride, self-will, self-absorption, double-mindedness, dishonesty, sexual excess, overeating, overdrinking, overactivity of any sort, all destroy attention and all cut the nerve of effective prayer. Just as sleep is upset by any serious mental disturbance, so attention is dispersed when unfaced sin gets the ascendancy. If prayer is attention, then it is naturally attention to the highest thing that I know, to my "ultimate concern," and this human prayer means a moving out of a life of inattention, out of the dispersion, out of "the Gethsemane sleep" into the life of openness and attention to the highest that I know. God can only disclose the divine whispers to those who are attending. Dorothy Hutchinson once quoted a

What things most distract me from prayer?

What one or two practices can I cultivate to develop spiritual awareness?

Senegalese proverb which says that "the opportunity which God sends does not wake up him who is sleeping."[3]

Recognizing the natural weakness of this made-of-dust human body and the spiritual weakness of sin, we must be intentional in cultivating spiritual practices that help us "tune in" to the Lord. Spiritual alertness will not come naturally. It is an acquired characteristic.

Our flesh is weary.

When Jesus came back from praying, he found the disciples sleeping because their eyes were heavy. Luke's account says that the disciples were worn out with grief. Some people think that this was simply because of the Passover meal and drink. Passover was not the most luxurious meal as you know, with the bitter herbs and all, but it was a rather heavy meal, and several cups of wine were drunk. Admittedly, the wine was diluted wine, but when combined with the emotions of the week, it made for a potent sleeping potion.

When am I most weary?

Are there particular times of the year, days of the week, or times of the day that are especially difficult?

The flesh is weary. Not only was it created weak, it wears out. I believe Vince Lombardi, the famous football coach of the championship Green Bay Packers, is the one who said, "Fatigue makes cowards of us all." I think many of us have been in situations where we just found ourselves overwhelmed. After a good night's sleep or a time of rest and rejuvenation, we came back. Prayer is a means for rest and renewal. Combined with proper rest, we gain strength to face whatever life brings.

What refreshes me?

How can I cultivate refreshing practices to renew me in these times?

We are selfish.

Let's be brutally frank: We are self-centered. We resist the demands of discipleship and faithfulness. Prayer is God's method to bring the flesh under the control of the Spirit. The very fact that Jesus prayed meant he would make it. In prayer God pours his power into our parched life, filling us with the rivers of living water: spiritual energy. Prayer is the pathway to the heart and mind of God. We keep watch, not only to be in fellowship with Christ, not only to protect ourself and arm ourself against the temptations and trials of life, but we keep watch in order to enter into the heart of God.

What was the substance of Jesus' prayer? The will of God. We ask, "Father, what is your will? Father, what is your heart? What is my role in your plan?" And God reveals it. Jesus' attitude is one of complete surrender to the will of God. When Jesus says, "If it is possible, may this cup be taken from me," he isn't making a demand. He's searching the heart and mind of God. He surrenders to God immediately: "Yet not as I will, but as you will." As we pray, we come to sense the heart concerns of God and feel the pain of the world in need.

There's a rather puzzling and provocative verse in Colossians 1:24, where the apostle Paul says, "I am glad when I suffer for you in my body, for I am completing what remains of Christ's sufferings for his body, the church." That does not mean that the suffering of Christ on the cross was inadequate or incomplete. It means that, as we come alongside Christ in the mission of the world, we will feel the pain of the body of Christ. We will feel the pain of disappointment and of being let down. We will feel the pain of a world in need and having limited resources or people who aren't motivated to go forward and meet that need. We will feel the pain of recognizing our own sleepiness. In prayer we are invited to enter the heart of God.

SEEKING GOD'S GLORY

In 1540 Martin Luther's good friend Frederick Myconius became deathly sick. He himself and others expected that he would die within a short time. One night he wrote with trembling hand a fond farewell to Luther, whom he loved very much.

When Luther received the letter, he sent back the following reply immediately: "I command thee in the name of God to live because I still have need of thee in the work of reforming the church. . . . The Lord will never let me hear that thou art dead, but will permit thee to survive me. For this I am praying, this is my will, and may my will be done, because I seek only to glorify the name of God."

Myconius had already lost the faculty of speech when Luther's letter came. But in a short time he was well again. And, true enough, he survived Luther by two months![4]

How many of us pray that boldly? Why could Luther pray that boldly? Because he kept watch.

O. Hallesby writes in his famous book entitled simply *Prayer:* "Nothing makes us so bold in prayer as when we can look into the eyes of God and say to him, 'Thou knowest I am not praying for personal advantage, nor to avoid hardship, nor that my own will in any way should be done, but only for this, that thy name might be glorified.' "

Our times of great weakness can awaken great boldness. If I were to pray as boldly as Martin Luther, what would be some of my prayers?

That's what Jesus prayed for. "Father, thy will be done. Thy name be glorified." And that's the invitation to you and me, to watch. To keep watch with him.

What about You?

Take time to write them in your journal. Don't censor yourself. Pour out your heart and review them with God later. Be bold!

Prayer is our lifeline to God. What would it have meant to Jesus Christ if his disciples had been alert? What would it have meant to them? What would it have meant to the course of their own personal histories if they had kept awake?

Prayer is our wake-up call from God. It brings us immediately into fellowship with the living Lord. It brings us immediately under the protection of the living Lord. And it allows us to understand his will. Can you wait and watch with the Lord? As we keep watch with him, we will watch Christ do great things.

Notes

1. *The Spirit of Discipleship* (San Francisco, Calif.: HarperSan Francisco, 1988), 26.
2. Tim Hansel, *What Kids Need Most in a Dad* (Old Tappan, N.J.: Power Books, 1984), 75.
3. Douglas V. Steere, *Prayer in the Contemporary World* (Wellingford, Pa.: Pendle Hill Publications, 1990), quoted in Donald Postema, *Space for God* (Grand Rapids, Mich.: Bible Way, 1983), 102.
4. O. Hallesby, *Prayer* (Minneapolis: Augsburg, 1931), 130–131.

CHAPTER 20

"Why do you doubt?" Doubt: A Starting Place

Luke 24:38

I WAS SITTING in my honors English class as a senior in high school. We were discussing a poem in which we read the following lines:

> Was he happy?
> Of course he was.
> If not, surely no one
> Would have told him.

Our teacher began to speak about how presumptuous it is for us to try to tell another person what will make him happy. Then she said, "I don't feel I have any right to judge another person, and that's why I make such a lousy Christian." At this she turned and looked right at me and said, "Right, Doug?" I was stunned. I looked back at her and said, "What?" And she said, "I don't think I can judge other people, and that's what Christians have to do. Right? You have to tell other people they're not happy. But how can Christians be so sure?" At that point began a discussion that lasted the rest of the class period.

How *can* we be sure? That is the big question, isn't it? I remember another class, just a year or so later. "My job is to get you to question every thing you ever believed," began the professor in my college introduction to philosophy class. You could see he really enjoyed the shock wave that his words sent through the class. I'm not certain how many students entered with a vital faith, but I know that very few survived with their faith intact by the time that term ended.

The interesting fact is that Jesus comes to us and says, in effect, "How can you *not* be sure? When you look at my creation, when you consider the incredible influence that my followers have exerted over history, when you examine the integrity of my word, when you hear the testimonies of credible witnesses who have seen me work in their lives, when you stop and listen to your own heart—how can you doubt?"

Doubt is more than a matter of intellectual concern. It is a significant factor in our spiritual vitality. The person who tries to follow Jesus but is plagued with doubts is like the soldier who questions both the validity of the war he is in and the commanders who lead him. He feels the pressure but lacks the confidence necessary to fulfill his responsibility. It's like an athlete who doubts her coach or a student who questions his teachers and advisors. Doubt corrodes our confidence in God and compromises our obedience.

It may be some encouragement to know that the disciples were the first skeptics. They themselves were subject to doubt. When the disciples were confronted with the new reality of the Resurrection, their doubts did not evaporate immediately. They clung like the grogginess that hampers a person roused from a deep and troubling sleep, and the disciples were left in a spiritual stupor. The frequency and nature of Jesus' resurrection appearances themselves indicate the necessity of confronting doubt as a prelude to ministry.

As we consider the following account, remember that Jesus had just appeared to his two followers on the road to Emmaus. They had not recognized Jesus when he joined them as they were walking along that road. When he broke bread with them, they suddenly recognized him. He vanished, and they ran back to tell their friends.

While they were still talking about this, Jesus himself stood among them and said to them, "Peace be with you."

They were startled and frightened, thinking they saw a ghost. He said to them, "Why are you troubled, and why do doubts rise in your minds? Look at my hands and my feet. It is I myself! Touch me and see; a ghost does not have flesh and bones, as you see I have."

When he had said this, he showed them his hands and feet. And while they still did not believe it because of joy and amazement, he asked them, "Do you have anything here to eat?" They gave him a piece of broiled fish, and he took it and ate it in their presence.

He said to them, "This is what I told you while I was still with you: Everything must be fulfilled that is written about me in the Law of Moses, the Prophets and the Psalms."

Then he opened their minds so they could understand the Scriptures. He told them, "This is what is written: The Christ will suffer and rise from the dead on the third day, and repentance and forgiveness of sins will be preached in his name to all nations, beginning at Jerusalem. You are witnesses of these things. I am going to send you what my Father has promised; but stay in the city until you have been clothed with power from on high." (Luke 24:36-49, NIV)

What Can We Do with Our Doubts?

It seems to me that we have three options when it comes to dealing with our doubts. First, we can allow our doubts to drive us to despair. When people cannot believe or don't know what to believe, they can despair of life altogether. This was the first reaction of the two on the road to Emmaus. They were sinking into spiritual depression, leaving Jerusalem in spite of the rumors of the Resurrection because they could not find a footing for faith. They may have wanted to believe, but a strange magnetism drew them away.

A second response is to allow our doubts to excuse us. To excuse our irresponsibility and inattention to God. This was the reaction of those gathered at Mars Hill in Acts 17 when Paul proclaimed Jesus' resurrection to the intellectuals of Greece. They were curious but not convicted. The agnostic who cannot be certain often uses that as an excuse to do whatever he or she pleases.

But there is a third choice. I can allow my doubts to stir me to action. Doubt can become a starting place.

Now a person really needs no counsel about falling into despair. That comes naturally. And a person needs no counsel about how to live irresponsibly. That, too, comes naturally. But it takes courage and wisdom to choose the way of facing our doubts and allowing them to lead us to something more.

What doubts have troubled me on my journey of faith?

How have I responded to them?

Living in an Age of Doubt

Doubt is not new in matters of faith. In fact, doubt lies at the very heart of life and of faith. I have been a doubter. I vividly remember awakening one morning after I'd been a Christian for several years and saying to myself, "What if this *isn't* true? What if the Resurrection never happened?" It was a soul-shaking moment, difficult to explain to those who have never experienced it. It's sort of like the little child who is suddenly afraid she's really adopted and that her parents have deceived her. Or like discovering that a dear friend has been living a lie. Such doubt can be devastating.

This doubt compelled me to begin an earnest search to validate my faith. Four or five books and the counsel of my pastors and wise friends who were not threatened by my questions got me through this time.[1] As I moved through the process of exploring the intellectual foundations of my faith, I felt a growing confidence and certainty that went beyond mental assent. I began to believe it in my very bones!

In fact, I see now that my intellectual crisis became a major spiritual motivator, shaping my ministry as one that makes intellectual credibility a primary factor in both outreach and discipleship.

Ours has been called the age of anxiety. The Germans call it *angst,* a vivid word depicting the feeling of desperation born of uncertainty and fear. Why is there doubt in our day? There are a number of explanations that could be given as to the cause of anxiety, such as the pace of change, the complexity of problems we face, or the major philosophical, social, and moral shifts we've seen in our culture. Over the last two hundred years especially we have seen a number of factors give rise to doubt. I'll touch on just a few of them briefly.

First, the twentieth century saw two world wars such as the world had never seen. The optimism of evolutionary progress was shattered by the revelations of death camps in one of the most sophisticated nations in the world. Human beings are not getting better and better. Beneath a thin veneer of civilization lurks a frightening beast. In addition to the shattering of human optimism, our capacity for self-destruction increased exponentially as nuclear weapons made annihilation a real possibility.

The twentieth century also saw a radical shift from what had been understood as fixed points of security and unquestioned standards of truth. Einstein's Theory of Relativity spread from a scientific theory to a moral and philosophical operating system. Instead of viewing Truth (with a capital *T*) as a single entity to be objectively known, truth in the eyes of many has become plural "truths" (with a lowercase *t*). Through travel and exposure to other cultures we have been led to believe that truth comes to us in a variety of forms. Different people very sincerely believe different things. In addition to the affirmation of pluralism, the spread of enlightenment ideas in philosophy and science means that we have become highly empirical, highly rationalistic, and antisupernatural. If we can't taste it, see it, touch it, hear it, feel it—if we can't measure it—how can we know it's true?

The diminished credibility of institutional religion has also undermined our confidence. Ironically, the church itself has done a great deal to destroy people's confidence in God and in faith. The state church in Nazi Germany, on the whole, supported Adolph Hitler. Church leaders have undermined their credibility by not leading lives of moral purity and integrity. They have failed to uphold the integrity of God's Word. The dramatic shifts in cultural influences, especially since the 1960s, give rise to doubt and the intense criticism of the Bible. We have surrendered the sanctuaries of security, such as faith in a God who is both transcendent and immanent, a sense of purpose embedded in the order in the universe, and reliance on the Bible as a trustworthy revelation. We have surrendered these sanctuaries of security for the harsh barren landscape of what the existentialist may call a courageous despair—but what most people simply experience as emptiness.

In this climate, people who do not understand the gospel portray false versions of it. They do not see the truth claims of Christ or the integrity of Christ, which calls forth the best from us. Instead, they draw their perceptions from the failures of the church and the distorted teaching of some leaders. We see this in Bertrand Russell, who says in his essay "Why I Am Not a Christian":

> Religion is based, I think, primarily and mainly upon fear. It is partly the terror of the unknown and partly, as I have said, the wish to feel that you have a kind of elder brother who will stand by you in all your troubles and disputes. Fear is the basis of the whole thing—fear of the mysterious, fear of defeat, fear of death. Fear is the parent of cruelty, and therefore it is no wonder if cruelty and religion have gone hand in hand. It is because fear is at the basis of those two things. In this world we can now begin a little to understand things, and a little to master

> them by help of science, which has forced its way step by step against the Christian religion, against the churches, and against the opposition of all the old precepts. Science can help us to get over this craven fear in which mankind has lived for so many generations. Science can teach us, and I think our own hearts can teach us, no longer to look around for imaginary supports, no longer to invent allies in the sky, but rather to look to our own efforts here below to make this world a fit place to live in, instead of the sort of place that the churches in all these centuries have made it.[2]

Russell's argument turns on the fact that science, not religion, is the only road to truth. Yet he forgets that science itself was born of the faithful seeking to understand God's creation. Johannes Kepler (1571–1630), a German astronomer and mathematician, is considered the founder of modern astronomy. He formulated three laws to clarify the theory that the planets revolve around the sun. Kepler said, "O God, I am thinking Thy thoughts after Thee." But modern science has rejected God and the supernatural. We have forgotten that science and knowledge cannot save us. "We have too many men of science, too few men of God. We have grasped the mystery of the atom, and rejected the Sermon on the Mount. The world has achieved brilliance without wisdom, power without conscience."[3] The sad fact is that brilliant scientists could lead us to the ultimate in racist nightmares, using genetic engineering and discrimination to control human destiny. I don't want to sound hysterical, but we must acknowledge the reality that science, unfettered by moral values, may not only explore life but may also administer death.

As I talk with people nowadays, I find many are intellectually resistant. They have been nursed on skepticism and weaned on cynicism. They are slow to believe anything in this age of enlightened disappointment—because they don't want to be hurt again. People don't want to believe too much. If you put too much hope in something and it crumbles, you'll be worse off than if you'd just walked through life rather timidly. I find people walking through life very timidly. They're not ready to take a stand. They're not ready to claim their spiritual inheritance because doubt has eroded their confidence.

How have I seen cultural factors and trends affecting my intellectual and spiritual confidence?

What sources of authority influence me most?

From guilt to doubt

People in previous generations used to be overwhelmed with guilt, with the burden that they had fallen short of the ethical standards of life. They felt badly that they'd fallen short of God's ideal and feared that they wouldn't make it to heaven. We of recent generations don't wrestle much with guilt. Instead, we wrestle with doubt. *And the very forces that have undone our guilt have nurtured our doubt. The very things that have freed people from their sense of moral failure are the same things that feed the doubt that haunts their lives.*

For example, the authority of intellectual and moral absolutes that used to judge us as wrong or guilty have been traded for a relativism that leaves us guiltless—but *uncertain.* People today don't take an absolute stand on issues. They say, "Hey, if it's true for you, that's all that matters." As a result, you may not feel guilty, but you also don't know where to stand anymore. How do we know what's right? Likewise, the God of standards who created the world has been replaced by mechanical processes that convey no inherent values. A basic tenet of evolutionary philosophy that pervades our culture makes us no more important than any other life form. We may be logical and scientific, but as a culture we no longer operate from a standard moral base. No wonder doubt has eroded the sure footing of our faith.

Let me say it again: The very forces that have undone our guilt have nurtured our doubt. But you need to know that doubt isn't new. The source of our doubts may be different, but the reality of doubt hasn't changed. What matters most is our response. In the Bible we see that Abraham doubted he would be a father in his old age. Sarah, his wife, doubted that she could become a mother, since the time had long since passed that she could bear children. Moses doubted that either Pharaoh or the Israelites would believe that he had been sent by God to deliver the Hebrews. The Israelites continually doubted that God would provide for them. Although God gave them manna from heaven and water from rocks, they doubted him on a daily basis. Gideon doubted that he mattered to God or that God could use anyone like him. Zechariah doubted that he and his wife could have a child. Doubt is part of our faith development. It's part of living. Paul Tournier has said, "The person who claims never to have doubted does not know what faith is. For faith is forged through doubt."[4]

Have I experienced my doubts leading me to a new level of faith?

If so, when and how did that happen?

Why Do We Doubt?

We have seen that there are a number of cultural factors that encourage doubt in our day. I have also found that, in addition to these, there are two primary reasons that doubt arises in our life. These factors have sown seeds of doubt throughout the generations.

We doubt when things don't match our customary expectations.

All of us have expectations. We have expectations about what God is like, what life should be like, what relationships should be like, and what faith should be like. And when things do not match with what we expect, we doubt.

The disciples had been with Jesus for three years. But when news of the Resurrection came, they doubted. They were the first skeptics. They were surprised that God would do something they didn't expect. Honestly, in their deepest souls they didn't believe Jesus would come back from the dead.

I was talking with a woman recently whose sibling had committed suicide. Naturally, this shook her to the core. "I just don't know what to believe anymore," she said, "I always thought that the Lord wouldn't allow this to happen in my family. I have prayed for them for years." Her anguish can't be put into words. I don't honestly know how I would respond emotionally and spiritually in such circumstances. But I am learning much from walking alongside her and her family. In spite of her doubt, her faith is actually growing. It is growing because she is seeking not so much for answers but for assurances of God's love and care in the midst of this. She isn't looking for explanations but for God's embrace. And God is giving that assurance.

You may have experienced doubts when

- you felt the first blast of a temptation far more intense than you ever thought a Christian could have;
- you saw a "problem" in the Bible that you couldn't resolve immediately and didn't know where to turn for an answer;
- you experienced the loss of something or someone dear to you, such as a pet, a loved one, a job, a marriage; or
- someone lied to you and let you down.

What are some of my basic expectations about life, faith, and God?

How have those expectations been disappointed?

How has that disappointment affected my spiritual life?

Our experiences can lead us to rethink our assumptions, reorder our priorities, and reexamine our faith. Those who do so find themselves moving to a deeper level of maturity. For reasons we can only partly understand, doubt and suffering are stepping-stones to growth. This was true even of Jesus, as is stated in Hebrews 5:8: "So even though Jesus was God's Son, he learned obedience from the things he suffered."

We doubt when things don't match our customary experience.

Jesus appeared in the room with the disciples, but they still doubted (see also Matthew 28:17), even after all he had told them about what would happen. The Resurrection didn't match their experience.

Our experiences shape our faith to some extent. John the Baptist had baptized Jesus and exclaimed, "Look! There is the Lamb of God who takes away the sin of the world!"

(John 1:29). He had inaugurated Jesus. But then John was thrown into prison by Herod. As word reached John of Jesus' ministry, it didn't match what John expected. So John sent his disciples to Jesus to ask, "Are you the Messiah we've been expecting or should we keep looking for someone else?" (Luke 7:19). John the Baptist was filled with doubts.

Thomas, who had heard the reports of the disciples, was filled with doubt. The disciples, who heard others telling of their encounter with the risen Lord, were filled with doubt. What we see here is that doubt afflicts not only unbelievers who say, "I don't believe that stuff." Doubt afflicts believers—especially after their initial affirmation of faith. Belief falls prey to questions when life gets hard.

A statistic I read recently stopped me in my tracks. It reported that 80 percent of all young people who are involved in church through high school will drop out and most likely not be involved again. Eighty percent. Why? Simply because they weren't prepared to handle the doubts and difficulties that come with adulthood. We need to cultivate a faith that loves God with the mind. We are to build a foundation that includes intellectual understanding, training in spiritual discipline, and a commitment to community. The person who doesn't develop an intellectual understanding of subjects, such as other religions and the relationship of science and faith, may well be swept away by the secular currents. Some never come back.

How do I handle the intellectual challenges to my faith?

I was talking with a dear friend who lives in another state. I asked him how their children were doing, and he said, "Two of them are far from the Lord, Doug." I knew their children and how special they were. I would have expected them to be strong and stay committed. But their college experiences seemed to have knocked them out of their Christian orbit. My friend is just praying that they will come back.

How have my family and friends responded as they have grown up?

Theologian Paul Tillich gives us a glimpse of hope that all is not lost when he says, "Doubt becomes the means for penetrating the depth of your being, the depth of all being."[5]

Doubt tests all the untested assumptions on which you have built your life. Doubt is like the earthquake that shakes the foundations, revealing what is solidly built and what needs to be retrofitted. The shaking reveals what you really need in order to stay strong. Truth is often hidden in the midst of doubt.

What are my life experiences, and how have they shaped my faith?

What things have happened to shake away all but my fundamental beliefs?

How Did Jesus Handle Doubt?

So what did Jesus do with his disciples? What does Jesus do with all people when they struggle with the reality of doubt?

Our doubt is overcome when our expectations are shaped by God's Word.

What am I supposed to expect out of life? What am I to understand about Jesus? What am I supposed to understand about who I am and what I am supposed to do? Jesus' strategy with John the Baptist and with all of his disciples was to take them back to Scripture. In Luke 24:26-27 we read that Jesus told them, "'Wasn't it clearly predicted that the Messiah would have to suffer?' Then Jesus quoted passages from the writings of Moses . . . , explaining what all the Scriptures said about himself." And he went on and told the story. Let your expectations be shaped by God's Word, not by public opinion or anything else.

Recently I was thinking about fairness. I've had several situations recently in which I said to the Lord, "It's just not fair!" As I prayed and reflected in my journal, I realized that *fair* is not a big part of God's vocabulary. Almost immediately, three Scriptures came to mind. The first was the parable of the workers in the vineyard, who were paid equally (Matthew 20:1-16). They all got the same wage, no matter how long they had worked—that's not exactly fair. The master says, "Am I not allowed to do what I choose with what belongs to me?" (v. 15, RSV). Then I thought of the parable of the Prodigal Son (Luke 15:11-32). The elder brother's sense of fair and unfair was soundly rebuked. Last, I thought of Jesus' dialogue with Peter in John 21:21-22. After Jesus had predicted Peter's death, Peter looked at the "other disciple," whom many assume is John, and asked Jesus, "What about him, Lord?" Jesus replied, "If I want him to remain alive until I return, what is that to you? You follow me!" Jesus wasn't concerned with equalization. His Word has given me much that challenges my expectations of fairness. Above all, I see that my criteria of fairness are no excuse for avoiding my unique call as a disciple or as a basis for questioning God's grace.

Those who study God's Word find that God's truth brings to them a doubt-taming strength and a mind-reassuring confidence.

Our doubt is overcome when we experience Jesus directly.

Faith goes beyond intellectually understanding the Scriptures, however. While our doubt is overcome as our expectations are shaped by God's Word, Jesus also invited his disciples to experience him directly. Jesus' encounters with the disciples had a definite physical dimension to them. He said, "Here, touch me. Here, feel, put your hand in my side. Do you have anything to eat?" And the resurrected Lord ate a piece of fish. Our doubt is overcome as our heart is assured by God's touch.

William Dixon lived in Brackenthwaite, England. He was a widower, who had also lost his only son. One day he saw that the house of one of his neighbors was on fire. Although the aged owner was rescued, her orphaned grandson was trapped in the blaze. Dixon climbed an iron pipe on the side of the house and lowered the boy to safety. His hand that held on to the pipe was badly burned.

Shortly after the fire, the grandmother died. The townspeople wondered who would care for the boy. Two volunteers appeared before the town council. One was a father, who had lost his son and would like to adopt the orphan as his own. The other was William Dixon, who was to speak next; but instead of saying anything, he merely held up his scarred hand. When the vote was taken, the boy was given to him.[6]

Although I am completely committed to nurturing a

credible faith based on sound thinking, I also know that there is no proof more powerful than the Lord's direct touch on our life. When we see his hands, we know his love beyond all doubt.

How does that happen? In my experience it happens differently with different people. A man I'll call Dave came in to see me during a time of intense struggle. He had been through a difficult divorce that left him with continuing significant financial commitments. He also was being kept from seeing his teenage daughter. I asked him to share his story.

> I had experienced a lot of stress over the past couple of years and that stress manifested itself in some physical ailments, not the least of which was a very serious case of tendinitis in my right elbow. It started in August, and over the next three or four months it got worse and worse. Eventually, my arm was put into a cast to immobilize it. It was so painful that I couldn't go through my everyday activities without taking lots of pain medication. I couldn't concentrate, and I couldn't sleep.
>
> To top things off, in December I got a notice that I had to go back to court with my ex-wife regarding finances. I also chose at that time to ask the court to intervene in this custody conflict that I've been going through for the past year. So, the anticipation of that court hearing was just something else that added to all the anxiety I was feeling at the time.
>
> Many members of the church have prayed for me and my daughter. But I suppose my own doubt manifested in anger and frustration and hostility toward the situation just wouldn't let me let go and let the Lord take care of it. Well, as the situation continued, my lovely wife, was very sensitive to the effect that this was having, both on me as well as on our marriage. And so about a week prior to my court date she called Doug and said, "Would you talk with

> Dave for a while?" So I went in on a Thursday afternoon before I was to go to court the next week and poured out all of my hurts, my frustration, my anger, everything that I had been going through. At the end of the session he had a prayer for me, and at the end of the prayer, almost parenthetically, Doug said, "And you know, Lord, Dave's arm is hurting him. He really doesn't need that added pain on top of everything else." Doug prayed that my arm would be healed. I have to tell you that all of that time my arm had been throbbing. I could barely tolerate the pain.
>
> The next day was uneventful. I went to work as usual. But on Saturday morning something pretty miraculous happened. I awakened, headed toward the bathroom to get my normal handful of pain medication for my arm, and I realized that my elbow wasn't hurting at all. So I felt all around and found just one little spot on the edge of my elbow that would hurt if I pushed on it. That little spot is still there today, more than a year later. It's a reminder to me of what the Lord did on that particular day. The relationship with my daughter would still take many months to resolve. And I still haven't resolved the financial situation. Nonetheless, I'm very positive that the Lord has a plan. He is in control and will do just what needs to be done. Whenever I doubt, all I do is just touch that little spot on my elbow, and it reminds me of his power.

What a powerful story! There are no easy answers. The pain isn't all gone, but the person of Christ is right there carrying us through the pain.

Why do you doubt? Honest doubt is a respectable place to start with God. But it's never a destination. *The doubters in the Bible had the courage to admit their doubt and then continue with God until things could be made clear.* Dave had the courage to say, "My life is being torn apart," but he came and opened himself to God—and God made it clear.

What about You?

Martha Wynn was a feisty woman in her eighties who was a member of our congregation. Even after the age of eighty she was volunteering in our church office. She's what I call a salty saint. She would often walk by my door and peek in, saying, "I don't mind being nosey. I deserve to be at my age." We would often chat about my sermon. In one Sunday morning's sermon I had said, "You know, the most amazing truth is not that we believe in God but that *God believes in us.*" The next day Martha stopped at my door. "You really got me thinking yesterday. I realize my greatest doubts are not about God but about me. I love God with all my heart, but I sure have problems with myself. So, Doug, I wrote this poem last night for you. I tried to tell you what I mean." And then this wonderful woman gave me this poem:

Thomas and I

Thomas knew you well, noting small things.
The contour of your beard, your sudden laugh,
The gentle hands, the way your eyes caught fire
At the desecration of a temple or a life. He more than most
Echoed your fervor when he prayed, "Thy kingdom come."
Yet Thomas doubted.

Not you! It was himself he disbelieved.
And his companions, fearing their anguished need
Induced illusions. You did not rail at him,
But gently, with a smile exposed your wounds
For added certainty of touch as he had asked.

Lest I confuse my aching wants with your commands,
Show me your hands.[7]

Martha has now seen the Lord's hands. She died a couple of months after sharing that poem with me. I am so thankful for her feisty intrusiveness that let me into her heart.

Martha's words can say a lot to us. On this journey of faith, we are invited to let our doubts take us deeper.

What doubts are threatening to eat away at your soul? Are they doubts about God—or about you? Are your doubts and fears related to your motives and abilities? to the distraction of past failures? to the anxiety of future expectations?

Let them go. Just leave them with the Lord Jesus. And take the next step on your journey with God.

NOTES

1. Among the books that helped me most were C. S. Lewis, *Mere Christianity;* J.N.D. Anderson, *Christianity and the Witness of History;* Frank Morrison, *Who Moved the Stone?* F. F. Bruce, *The New Testament Documents: Are They Reliable?* and Josh McDowell, *More Than a Carpenter.*
2. Bertrand Russell, "Why I Am Not a Christian" (New York: Simon and Schuster, 1957), 22, quoted in R. C. Sproul, *The Psychology of Atheism* (Minneapolis, Minn.: Bethany Fellowship, Inc., 1974), 49.
3. Omar Bradley, in Tony Castle, ed., *The New Book of Christian Quotations* (New York: Crossroad, 1984), 215.
4. Paul Tournier, *The Person Reborn* (San Francisco: Harper & Row, 1966), 106.
5. Paul Tillich, "God's Pursuit of Man," in Clyde E. Fant Jr. and William M. Pinson Jr., *20 Centuries of Great Preaching* (Waco, Tex.: Word Books, 1971), 10:66.
6. Neil Strait, "He Merely Showed His Hands" in Paul Lee Tan, *Encyclopedia of 7700 Illustrations* (Rockville, Md.: Assurance Publishers, 1979), 1939.
7. Shared with the kind permission of Martha's children, Ms. Pat Wynne and Mr. Robert Wynne.

CHAPTER 21

"Who do you think you are?" The Danger of Secondhand Faith

Acts 19:14

BILL WAS A grandiose, loud-talking New York City alcoholic. Nearly forty, he was feeding his habit by stealing grocery money from his wife's purse and sometimes by panhandling. Several times he had been hospitalized, but he always started drinking again, no matter what resolutions he made.

One November day an old alcoholic friend, Eddy Thatcher, paid Bill a visit. Thatcher was sober and had come to tell Bill why. He had had a religious experience. Members of an organization called the Oxford Group had visited him in jail, where he had been incarcerated for drunkenness, and he had yielded his life to God. The desire to drink was gone, he said. His life was changed.

After several visits, Thatcher convinced Bill—who was quite averse to religion—to attend a meeting at a Manhattan rescue mission sponsored by Calvary Episcopal Church, local headquarters of the Oxford Group. Bill stopped at several bars on the way and was quite drunk when he arrived. He was, however, sufficiently moved by the testimonies to go forward and testify at length to his own changed heart. This change lasted less than a day. Bill went on a three-day binge and was hospitalized again.

Thatcher visited the hospital and, at Bill's request, repeated his formula for conversion: "Realize you are licked, admit it, and get willing to turn your life over to the care of God."

Bill fell into a deep depression after Thatcher left. As he was later to describe it:

> I still gagged badly on the notion of a Power greater than myself, but finally, just for the moment, the last vestige of my proud obstinacy was crushed. All at once I found myself crying out, "If there is a God, let him show himself! I am ready to do anything, anything!"
>
> Suddenly the room lit up with a great white light. I was caught up in an ecstasy there are no words to describe. It seemed to me, in the mind's eye, that I was on a mountain and that a wind not of air but of spirit was blowing. And then it burst upon me that I was a free man. Slowly the ecstasy subsided. I lay on a bed, but now for a time I was in another world, a new world of consciousness. All about me and through me there was a wonderful feeling of Presence, and I thought to myself, *So this is the God of the preachers!* A great peace stole over me and I thought, *No matter how wrong things seem to be, they are all right. Things are all right with God and his world.*[1]

Bill never took another drink. And he has helped thousands resist the self-destructive power of alcoholism. This is the story of Bill Wilson, known best as "Bill W." in Alcoholics Anonymous lore. He was unquestionably the most influential person in the development of Alcoholics Anonymous.

It's one thing to know about God but an entirely different matter to know God and experience God's power personally. Those who only know about God may be like Bill was initially, averse to "religion" because they don't see its relevance. To them, it's just a bunch of sentimental folklore that gets in the way. But those who truly encounter God, as Bill did, are changed forever. The tragedy is that most people live their lives by hearsay instead of by firsthand experience. That can have drastic consequences, as some first-century Jewish exorcists learned.

> **God did extraordinary miracles by the hands of Paul, so that handkerchiefs or aprons were carried away from his body to the sick, and diseases left them and the evil spirits came out of them. Then some of the itinerant Jewish exorcists undertook to pronounce the name of Lord Jesus over those who had evil spirits, saying, "I adjure you by the Jesus whom Paul preaches." Seven sons of a Jewish high priest named Sceva were doing this. But the evil spirit answered them, "Jesus I know, and Paul I know; but who are you?" And the man in whom the evil spirit was leaped on them, mastered all of them, and overpowered them, so that they fled out of that house naked and wounded. And this became known to all residents of Ephesus, both Jews and Greeks; and fear fell upon them all; and the name of the Lord Jesus was extolled. Many also of those who were now believers came, confessing and divulging their practices. And a number of those who practiced magic arts brought their books together and burned them in the sight of all; and they counted the value of them and found it came to fifty thousand pieces of silver. So the word of the Lord grew and prevailed mightily. (Acts 19:11-20, RSV)**

One of the great pitfalls in life is being a spectator when you are meant to be a participant. I'm not talking so much about watching sports on TV but about watching the ordinary, common things of life from the sidelines, when we are meant to be on the field. How many of us are moved by the tenderness of a television commercial about friends reconciling or families being in touch over the holidays, but we don't take the initiative to reach out to our loved ones? Or we are moved by the inspiration of people whose lives are making a difference, but we don't move into action. Vicarious experience in the spiritual life is unsatisfactory.

We visited the Johnson Space Center in Houston several years ago and saw what the astronauts eat. I don't envy the astronauts, who get their food in pellets. I'm sure I would not want to eat that way. True, those pellets contain all the nutrition the astronauts need, but it's already been processed. I not only want nutrition, I want the experience of the food. I want the enjoyment of real food. A processed, secondhand faith is a lot like food pellets. We were made to taste and see for ourself that the Lord is good.

We're Not Safe with a Secondhand Faith

In this passage of Acts we will learn about the danger of a secondhand faith. As we consider this account, though, we are confronted with aspects of the evil world that may be far from our experience—demonization and exorcism. More than that, we may simply dismiss them as prescientific superstition and fail to consider seriously the message for us today.

Colin Brown, a professor at Fuller Theological Seminary, tells the story of the seventeenth-century king of Siam (Siam was the old name for what is now Thailand) meeting with the Dutch ambassador for the first time. It seems that they were having a very pleasant conversation. The king was learning all about life in far-off Holland. Enthralled as he was, the king had an immediate negative reaction against the ambassador when he began to talk about winter. The king of Siam had lived all of his life in the tropics, and when the ambassador said the water would get so hard that an elephant could walk on it, the king of Siam lost all belief in this man. He said, "Hitherto I believed the strange things you have told me because I look on you as a sober, fair man, but now I am sure you are a liar!" You see, the experience of winter was out of the realm of reference for the king of Siam, and so he immediately wrote off the Dutch ambassador as a liar.[2]

We often dismiss that which is outside our own experience. But there is much more to life than what you or I may have seen or experienced up to this point. The Bible teaches us that we will face spiritual conflict with God's enemies. Spiritual conflict is real. The battle of the universe is being waged among us. It's been waged on this planet—not simply between God and Satan, but between God's people and the people of evil in this world. Demonization is evidence of that conflict.

Many of us are used to phrases like "demon possession" or even "demon oppression." I prefer the word *demonization.* It's biblical. It's a transliteration of the Greek. The people were demonized. This term expresses a level of influence. It isn't so much a matter of property, as indicated by the term possession, but a matter of the level of influence that evil has over people.

What do I believe about the nature of demons and evil?

How have I come to these beliefs? How does that affect my spiritual life?

What's the significance of exorcism? Exorcism was a regular aspect of Jesus' ministry. We can't read in the Gospels without coming across Jesus casting out demons. Listen to Jesus' own words in Luke 11:20: "But if I drive out demons by the finger of God, then the kingdom of God has come to you" (NIV). The demonic activity that arose and the deliverance that Jesus brought are evidence that he was God over all the kingdoms. He had come to break the power of the evil one, "to destroy these works of the Devil" (1 John 3:8). It was a breakthrough. Redemption was no longer only a future but a present reality in people's lives. In this struggle, Jesus himself broke Satan's power and continues to do so. In other words, the reign of God—which the Jews look at as an eschatological or future reality—had broken into the present.

When you and I begin to take faith seriously, it often pushes us beyond the limits of our comfort zone. It challenges our neat categories of life. It forces us to examine our prejudices and assumptions. Many people are put off at this

"The reign of God has broken into the present. . . ." What practical difference could this assertion make in my life today?

What would be different about my attitude and activities?

point and stall in their growth. Those who press on, however, break through into a much richer experience of their faith. In this case, we can break free from the fear of evil and learn about our security in Jesus Christ.

Shielded by Jesus' authority

The sons of Sceva were typical Jewish exorcists, who would simply recite incantations using the names of every god they could remember. They would list these gods on the theory that one would be more powerful than the demon and drive it out. Now they were adding Jesus' name to the list. Jesus, however, used a radically different approach when confronting demons. Unlike contemporary exorcists, Jesus used little or no ritual. A mere word of command was often the only means employed. He said to the demon in the boy who was throwing himself into the fire, "I command you, come out of him!" and the demon was gone (Mark 9:25, NIV). This gives us an overwhelming impression of Jesus' authority.

I remember talking with a student teacher who told me about losing control of her class on one of her first days. Her elementary school students were doing whatever they wanted, and she couldn't regain order. Then in came the teacher. She happened to be a very strong teacher. She walked into the classroom and everything stopped. Discipline was administered. Her simple presence brought the authority that the student teacher had yet to learn. Likewise with Jesus. When he said something, it was done.

Jesus had exercised authority over the physical and spiritual evil in people. But he did so out of compassion, not for his own power needs. He didn't perform exorcisms as his primary itinerant ministry. He did this as a way of loving people—of healing and restoring them. He also imparted this same authority to his followers (see Matthew 10:1).

What about today?

Jesus' miracles then, including exorcism, were visible evidences of the coming kingdom of God. But what about today? A lot of us have grown up thinking that what happened in the Bible happened way back then but it certainly doesn't happen today. There's abundant evidence to the contrary, however.

I read of a church in my own rather traditional denomination that held a conference on prayer attended by more than seven hundred people. They reached a point in the program where the people broke up into groups of ten to pray. As they were moving to different areas of the facilities for their prayer time, a woman came onto the church campus.

> The woman's face was aged beyond her years. She was skin and bones although money for food was not a problem. Sleep had been impossible for weeks. A quest for help from self-styled spiritualists had driven her deeper into her problem. She was about to respond to a command to do something that everything in her rational mind resisted. The problem had begun very innocently. As a lark the woman had been taught spirit writing by an occult. And her loneliness had driven her to communicate to the spirit pal, as she called him. She had asked for his name on a Ouija board. A-L-B-E-R-T had been spelled out in response. Daily conversations were carried on for weeks. Intimate questions had been asked. Directions for life requested. Always there was a clear answer. Then her spirit became anything but a pal. He spelled out her sister's name. J-A-N-E. Simple, benign suggestions about her at first. Then a horrible command.
>
> M-U-R-D-E-R-J-A-N-E. Murder Jane. How and when were detailed through the Ouija board. With trembling fingers she had spelled out the words, "Who are you?" And the answer came back swiftly, moving her hands deliberately, E-V-I-L. Frantic and almost out of her senses, the woman came for help, stuttering out her plight and great anguish. They took her into the sanctuary. And there two elders

> and I laid hands upon her. The wife of one of the elders knelt before the disturbed woman seated in the pew, taking her hands in a loving clasp. We told her about Jesus Christ and his love for her and the power of his name to liberate people from evil. Then the elder and I laid our hands on the woman's head and prayed for her release. I will never forget the transformation on her face after we prayed. Her eyes lost the glassy, wild look, her body slumped in quiet peacefulness. That night she slept for the first time in weeks. The next day she was back to take part in our conference. She still has my Bible with verses underlined to direct her to the Savior and his power. The Lord had given the first fruits of the prayers of his people.[3]

Even if I haven't had experiences such as those described above, how do I respond to the promise of my authority in Christ?

Do I live confidently in light of this reality?

Or am I shy and reluctant to "claim my birthright"? Why?

The pastor in this account was Lloyd John Ogilvie. It happened at Hollywood Presbyterian Church in the early 1970s. And it's written in Lloyd Ogilvie's book *Drumbeat of Love* on the book of Acts. In the early 1990s, Dr. Ogilvie went on to become chaplain of the United States Senate. He has seen that elephants can walk on water! He saw that God can gain victory over the devil. You and I need to realize that we will face spiritual conflict. Whether or not we have ever faced such a conflict, we know that in the world and the flesh and the devil, we will meet people who conspire to tempt and destroy. And the message is this: We are not safe with a secondhand faith.

Knowledge of Jesus—or Knowing Jesus?

The sons of Sceva made a tragic assumption. They assumed that knowledge of Jesus was the same as knowing Jesus. But those are two very different realities. They tried to use Jesus' name without believing in him. Without trusting him, without relying upon him. The evil spirit challenged their presumption (Acts 19:15).

To me this passage has a certain dark humor. Let me set up the scene. The sons of Sceva parade around this person, reading melodramatically through their very impressive incantation. As they conclude, they say, "And, by the way, in the name of Jesus whom Paul preaches, we adjure you to come out." Now, with your sanctified imagination, picture this demon sitting back behind a desk, with his legs propped up, lighting a cigarette, taking a long drag, and blowing out the smoke. He eyes the seven sons of Sceva one by one. Then he says, "I know Jesus, and I know Paul, but who are you?" Then he stands up, crushes the cigarette on the ground, and leaps on these unsuspecting guys, mauling them and tearing their clothes from them! They run out of this house naked and wounded. I imagine they found a different profession after that! It wasn't as safe as they thought it was.

First of all, the demon says, "I know Jesus." The demons knew Jesus. James 2:19 says, "You believe that there is one God. Good! Even the demons believe that—and shudder" (NIV). We read in the Gospel accounts that when Jesus would come near the demons, simply his authority and his presence would intimidate them. They would cry out, "What do you want with us, Jesus of Nazareth? Have you come to destroy us?" (Mark 1:24, NIV). And Jesus would give his orders, and they would have to obey. The demons know Jesus.

But what's really astonishing in the Acts passage is who else they know. They know Paul. How do they know Paul? I guess word gets around through the demonic network! "Hey, watch out for Paul. If he comes, you're out of here!"

WE ARE MARKED PEOPLE

The point is that Jesus' followers are marked people. Did you ever think of that? The evil ones know who you are if you are in Jesus Christ. That is an astounding reality. Did you know you have that kind of authority if you are his follower?

But imagine this scene. You are confronted by an evil one, and it says, "Who are you?"

"Well, I go to church," you respond.

"I know, but who are you? I've never heard of you. Who are you to act by an authority that is not yours?"

"But I believe in God."

"So do I!!" He cackles. "But that doesn't make me on his side!"

"Well, I was brought up in the church."

"Yeah, but you don't live under his authority. I've never seen you lay your life on the line for another person. You take his name on your lips, but I've never seen you lay down your life for your brothers and sisters. I've never seen you give money that was marked as if it were under his authority. You tip God, you don't tithe. You don't have that . . . that . . . radiance that his real followers have. Who do you think you are?"

The Power Is in the Relationship, Not in the Magic

There is no secondhand faith, and there is no secondhand power. We can't simply know who Jesus is and use his name like an incantation. If we do, the demons will know the difference. More important, God knows the difference. There's a sobering passage in the Sermon on the Mount when Jesus says,

> "Not all people who sound religious are really godly. They may refer to me as 'Lord,' but they still won't enter the Kingdom of Heaven. The decisive issue is whether they obey my Father in heaven. On judgment day many will tell me, 'Lord, Lord, we prophesied in your name and cast out demons in your name and performed many miracles in your name.' But I will reply, 'I never knew you. Go away; the things you did were unauthorized.' " (Matthew 7:21-23)

We will only have power over evil in this world if the power of Christ is working in us. When you get right down to it, all that matters is knowing God. "And this is eternal life, that they know thee the only true God, and Jesus Christ whom thou has sent" (John 17:3, RSV).

This is a very deep concern to me because I care a great deal about passing on our faith to the next generation. We want to nurture our children in the Lord. But all children—our good, churchgoing children included—must place themselves under the authority of Christ by accepting him as Lord and Savior. When evil comes against our children, our prayers will help, but those children need to belong completely to Christ in order to have power over the evil that will come against them. If we, as parents or as churches, are not earnest and intentional about bringing the next generation to that personal salvation, these kids will end up with a secondhand faith. The greatest tragedy is that they'll feel very secure when they really aren't.

Are there people in my life (family members, friends) who, as best as I can discern, do not yet know the Lord personally?

How can I pray for them and share my faith with them in ways that will be received?

A lesson from the Cavaliers

One of the most influential groups of Christians who have ever walked the earth were the Puritans. The Puritans exercised incredible influence in England in the seventeenth and eighteenth centuries. They were the best educated segment of English society. Their commitment to God's Word was beyond question. Read their diaries, study their theology, examine their works, and you will find sharp minds, earnest faith, and tireless commitment. When they sailed to America, theirs was the primary influence shaping the culture and the government of the colonies that later became the United States of America. Yet, their children did not follow in their footsteps. In fact, their children moved defiantly in the opposite direction. The children of the Puritans are called the Cavaliers. (Don't confuse that with the Cavaliers who were in Scotland and England at another time.) They were the least educated generation until today's so-called Generation X.

There are many other correlations with our own situation today. The Cavaliers represented the greatest single-generation decline in American history. They lived a corrupt and violent lifestyle with many of them getting into witchcraft and routine violence. The Cavaliers were filled with religious skepticism, and they lacked spiritual fervor. They did not accept the lordship of Christ. Materialism birthed spiritual malaise and a false sense of security. In an effort to maintain some link between the church and the next generation, the Puritans devised what was known as the halfway covenant for the Cavaliers, enabling them to join the church and participate in church leadership without embracing the whole concept of discipleship and commitment that was held by the Puritans. The children of the Puritans had a secondhand faith, a nominal faith.[4]

Faith—or an heirloom?

A nominal faith is a faith in name only—faith that is a family heirloom. In our home we have an antique coffee grinder. It's one of those old wooden ones with the metal crank on top. I've never once ground coffee beans in it. It's a family heirloom. We don't use it—we just look at it. And secondhand faith is like that—a sentimental practice. It's a family tradition you practice for old times' sake, not a living reality that is woven into the warp and woof of your daily life.

Faith is a sentimental reality for many people, used only at baptisms, weddings, and funerals. In pastoral ministry we have a little adage for the times when nominal Christians "call upon our services" (at least, that's how they approach us, as service providers). We pastors are often called upon to "hatch, match, and dispatch," or, in other words, to baptize, marry, and bury people. These are, of course, the central experiences of life, and we *are* grateful to be able to bring God's presence into them. I am grateful for every opening to share the gospel of Jesus Christ. But when these are the only times people turn to faith, it's like calling a friend only when you need something from him. That's missing the whole point of friendship. And nominal Christians are missing the whole point of faith. Someday they will hear this question: "Who do you think you are?"

There when we want it

The danger of a nominal faith is that you presume that God will do anything when you want it done—while you refuse to do what God wants. We cannot draw our identity nor our security from a secondhand faith. We can only know Jesus in a firsthand way.

Who are you? Do you have a secondhand faith or a firsthand faith? Do you simply repeat the name of Jesus because you've watched others do it? Maybe they're people you know and respect. Or are you a follower of Jesus? And how do we confirm that? If you are in a spiritual battle would you be identified: "Jesus I know, and Paul I know, and I've heard of you"? Can you imagine that? It isn't enough to say the name of Jesus; you must believe in him!

THREE CRUCIAL ASPECTS OF REAL FAITH

Faith is not simply wishful thinking. Nor is it, as H. L. Mencken defined faith, "an illogical belief in the irrational." Biblical faith has three primary elements.

Faith consists of knowledge of the facts.

Faith is rooted in facts as substantial as any of the facts we accept from science and history and any other branch of human learning and life. What are the facts? The facts are that God sent his Son, Jesus Christ, to redeem the world from sin. And that Jesus Christ gave his life for you and me, erasing all of God's charges against us. He was raised again from the dead and sits at the right hand of God. And if you put your faith and trust in Jesus Christ, all your sins will be forgiven. Those are the facts of the gospel. Do you know these ABCs of the faith?

Faith consists of intellectual assent to the facts.

You may know the facts, but do you believe them? Do you believe Jesus Christ is the Son of God? Do you believe he died for your sins? Do you believe that when God looks at you now in Christ he says, "My child, come in"? Intellectual assent is important. I know the facts of Mormonism, I know the facts of Hinduism and of Buddhism. But I do not give intellectual assent to those facts or to any other religious system. My mind is fully satisfied with the intellectual credibility of the Bible and the integrity of the gospel.

Faith consists of total trust in the facts.
The third essential element to faith, however, is putting your total weight on those facts. Real faith says, "I'm going to count on this!" For example, when we put our money at risk, we send a message about what we really believe. My dad, who is a conservative man economically, said, "Doug, never put any money in the stock market you can't afford to lose." So, I've never put any money in the market! You could say to me, "Doug, you really don't believe in the stock market. You may intellectually assent that a lot of people have made a lot of money there, but you've never put your money at risk." If you really believe (and have the resources) you will show that faith by totally trusting, investing your money.

You exercise total trust when the doctor gives you a medication and says, "Here take this, and in ten days the antibiotic will cause the bacteria to leave your system." You might know the pills are good for you and intellectually assent to the fact that they should help you get better, but if you refuse to take them, you don't have true faith. Faith leads to action.

Have you really put your faith and trust in Jesus Christ? One day you will die. It's not a matter of *if* but of *when.* You will die, and you will stand before God, and he will ask you why he should let you into heaven. Then it will not be enough to say, "My mom believed, my dad believed, I went to church." The big question will be, "Did you know me?" Because of my faith in Jesus Christ, evil and good alike will say, "I know Doug Rumford." My name is written in the Book of Life. Is yours?

Firsthand Faith Results in a Changed Life

A number of people in Ephesus had said they were followers of Jesus, but after this incident with the sons of Sceva there was quite a stir in the church. That's why there is more to this story than the seven sons of Sceva being defeated. In fact, what looked like a demonic victory resulted in a far greater victory for the cause of Jesus Christ.

What happened? Well, firsthand faith resulted in changed lives. We need to remember that Ephesus was notorious for its occult literature, the kind you find in the bookstore under astrology and New Age religion. They had books about magic, divination, astrology, casting spells, telling fortunes, contacting the dead, interrupting the dreams, and predicting future events. They had tutors to instruct them in the black arts. But they had to be taught that this was forbidden by God. We read in Deuteronomy 18:9-14:

> When you arrive in the land the Lord your God is giving you, be very careful not to imitate the detestable customs of the nations living there. For example, never sacrifice your son or daughter as a burnt offering. And do not let your people practice fortune-telling or sorcery, or allow them to interpret omens, or engage in witchcraft, or cast spells, or function as mediums or psychics, or call forth the spirits of the dead. Anyone who does these things is an object of horror and disgust to the Lord. It is because the other nations have done these things that the Lord your God will drive them out ahead of you. You must be blameless before the Lord your God. The people you are about to displace consult with sorcerers and fortune-tellers, but the Lord your God forbids you to do such things.

For whatever reason, the Ephesian believers had not made a clean break with their past. Their old ways had clung to them. But in this incident, they saw the power of God demonstrated, and they repented. They no longer tolerated the evil practices that had distracted them and violated God's will for their lives. In doing so, these believers moved beyond a nominal faith to a committed faith. They brought all their books to be burned.

When did I make the decision to put my total trust in Jesus Christ?

Have I ever written that story?

If I were to begin it now, I would write . . .

Are there any of these practices in my life currently?

Have I practiced them in the past?

I want to renounce them and make a clear break with them now, praying for God to forgive, to cleanse, to break the bonds of evil . . .

That's a powerful testimony. I believe they brought their books to be burned for at least three reasons. First, they wanted to show their resolution and their commitment. They were not going to allow evil to have power over them again. They were committed to following Christ. They burned their books as a public demonstration of making a clean break with evil practices.

Second, burning the books removed the temptation to revert back to their old ways once the initial enthusiasm for the faith waned. If they had kept the books, there was danger that they would lose their resolve or become curious again and return to them. Those who truly repent of sin will keep themselves as far as possible from the occasions of it.

Third, burning the books also prevented others from being harmed by the teachings. The Ephesians burned their books of magic because they didn't want anybody else to be led into that kind of deception and life-destroying behavior. If you've got evil things, don't give them to the thrift store!

I had a friend who had a collection of *Playboy* magazines. When he became a Christian, he faced a dilemma. He knew it was spiritually unhealthy and morally wrong to buy or look at such magazines. But the collection was valuable. He said, "Maybe I'll sell it because it's very valuable, and I'll even give all the money to the church." How do you think I counseled him? I said, "Burn them! You can't pass that junk along to other people!"

What about You?

Real faith involves your whole life. When you and I trust God, there is no holding back. No tolerating our pet sins. No excluding God from certain areas of our life—because those areas that we exclude from God become avenues for evil. This passage, which may have given us the greatest reason for concern, also gives us the greatest reason for hope. We cannot draw our identity from a secondhand faith. We can only know Christ firsthand.

So I ask you, Who are you? Does Jesus know you by name? Would the evil ones know you by name? Or have you been living on spiritual food pellets when you could have a vital living feast day in and day out with Christ? Are you like one of the Cavaliers, hiding behind your parents' faith or hiding behind the previous generation? Are you simply going halfway?

You may have known the Lord for years, but your experience of faith has become routine. Your best times are simply a memory. Maybe you're living as if you have a secondhand faith. It's never too late to change. In fact, now's the perfect time.

Notes

1. Tim Stafford, "The Hidden Gospel of the 12 Steps," *Christianity Today,* 22 July 1991, 14.
2. C. Peter Wagner, *How to Have a Healing Ministry* (Ventura, Calif.: Regal Books, 1988), 143–144.
3. Lloyd John Ogilvie, *Drumbeat of Love* (Waco, Tex.: Word Books, 1976), 239–240.
4. Ralph Moore, *Making Friends: Embracing & Empowering Gen X,* The Pastor's Update Audio Series (Fuller Theological Seminary, 1996).

[illegible]

... regularly at conferences for men, couples, and [illegible]

... received his doctor of ministry degree from [illegible] Theological Seminary; he earned his master of divinity [illegible]

ABOUT THE AUTHOR

Dr. Douglas J. Rumford has pastored the eleven-hundred-member First Presbyterian Church (PC-USA) in Fresno, California, since 1988. He previously served congregations in Old Greenwich and Fairfield, Connecticut. In addition to serving as a pastor for more than twenty years, Doug has written two other books: *Scared to Life* (Victor Books, 1994) and *SoulShaping: Taking Care of Your Spiritual Life* (Tyndale, 1996). He has also written a number of articles for *Leadership Journal* and other evangelical publications. He speaks regularly at conferences for men, couples, and churches.

Doug received his doctor of ministry degree from Fuller Theological Seminary. He earned his master of divinity degree from Gordon-Conwell Theological Seminary, graduating summa cum laude as valedictorian. He graduated magna cum laude, Phi Beta Kappa, with a bachelor of arts in English from Miami University, Oxford, Ohio.

Doug and his wife, Sarah, have been married over twenty years and have a daughter and three sons.

His goal in writing is to touch hearts and minds with the truth, grace, and power of God. “As I serve Jesus Christ, my greatest joy is bringing ideas to life that can change others' lives.”